The Old Hermit's Almanac

Cover note: the scroll on the back wall of the Old Hermit's observatory contains a quote from Marcus Cicero (106-43 B.C.): *Dum anima est, spes est,* usually translated as "Where there is life, there is hope."

The Old Hermit's Almanac

Edward Hays

FOREST OF PEACE
Publishing

Other Books by the Author:
(available through the publisher or your favorite bookstore)

Prayers and Rituals
Prayers for a Planetary Pilgrim
Prayers for the Domestic Church
Prayers for the Servants of God

Parables and Stories
The Quest for the Flaming Pearl
St. George and the Dragon
The Magic Lantern
The Ethiopian Tattoo Shop
Twelve and One-Half Keys
Sundancer
The Christmas Eve Storyteller

Contemporary Spirituality
The Gospel of Gabriel
The Lenten Labyrinth
Holy Fools & Mad Hatters
A Pilgrim's Almanac
Pray All Ways
Secular Sanctity
In Pursuit of the Great White Rabbit
The Ascent of the Mountain of God
Feathers on the Wind

The Old Hermit's Almanac

copyright © 1997, by Edward M. Hays

Library of Congress Cataloging-in-Publication Data

Hays, Edward M.
  The old hermit's almanac / Edward Hays.
   p. cm.
  Includes bibliographical references and index.
  ISBN 0-939516-37-3
  1. Devotional calendars. 2. Calendars. 3. Almanacs. I. Title.
  BV4811.H34 1997
  031--dc21   97-35596
              CIP

published by
Forest of Peace Publishing, Inc.
PO Box 269
Leavenworth, KS 66048-0269 USA
1-800-659-3227

printed by
Hall Directory, Inc.
Topeka, KS 66608-0348

cover art and design by Edward Hays
cover computer graphic art by Darrin NeSmith

Dedication

This Almanac of some of the famous and memorable days
in history is
dedicated
to the following
non-famous, but extremely memorable, days
that have influenced
this old hermit author:

August 1, 1812	March 14, 1946
March 31, 1816	March 26, 1947
January 5, 1825	October 23, 1947
October 22, 1842	April 30, 1949
October 1, 1850	January 28, 1950
December 10, 1853	July 6, 1955
November 26, 1862	September 7, 1955
October 11, 1878	December 14, 1957
November 20, 1893	May 31, 1958
January 28, 1895	August 8, 1959
May 31, 1912	August 6, 1964
November 23, 1917	May 31, 1971
September 1, 1919	February 20, 1972
October 6, 1920	May 31, 1972
December 28, 1921	July 31, 1973
January 5, 1925	January 24, 1976
January 23, 1927	June 16, 1979
January 6, 1931	September 15, 1979
September 8, 1931	May 1, 1981
October 11, 1931	February 8, 1982
January 10, 1934	December 27, 1983
July 2, 1935	July 1, 1995
August 13, 1935	July 31, 1998
October 2, 1939	January 1, 2000
January 19, 1941	September 8, 2001
July 24, 1945	May 31, 2008

Author's Acknowledgments

I acknowledge my giftedness in having this book, my twentieth, edited by Thomas Skorupa, who has been a part of each of my previous books. I am grateful to my longtime friend, Thomas, for his creative craftsmanship with words and his keen eye for continuity in the flow of my words and thoughts. Being co-creators, a good editor and an author share in shaping the soul of a book and in the romance of creation.

I am also fortunate that this book is the twentieth one to be published by the same publisher, whose name is also Thomas. I express my gratitude to my old and good friend, Thomas Turkle, for his professional competence, his care and his passion for perfection in the publishing of this latest book.

Yet another Thomas was involved in this book. I am grateful to Thomas Melchior, whose friendship I have valued for over forty years, for serving as the advisory editor and text reader of this book. This is the first of my books in which he has participated before publication, and I thank him for his wise insights, suggestions and assistance.

To these three men named Thomas, I express my fraternal appreciation and gratitude.

The borders and graphics in this book are gratefully used with permission from the Dover Pictorial Archive Series, Dover Publications, Inc. New York. They came from: Handbook of Early Advertising, Clarence P. Hornung; and 200 Decorative Title-Pages, Alexander Nesbitt.

Contents

1. New Year's Day and the Eighth Day of Christmas. **2.** Traditional Day the New Year Suddenly Becomes Old. **3.** Feast of Janus, the Roman God of Doorways and the Patron Saint of This Doorway Month of January. **4.** Enjoy Yourself — It's Later Than You Think Day. **5.** Toy Day. **6.** Traditional Epiphany, Twelfth Day of Christmas. **7.** The Seventh Day of the New Year. **8.** Don't Take Down Your Christmas Decorations Day. **9.** "God Speed" Day. **10.** Death Day of Buffalo Bill — Death of an Age, 1917. **11.** The Birthday of the Wool Sweater. **12.** "Stop All That Racket and Go Away" Day. **13.** Feast of the Holy Bed of St. Hilary of Poitiers. **14.** A Good Day to Break the Ice. **15.** Birthday of Dr. Martin Luther King, Jr., 1929. **16.** Celebration of the First Vatican — Feast of St. Priscilla. **17.** Birthday of Benjamin Franklin, 1706. **18.** Feast of the Lost Magi. **19.** Birthday of Robert E. Lee, 1807. **20.** Leandro P. Rissuto Day. **21.** Feast of St. Agnes, Partroness of Virgins & Girl Scouts. **22.** Pedestrian Prophecy Day, 1977. **23.** Birthday of John Hancock, 1737. **24.** Birthday of Fundamentalism, 1923. **25.** The Feast of the Conversion of St. Paul. **26.** The Birthday of the Tin Can, 1795. **27.** The Birthday of the National Geographic Society, Established on this Date in 1888 in Washington, D.C. **28.** End of the World Day — 133 Million B.C. **29.** The Nationalization Act Passage Day, 1795. **30.** The Unorthodox Feast of the Magi's Return Home. **31.** Cope with the Problem in a Nonviolent Way Day.

1. Feast of Holy and Humorous St. Brigid of Ireland, the Patroness of Nuns, Milkmaids and Fugitives. **2.** Groundhog Day and the Feast of the Purification, or Candlemas, the End of Traditional Christmas. **3.** Spiritual Weather Forecast Day. **4.** Birthday of Rosa Louise Parks, 1913. **5.** Feast of St. Agatha, Patroness of Buns and Bells. **6.** The Birthday of Babe Ruth, 1895. **7.** Pedestrian Prophecy Day, 1899. **8.** February Pentecost Vigil. **9.** Feast of St. Apollonia, Martyr and Patroness of Dentists and Those Afflicted with Toothaches. **10.** The Second Coming of the Groundhog. **11.** Nelson Mandella Released from Prison Day, 1990. **12.** Birthday of President Abraham Lincoln, 1809. **13.** Birthday of the Million, 1300. **14.** St. Valentine's Day, Feast of Friendship and Love. **15.** Non-Spectator Day. **16.** The Invention of Monkey Business, 5,000,000 B.C. **17.** The Discovery of the Planet Pluto, 1930. **18.** Be Salt Day. **19.** Clean Your Coffee and Tea Cup Day. **20.** The February Blahs Day. **21.** Death Day of Malcolm X, 1965. **22.** Birthday of President George Washington, 1732. **23.** Lenten Satellite Day. **24.**

Walpurgisnacht, Night of the Witches. **25.** Birthday of Showman Buffalo Bill Cody, 1846, and the Feast of St. Walburga of Germany, Healer and Abbess. **26.** Lenten Fast Day. **27.** Heart Home X-Ray Day. **28.** International Day of Reinvention. **29.** Feast of the Leaping St. Oswald of Worcester.

1. March Weather Forecasting Day. **2.** Birthday of Dr. Suess, 1904. **3.** Birthday of Alexander Graham Bell, 1847. **4.** Commemoration of the Divine Ding Dong. **5.** Lenten Lost and Found Day. **6.** Kything Day. **7.** The Birthday of Ebenezer Scrooge, 1842. **8.** Birthday of the Camel, 4,500,000 B.C. **9.** Grin and Bear It Day, 1775. **10.** The Feast of St. Adam of Eden. **11.** A New Lenten Sweet and Sour Dish Day. **12.** Chinook Wind Day. **13.** Pedestrian Prophecy Day, 1876. **14.** Birthday of Albert Einstein, 1879. **15.** Ides of March — a Day to Beware. **16.** Bathing in the Shannon Day. **17.** Feast of St. Patrick, Patron of Ireland and Parades. **18.** The Feast of Blessed Blarney. **19.** Feast of St. Joseph, the Husband of Mary and Father-Protector of Jesus, and Swallow Return Day at the California Mission of San Juan Capistrano. **20.** Construction of the Church of St. Basil, Moscow, 1555. **21.** Spring Equinox. **22.** End of the Forty Years War, 1014. **23.** The Feast of Sour Wine, Vinegar. **24.** Eve of the Feast of St. Dismas, the Good Criminal. **25.** Feast of the Annunciation and of Jesus' Conception. **26.** Fire Drill Day. **27.** The Feast Day of Your Conception. **28.** Birthday of Your Surname, 1100 A.D. **29.** Bobo Masquerade, Creating Order Out of Disorder Day. **30.** The Purchase of the Polar Bear Garden, Alaska, 1867. **31.** The Feast of the Non-Saint Etgall.

1. April Fools' Day. **2.** The Cart Before the Horse Day. **3.** It's Raining Cats and Dogs Day. **4.** Futurama Fun Day. **5.** Feast of St. Vincent Ferrer, Patron of Builders. **6.** Futurama II Day. **7.** Life on the Moon and Other Hoaxes Day, 1835. **8.** The Birthday of the Rainbow — the Dawn of Creation. **9.** Hallelujah Replacement Day. **10.** Celebration of the First Human Cannonball, 1877. **11.** Pointing at a Rainbow Brings Bad Luck Day. **12.** Alleluia Replacement Day. **13.** The Birthday of President Thomas Jefferson, 1743. **14.** Noah Webster Copyrights His Dictionary Day. **15.** "Women and Children First" Day. **16.** The Birthday of Holy Mother Eve of Eden. **17.** "Good to the Last Drop" Day. **18.** Inspection of Pandora's Box Day. **19.** First Use of Chemical Warfare in America Day. **20.** The Birthday of Hijacking, Chicago, 1926. **21.** Death Day of Baron von Richthofen. **22.** Dan Hartman's Electronic Jumpsuit Day. **23.** The Feast of St. George, the Patron of England, Horse Lovers, Knights and Defenders of the Weak. **24.** National Promote St. Elvis Day. **25.** Feast of St. Mark, Arbor Day and Baptism Day. **26.** "Now, It's Perfect!" Day, 11,941 A.D. **27.** Feast of "Tomorrow Should

Introduction

Important Information for the Owner of This Manual
Red-Letter Days and ✴ Star-Dates

Each day in *The Old Hermit's Almanac* is literally a red-letter day since each date is printed in red ink. Since the fifteenth century it has been the custom to indicate holidays, festivals and saints' days by marking them on calendars in red ink. With the passage of time, the expression, *red-letter day*, came to mean any memorable, happy day. Printing each day in this book of days in red ink was done with the hope that you might find each day of the year memorable in some way — or at least an occasion to reflect on the journey of life.

The memorable festivals and holidays, feasts of known, unknown and even secular saints noted in this Almanac are not the only *red-letter day* opportunities to celebrate the joy of life. Each of us has our own personal red-letter days that commemorate events of importance in our lives. Therefore, this Almanac has provided space at the end of each day's reflection, marked by a red star, for you to comment on your memorable days and occasions in your life. You can enter star-dates in your personal history, like birthdays, anniversaries of various important events (like your first date with your spouse), and Epiphany star-dates when you have especially experienced heaven's blessing. To record such past events is to relive those red-letter occasions and so to redline your life journey with meaning. Remembering is the heart of our Christian, Jewish and Islamic worship and faith life. As the church has its year of feasts, so your home church should also celebrate key events in your life with your own yearly calendar of personal feast days.

While each ✴ Star-Date space is limited to a line or two, you can make an abridged entry there and perhaps continue to write in the margins. *The Old Farmer's Almanac* of nineteenth century readers commonly displayed margins filled with personal entries of facts on farming, rainfalls and snowfalls, business ventures and family history: births, marriages and deaths. Let the ✴ Star-Date spaces invite you to continue this grand tradition in this Almanac intended for your use into the twenty-first century.

THE
MONTH
OF
JANUARY

This first month of the year is named after Janus, the two-faced Roman god of doorways. With one face he was able to guard the front entrance; with the other he watched the rear door. Janus not only presided over the entryway of the front door of the New Year, he was also the patron of janitors. The Dutch once called this first month of the year by the name *Lauwmaand*, the frosty month. Because hungry wolves were especially troublesome at this time of year, the Saxons called it *Wulf-monath*. After their conversion to Christianity, it was renamed *Se aeftera geola* (after the yule), and it was also called *Forma-monath*, the first month. This latter name most simply captures the nature of this month which again begins the cycle of time for another and new year.

New Year's Day and the Eighth Day of Christmas. On this first day of the year be sure to wear something new, or as the old superstition says, "You will not get much all year." Also, bad luck comes to all who clean their houses on this day: Beware of sweeping up dust or throwing out trash lest good fortune be swept away from you in the coming year. Beware of washing clothes on this day, or a member of your family may be washed away. Put a lucky penny in your children's pockets today, and in your own as well, so that good fortune will be in your pockets all year long.

1

Lost amidst the various celebrations of this holiday, the football games and family gatherings that welcome in the new year, is the **Feast of St. Clarus**, which also comes on this first day of January. By heaven's good fortune and great insight, Clarus is the perfect saint for New Year's Day, being the patron saint of those who suffer from myopia, who are shortsighted.

Rub your eyes today and ask St. Clarus, who was a French monk of the seventh century, to make you long-sighted so that you can see the big picture in life. Just as myopia causes distant objects to be blurred, myopia of the spirit causes you to lack discernment in planning ahead.

St. Clarus, aid us today that we might see clearly with both eyes, that we might be wise in planning ahead for the various possibilities hidden in this new year, and that we might behold all the blessings directly in front of us.

O good St. Clarus, whose name means *clear*, on this eighth day of Christmas, when the vision of so many is focused not on the family but only on a televised football game, give us the gift of clear vision.

❦

Also today, celebrate the **Opening of Ellis Island** in New York Bay in 1892 as a receiving station for immigrants, who ironically were the ancestors of many of today's promoters of strict anti-immigrant laws. Propose a toast today to your immigrant relatives and to the great and generous country that welcomed them here.

(The �֎ Star-Date spaces at the end of each entry in this Almanac are for your personal entries, your recording or reflection on significant occurrences in your life.)

✵

---

2 — Traditional Day the New Year Suddenly Becomes Old.

January 2 marks the cultural end of the holidays, being the day most people go back to work. This day marks the beginning of the *hollow days*, a parade of dull days of the same old thing, done in the same old ways. *Hollow days* are the result of the past continually conditioning the present. This new day in a new year will most likely be like every day of the past old year, since life is pressured to constantly repeat itself. This inclination to repeat is the reason why customs and habits resist change. Most of life, like this day, is governed by Newton's Law of Gravity rather than the Law of Gravy.

Resolve today and every day of this new year to be as new as possible. Life can only be new or taste different if you constantly add new ingredients to the *gravy sauce of life.* Those unable to introduce anything new into the days of this new year will fall victim to Newton's Law of Gravity, condemned to spend their days not on the *gravy* train but on the *grave* train.

✵

3

Feast of Janus, the Roman God of Doorways and the Patron Saint of This Doorway Month of January. Statues or pictures of Janus portray him as having eyes, a nose and mouth on both the front and back of his head! As god of the doorway he was to watch simultaneously over the front and the back doors, looking forward and backward at the same time.

While this new year is only a few days old, consider being like Janus. Look not only ahead to the coming twelve months of life but also back over the twelve months that exited three days ago. While it is not usually a compliment to be called two-faced, there is wisdom in being two-faced like Janus. We proceed best in life by looking back at our mistakes, errors in judgment and miscalculations in order not to repeat them today or in the future. At the same time, we need to look ahead as best we can and plan for the future.

Take a few minutes today to look backward at the year that became history three days ago. Ask yourself honestly what you wish you had done differently regarding your family life, your work and your spiritual life. With that information, look ahead and jot down some concrete corrections-in-course for your journey this year. You can record these insights in your ✵ Star-Date entry spaces throughout the coming months to remind you not to repeat last year's mistakes.

✵

4

Enjoy Yourself — It's Later Than You Think Day.
Once, these Twelve Days of Christmas were all days of celebration
and rejoicing. In light of the prophecies of doom for the year
2000 and beyond, consider celebrating and enjoying all 365 (366)
days of this new year. Bob Wadsworth, a contemporary visionary,
warned that the arrangement of stars on September 26, 1996,
depicted the beginning of the end, with a three and a half year
period of tribulation — that on March 10 of the year 2000, three
and one-half years later, the stars would show a gathering and
ascension to Christ of all 144,000 faithful still on earth in
preparation for approaching Armageddon.

⚜

For many years into the first half of the twenty-first century,
warnings of the Terrible End will pop up like dandelions in your
May lawn. Why wait till the year 2000, 2012, 2027 or any other
predicted day of Armageddon? Why rely on prophets of doom
to awaken you to enjoy the delights of this day? Today, rather
than making a *new year* resolution, make a *new life* resolution
to savor to the full both the sweet and sour of this and each day
of the new year.

�֎

5

Toy Day. If you're lucky enough to live with small children,
you can enjoy on this Eleventh Day of Christmas all the Christmas
toys throughout your house. Or if you have only "adult" toys to
enjoy today, you can reflect on the prophecy of this day's patron
saint, Marshal Ferdinand Foch. In the days when airplanes first
appeared, this great general and professor of strategy from the
French School of War said, "Airplanes are interesting toys, but
of no military value."

⚜

This pedestrian prophecy by Marshal Foch, once the supreme
commander of all British, French, American and allied armies
in World War I, failed to be proven true. However, Foch's prophecy
can inspire you to consider which of today's "toys of the rich"

might someday be as common as airplanes. Poor Marshal Foch should not be remembered just for this error in prophecy. Rather, take as your motto his famous statement during the critical battle of the Marne: "My left yields, my right is broken through; situation excellent: I attack."

✡

Traditional Epiphany, Twelfth Day of Christmas. 6
Now commonly celebrated on the Sunday between January 2 and 8, today is Epiphany's traditional feast day. It commemorates the arrival of the three Magi kings to adore Jesus, the Babe of Bethlehem. It was the original celebration of Christmas and still remains so in many Eastern European countries. Among the Russian Orthodox it is a feast of blessing and drinking water. This custom dates back to a pre-Christian Egyptian belief that on this day the gods turned water into wine.

Today this once-great feast in the Western world is often neglected, but you can enjoy it in your home as an occasion to reflect on the wonder of water and stars. Fill a glass, or glasses, with water and pray:

Dear God, we thank you that long ago you smiled
  and stars and comets dived into the oceans of this planet,
  fertilizing them with life.
With gratitude for the beautiful stars in the night skies
  and for the water of life piped into our homes,
  we toast you and one another: To Life!

✡

The Seventh Day of the New Year. Get lucky today, as 7
you reflect on whether your gift of a new year, with its pockets jammed with possibilities for newness, still feels new. Seven is a lucky number, and this seventh day will be full of good fortune if you realize the importance of every event of this day. Since everything in life contributes to the final outcome, nothing that you do, say or feel is insignificant. Look upon this day, and the

days to follow it, as an artist approaches a painting. Put your heart and soul into every detail, making each of life's event important regardless of how ordinary or insignificant it may seem.

Perform some hidden act of kindness today: Give a genuine smile to a stranger, choose the hard choice of telling the truth – make every act part of the masterpiece of your life. Bit by bit, piece by piece, you can construct a grand life. Blessed are those who are awake to the presence of God in every event of life. Blessed are those who agree to be co-creators with God in making their lives more beautiful and by so doing making the world more beautiful.

8 **Don't Take Down Your Christmas Decorations Day.** In ages past it was considered bad luck to remove your Christmas decorations – holly, evergreen, tree or crib – before February 2nd! "Woe to the house so foolish as to box up Christmas until the end of the forty days." If you've had a recent run of bad luck, accidents or ill fortune, the ancients would ask if your Christmas decorations are still up!

Also on this day in 1935: the **Birthday of Elvis Presley**, whose death continues to be doubted by many who believe in his countless sightings. This is a good day not to let your celebrations of Christmas die. As with the perpetual appearances of Elvis, be delighted by the surprise appearances of Christmas in the unexpected places of your life. Even if you take down your Christmas tree, keep your Christmas spirit up.

Consider making a donation of food or clothing to the poor today – in the spirit of Christmas.

"God Speed" Day. This ninth day of the new year may or may not be a Monday, but it's a good day to celebrate Plough Monday. The first Monday after the Twelfth Day of Christmas, Epiphany, was once celebrated by that feast name. In the time when all twelve days were kept as a holiday, this day marked the return of farm workers to the plough and to all their labors. As the ploughmen departed for work on this day, they did so dressed in white and singing a song with the repeating lyric, "God speed the plough." With the passage of time, this wish for success and prosperity dropped the last two words of the blessing and became simply "God speed."

9

Consider giving this old blessing today, even if the person you are blessing isn't going to use a plough. As a farewell blessing before a workday begins, "God speed" is more than wishing someone success. It can be a wish that God will break up the hard, crusty soil of the person's daily work which must be ploughed through, that God will be the energy for bringing prosperity out of failures and good out of evil. Hidden within these two words is the blessing, "God speed you through jammed rush-hour traffic and the snarls of bureaucratic red tape, and in all ways may God help you break open new ground."

Death Day of Buffalo Bill — Death of an Age, 1917. Bill Cody shocked his friends when he asked to be baptized as a Roman Catholic at the age of seventy. He was a Catholic for only one day before dying in 1917. Buffalo Bill was a Pony Express rider, an Indian scout and a Civil War soldier, all before the age of twenty! His nickname came from an eighteen-month period staring in 1867 during which he shot 4,280 buffalo to be used as food for the men building the American railroads. At age thirty-eight he organized his first Wild West exhibition that included such celebrities as Sitting Bull and Annie Oakley. His Wild West Show traveled the United States and even gave command performances for Queen Victoria and the crown heads

10

of Europe. With Buffalo Bill died one of the most romantic periods of American history. The expansion of the railroads, the immigrant invasion and the crisscrossing of the prairie with barbwire fences, closed the era of the Wild West.

⚜

Today, as in the early 1900s, an age is ending. We refuse to acknowledge that it's dying — just like those who longed to keep alive the Old West. Perhaps, like Buffalo Bill, we should create a show that displays all the nostalgic spirit, the flare and flamboyance of the second half of the twentieth century. Then again, maybe it already exists and millions go to see it. We call it Disneyland, a "land of yesteryear" with no slums, no poor, liter- and smog-free, filled with happy, youthful faces.

Each of us today has the option, like Sitting Bull and Annie Oakley, to star in such a grand exhibition. Actually we have two choices: We can star in a show of daily life called "The Good Old Days" or one called "Tomorrow Land." This second choice need not take us into a science fiction future but rather points to the tomorrow of which the prophets spoke and which Jesus said had already come. Jesus lived his life in God's time and invited his disciples to join him in that prophetic age of justice and peace. While most around him lived in a time of the Old Law, Jesus lived in the New Law of God, a time of justice for the poor and those on the margins of society, an equality that excluded no one from his friendship, a time of generous forgiveness and unconditional love for all. If you wish to do more than visit God's Tomorrow Land and desire to be a star like Annie Oakley, then daily live what Jesus taught: that the kingdom of God has arrived. Those who live in such a way truly live not in the Good Old Days but in the Good New(s) Days!

�֎

---

11 **The Birthday of the Wool Sweater.** If the bitter-cold north wind is howling at your windows and doors, be sure to dress warmly before going out. As you slip into your sweater, gives thanks and remember. Today, celebrate the birthday of woolen clothes over 6,000 years ago in Babylon. Next, thank the

Spanish explorer Coronado's expedition, which in 1540 brought a few Spanish sheep to New Mexico. Then thank the colonists at Jamestown who imported English sheep in 1609.

Today's well-heated offices and homes can easily make a wool sweater live up to its name, causing its wearer to *sweat* freely. This pullover began as a type of throw-over blanket used to make horses sweat after a workout. Later it was used as a garment by athletes and continued to live up to its name. Soon the fashion industry produced stylish pullovers as a source of warmth in cold and wet weather. The horse sweater is the great grandparent of today's flannel sweat pants and shirts.

Back in the days of the horse sweater, a common expression was "to sweat the truth" out of someone. When you look at the label on your sweatshirt, you may see that it was made in a third world country. This very fact should make you sweat! The reality of women and children working for pennies making those sweaters should make you sweat out a confession that we are all interconnected in a global social sin.

If you're thinking of buying a wool sweater, which can be very expensive, and are tempted to buy a cheap third-world substitute, consider again the confession that might be sweated out of it. Also, if you're doing anything involved with quality, take a few moments to reflect on this saying, "The bitter taste of poor quality lingers long after the brief sweetness of a cheap price is forgotten." Remember too that the best "sweater" to keep your children warm all day at school is to wrap them up in an affectionate hug and kiss before they leave home.

(Remember to use your ✯ Star-Date space in this Almanac to record important milestones in your personal or family history.)

✯

12

"Stop All That Racket and Go Away" Day. As the new year begins, consider briefly those who are disturbed when opportunity comes knocking at their doors. When an opportunity knocks at your door, regardless of how it is dressed, lay aside whatever you're doing, go to the door and welcome it. Great opportunities come to your door rarely, and even more rarely do they come back if no one answers when they knock.

Today, memorize and frequently refer to these lines from Shakespeare's *Julius Caesar*, Act IV:

> There is a tide in the affairs of men,
> which, taken at the flood, leads on to fortune;
> Omitted, all the voyage of their life
> Is bound in shallows and in miseries.

❧❀☙

The knock at your door in the coming days of this new year may be to awaken you to the fact that the tide is rising, that it's time to depart. Even if an opportunity comes knocking at your door dressed as defeat, as the end of a dream or a sorry mistake, open wide your door, and yourself, and invite this "opportunity" in.

---

13 Feast of the Holy Bed of St. Hilary of Poitiers.

Hilary was born with a silver spoon in his mouth, into a wealthy family in Gaul, which is now called France. He became a Christian at age thirty-five and against his strong objections was made a bishop in the year 350. The bed in which he died was given a place of honor in the cathedral of Poitiers and called "Hilary's Cradle." In the Middle Ages, it was widely believed that if anyone mad or insane could be enticed to spend the night in his bed, that person would rise up in the morning fully cured.

❧❀☙

Tonight, if you are troubled — "out of your mind" with anxieties — or mad — as in very angry with someone — consider making your bed into "Hilary's Cradle." Pray before retiring that whatever is driving you crazy, stinging you like a serpent (St. Hilary is also the patron of snakebites) will be cured as you sleep. Beds are places of nightly miracles, for sleep and dreaming hold the power to sort out issues, lessen the stings of life and heal the upset heart. Studies have shown that those who are prevented from a good night's rest and the ability to dream can eventually be driven insane. As you lay down tonight, give thanks for God's restorative gift of sleep – and also for your bed, the site of a million miracles.

✡

14

A Good Day to Break the Ice. From the days when England first became a navigational power, the river Thames brought ships up to London. In the dead of winter, however, the greatest fear was that the famed river would freeze over. With London's docks being over forty miles from the mouth of the river at the channel, the tides were unable to push brine far enough up the river to prevent a freeze. Small boats were unable to do their work because of the heavy ice that would typically form. In January, English boatmen were forced to "break the ice" before beginning to get down to the business of navigation. From the docks of London, this river-talk has become a common expression for any method of initiating some activity.

Taking time to break the ice is wise work before beginning any engagement of business or pleasure. Someone once said that doing business with Arabs requires at least one and a half hours: half an hour to say hello and to visit about each other's families and health, half an hour for the actual business, and then another half an hour to say good-bye.

Today, everyone is in a hurry, and we often feel a need to plunge directly into the icy waters of the business at hand and to jump out as soon as the business is completed. I believe you will agree that we do the same with God in prayer. Consider taking time today to "break the ice" with God as you chat about your family and life before you plunge into the "business" of prayer.

✡

15 Birthday of Dr. Martin Luther King, Jr., 1929.

This national holiday is a movable feast celebrated on the third Monday in January. This day in 1929 in Atlanta, Georgia, marks the actual birthday of the African-American Baptist minister who was the leader of the American Civil Rights Movement until his assassination in 1968. From the mid 1950s till his death, Dr. King's eloquent leadership was instrumental in ending the segregation of blacks in the South and elsewhere in the United States.

SSt. (secular saint) Martin Luther King, Jr. should be a hero not just to Black Americans but to peoples of all races. We should do more than take pride in his heroism and willingness to stake his life on the cause of equal rights for all — we should be inspired to continue that struggle. Be inspired by him whenever you are told to be patient with existing inequalities. Today, recall his words in a speech at the beginning of the Montgomery, Alabama, bus boycott, "We have no alternative but to protest. For many years we have shown an amazing patience. But we come here tonight to be saved from that patience that makes us patient with anything less than freedom and justice."

Today, ask God to grant you that kind of heroic impatience with the continued inequalities present in almost every aspect of our lives. Also today, examine your own racial — and other — prejudices.

16 Celebration of the First Vatican—Feast of St. Priscilla.

Priscilla was the wealthy Roman widow of Mancius Glabrio who allowed St. Peter of Galilee to use her home on the Via Slaria as his headquarters in Rome. Beneath the site of her home is a catacomb, named in her honor, in which she is buried. Priscilla is the patron saint of all widows.

This January day thus provides us with an opportunity to celebrate a much needed feast in our calendar of holidays. We have a mother's and a grandmother's day, why not a widow's day? While they are no longer as defenseless and victimized as in the ancient world, where to be "manless" was to be among the weakest of the weak, widows today deserve a special day in their honor.

Also use this day to playfully ponder how the Catholic Church might have evolved differently if its head bishop had followed Peter's example and always remained a guest in someone else's home — and a woman's home at that!

✴

Birthday of Benjamin Franklin, 1706. The various **17** accomplishments of this genius, this jack-of-*all* trades and master of *many*, were surpassed in his day only by Thomas Jefferson. The publisher of a newspaper (the first to have cartoons and to use maps to illustrate news stories) and the author of *Poor Richard's Almanack* for every year from 1733 to 1758, he is the secular patron saint of almanac authors. His almanac was filled with his many insights and poetic pearls of wisdom, like "God helps those who help themselves" and "Early to bed and early to rise makes a man healthy, wealthy, and wise." Franklin was also a scientist; his often-pictured experiments with electricity using a kite led him to invent the lightning rod. In addition, he invented bifocal lenses for glasses and the Franklin stove that produced more heat while using less fuel than other stoves in that age. Although the space of this almanac does not allow us to list all his honors or his political and civil achievements, we have ample reason today to honor this American genius and patriot.

❧❀❧

In 1789 George Washington wrote this to Franklin: "...you must have the pleasing consolation to know that you have not lived in vain." How wonderful if these same words could be said of you and me at the end of our lives. Do something today — even if unseen by others and not as famous as the lightning rod

— that will give you the consolation to know that you have not lived in vain.

✵

---

18 **Feast of the Lost Magi.** By tradition this day celebrates the story of how the Three Magi, on their way home, couldn't agree on which star to follow, and so parted company. Magus Melchior followed a bright star in the northwest sky, claiming it was the one which would lead the way home. King Caspar followed an equally bright star in the northeastern sky, moved by the fierce conviction that it was the right guide. King Balthasar parted company with the other two and continued to follow a bright star high in the middle of the northern sky. (Note: The end of this Lost Magi story can be found in an upcoming entry in this Almanac. Don't go in search of it; just let its appearance be a surprise gift.)

~≈✺≈~

January 18 is the feast day of those following the wrong stars in life, or who are afraid they are doing so. A good question for today is, "Which star, heroine or hero, vision or dream, are you presently following?"

✵

---

19 **Birthday of Robert E. Lee, 1807.** This is a feast day of losers in life, a day that should become a new American holiday, celebrated with parades and holiday spirit. While ticker-tape parades understandably honor winners of Super Bowls and elections, we also need a celebration for losers. General Robert Edward Lee, commander of the Confederate armies, who lost the Civil War, once said that duty is the sublimest word in the English language. A model of nobility, Lee is a secular patron saint for losers.

Viscount Wolseley, a distinguished British soldier, said of Lee, "I have met many of the great men of my time, but Lee alone impressed me with the feeling that I was in the presence of a man who was cast in a grander mold and made of different and finer metal than all other men."

Lee is a hero to be admired and an example to be followed, especially in our culture that values only winning – whether a game, an argument, a contract or the love of another person. Defeat is among the most painful of life's afflictions. Some will go to great lengths to never lose or even admit a mistake, so great is their need to be winners – or, perhaps, to not be losers. Today in some way, large or small, you will lose. As you do, remember General Robert E. Lee and surrender with dignity and honor.

20

Leandro P. Rissuto Day. In 1959, with only $100, Leandro and his parents started a company to market hair rollers for beauty salons. They soon realized that if a way could be found for hair salons to speed up the hair drying of clients, drooping revenues could be increased. Leandro Rissuto to the rescue! In 1971 he introduced the first handheld hair blow-dryer in the United States. On what for most of the readers of this book is a cold winter day, Leandro's invention insures that you won't go outside in the bitter cold with a wet head.

In addition, more than a dry head of hair is possible with Rissuto's creation. Among your hair dryer's many uses are: defrosting frozen pipes, a too common occurrence in this winter season; drying wet boots and shoes (using a low setting); unfreezing windows frozen shut; thawing a frozen lock on your car. And for a special treat on a cold winter's night, use your hair dryer to warm your cold sheets so you can climb into a toasty-warm bed.

The spiritual life and the practical life are one, and the wise person removes the line between them. Hair dryers can be tools for erasing that line. Having cabin fever or being in the doldrums is common in these gray days of winter. *Doldrums* originally referred to the area where sailing ships were stalled because of a lack of wind — perhaps the word is a blending of *dull* and *tantrums,* since the lack of a wind to energize your sails could lead to tantrums. So if you find yourself down in the dumps, becalmed "without a wind," consider praying with your hair dryer!

Say a prayer to the Holy Spirit, perhaps even sing to yourself the old hymn "Come, Holy Ghost," setting your hair dryer on low and blowing your hair in all directions. As you do, let your sails be filled with your homemade holy gale. Enjoy the mirth of "making wind" with your hair dryer; let it encourage you to use your good humor as a spring breeze to lift the spirits of others on this winter doldrums day.

✳

---

21 Feast of St. Agnes, Patroness of Virgins & Girl Scouts.

In 304 Agnes rejected the marriage proposal of the Roman governor's son, saying she had chosen Christ as her beloved. For refusing to be married, she was stripped naked and led publicly through the streets to a brothel, there to be used by one and all. Yet her courage and purity were such that no man presumed to come near her. Afterwards she was sentenced to die by beheading.

Since her name sounds like *agnus,* Latin for "lamb," on this day the pope annually blesses two lambs in Rome. The wool from these lambs is used to make a pallium, a white woolen yoke which is worn at liturgical services by Catholic archbishops as the sign of their office.

It was once a practice on St. Agnes' feast for unmarried girls to dream of their future husbands. They would see "the man of their dreams" if on the eve of Agnes' feast they would fast for twenty-four hours and then eat an egg with salt just before bedtime.

❧❀❧

Age-old observances aside, Agnes the Brave can be a perfect patron saint for all of us today whose beliefs are challenged, especially those of us who often choose silence instead of speaking out. In the presence of hate and discrimination, most of us lack the courage to speak out boldly, as did Agnes, for what is right. Though few if any of us will be called to glorious storybook martyrdom, may St. Agnes inspire us to embrace a "Monday martyrdom," a workaday willingness to be ridiculed for our beliefs.

✳

Pedestrian Prophecy Day, 1977. This shortsighted prophecy was made relatively recently, in 1977: "There is no reason for any individuals to have a computer in their home" — Ken Olsen, president, chairman and founder of Distal Equipment Corporation.

22

❧❦❧

The future today isn't what it used to be! For one thing it arrives much more quickly than ever before. If your future looks drab and limited, perhaps it is because it is only an attic filled with dusty yesterdays. As you look at your life on this day, what do you feel is impossible? Make a short list of these impossibilities; then remember Ken Olsen's statement and look at that list of impossibilities a second time.

✳

Birthday of John Hancock, 1737. As president of the Continental Congress from 1775 to 1777, Hancock won fame for the brash boldness with which he signed the Declaration of Independence. His name written in beautiful penmanship was the first of those who placed their lives and fortunes on the line to proclaim their dream of independence from the English Crown. On June 12, 1775, the British offered a pardon to all colonists who would surrender their arms. There were only two exceptions to this amnesty: Samuel Adams and John Hancock. If either were captured, he was to be hanged — the price of being controversial and prominent. Yet his boldness won him a lasting name in history.

23

❧❦❧

Even to this day, when asked to sign your name, the frequent request is: "Put down your John Hancock." Like your fingerprints, your signature is unique and should be written boldly and proudly, even if only on a credit card charge slip. When we type a letter or send a purchased greeting card with a printed verse, we usually still handwrite our name at the bottom. Yet handwriting itself is a dying art, and we might ask if even these last relics of an ancient art form will soon disappear. Will the ever present computer in the home or school or on the lap cripple the art of handwriting? Will tomorrow's adults lack the skill and beauty of handwriting known in previous pre-technological ages and modeled in the signature of John Hancock? The Word made flesh is God's wondrously beautiful signature in Jesus and in the infinite variety of us human beings. Your signature is a sacrament of that incarnation. So, like John Hancock, write it boldly and beautifully.

✺

24 Birthday of Fundamentalism, 1923.

On this day in 1923 William Jennings Bryan, the famous orator from Nebraska, stirred up controversy over the question of evolution while addressing a group of ministers in St. Paul, Minnesota. The theory of evolution, he said, is a "program of infidelity masquerading under the name of science." The debate was quickly picked up by newspapers, which gave the names "fundamentalists" and "modernists" to the two opposing sides.

In the year 1858 Charles Darwin and Alfred Russell had independently published the theory of evolution, which held that all life-forms on earth descended from common prehistoric ancestors. Evolution, or the natural selection theory, is based on scientific research in genetics and paleontology (the study of fossils, the remains of prehistoric skeletal structures). Fossils show that over the course of history some species have completely died out and that others, including humans, appeared much later in time, having evolved from previous or lower life-forms.

In 1925, John Scopes, a public school teacher, was arrested and tried for teaching evolution, which was against the Tennessee state law, a law not repealed until 1967. Scopes' lawyer was C.S.

Darrow, and William Jennings Bryan aided the prosecutor. Scopes was convicted but released on a technicality.

✦

The debate continues to this day, with religiously good people profoundly convinced that the theory of evolution is evil and contrary to the Bible. Abundant scientific evidence of the evolutionary development of the earth and creatures does not alter the conviction of fundamentalists, who regard evolution as "infidelity" to God's word. The most literal hold that in the first six days of creation God created every type of creature that has ever lived. In the sixteenth century Martin Luther declared, "I hold animals took their being at once upon the word of God." Luther taught that while an individual bird may die, its species cannot.

In the early years of the debate a rich variety of arguments was given by various clergy to explain the prehistoric bones increasingly being discovered by the sixteenth century. One interesting suggestion was that they were bones of creatures who had dillydallied on their way to Noah's Ark and so were lost in the great flood. (This idea even bent the Biblical texts, since God told Noah to bring two of *every* living creature into his ark.) Others theorized that the skeleton bones were not really bones, but were stones created by God that only looked like bones, and that they were test creatures that were discarded by the Creator. Still others held that fossils were God's blueprint shapes of future creatures. While these and other creative explanations abounded, all agreed that the Bible held the literal truth, and these supposed creatures had never existed, that the animals presently on earth had to be the very same species that had come out of Noah's Ark.

As early as a hundred years before the birth of Jesus, Lurcretius, a Roman poet-philosopher, wrote about the fossils of prehistoric animals. Although he never saw an actual dinosaur bone, Lucretius declared that "Everything is on the move. Everything is transformed by nature and forced into new paths." Lurcretius' view of fossils and evolution was condemned as heresy by the Catholic Church in the fourth century. In 1997, however, some fifteen hundred years later, Pope John Paul II affirmed the likelihood of this once heretical belief!

⚜

Use a few moments today to reflect on this fact: It is estimated that at least ninety-nine percent of all species that ever lived are now extinct! After more than 2,100 years since the writings of Lurcretius, are you ready to acknowledge not only the possibility of evolution, but perhaps even more startling revelations of science?

✴

25 The Feast of the Conversion of Saint Paul. Today celebrates being knocked off our high horses as was Saul of Tarsus on his way to Damascus. Saul was delegated to go to Damascus to arrest members of the *Jesus sect* and to bring them back in chains for trial. On the way to Damascus, however, an explosion of light threw him off his horse. As he lay on the ground blinded, he heard a voice say to him, "Saul, Saul, why do you persecute me?" When Saul asked who was speaking, the voice replied, "I am Jesus, whom you are persecuting" (See Acts 9: 1-5). Saul converted and became St. Paul, considered along with St. Peter to be the cofounder of Christianity.

⚜

Are you ready to be knocked off your high horse today and converted from some firmly and passionately held belief? Many are those who hold so tightly to their present religious beliefs that they have glued themselves to their saddles to prevent even God from throwing them off their horses. Saul's blindness was temporary, lasting only three days. Some fanatics, alas, remain as blind as Saul, glued to their saddles, as they ride onward unconverted. Reflect, on this feast day of radical conversion, whether you hold any belief or philosophical position that you would refuse to change even if God asked you to be converted to a new belief.

✴

The Birthday of the Tin Can, 1795.

26

In most of the United States on this January day snow covers the backyard gardens of those who still have a garden. If we want a dish of peas, however, all we do is open a can. Pause, today, with can opener in hand, and give thanks to Nicolas Appert for his invention of the tin can.

Napoleon firmly held the belief that armies marched on their stomachs. They also marched during the winter. In 1795, therefore, Napoleon offered a prize for the best practical way to preserve food for use by his armies. First prize, (one wonders what was second or third) was won by the French inventor, Nicolas Appert.

❦

Prayers before meals are rare today. If we were not blinded to the marvels of daily life, being able to eat fresh vegetables or canned foods in the midst of winter would cause us to break out in praise. Few kings and queens of olden days could have such wonderful meals as the average person eats today. Before you pick up your fork to eat any meal today, pause for a moment. Take time to look at what is on your plate; then consider how it came to be there. You will not likely find it difficult to pray in thanksgiving.

✦

The Birthday of the National Geographic Society, Established on This Date in 1888 in Washington, D.C.

27

The National Geographic Society was founded on this day in 1888 and soon thereafter sponsored expeditions to the North and South Poles by Robert Peary and Richard Byrd respectively. It is now the largest scientific organization in the world, dedicated to the spread of geographic information among all Earth's peoples, from one pole to the other.

❦

The National Geographic Magazine is famed for the beauty of its photographs of various exotic places throughout the world.

Consider, today, viewing your home, your way to work and even your workplace through the lens of a camera of a *National Geographic* photographer. See with new eyes how beautiful is your world. You might also consider taking a short expedition and exploring something nearby that you have never visited before. Leave home on this expedition with the same enthusiasm and promise of a Peary or Byrd.

✴

28 **End of the World Day — 133 Million B.C.** The International Nautical Congress of Fish and Marine Reptiles today declared the End of the World! This prediction came as the vast oceans covering much of the earth dramatically began to disappear. As these large water areas were drying up, the approach of ancient Armageddon seemed immanent. Then, after a transitional time during which the huge sea beds were barren and exposed, the earth started once again to blossom in a colorful transformation as thousands of species of flowering plants arose from the wasteland. Instead of the end of the world, it was a floral revolution!

❧⚘☙

Today, when cult or religious groups ring the panic alarm for the end of the world or the death of some institution, church or group, remember this day 133 million years ago and do not panic. Instead, find hope in earth's *long* history. The time of transition may seem long and painful, but today light a candle of hope and rejoice that God, ever the Re-creator, can reshape worlds, institutions, and even you, out of death into new forms of life. Unlike the once-exposed, dried-up ocean beds, you, however, have free choice. You can choose to hinder or to cooperate as a co-creator with God's creative and recreative design.

✴

29 **The Nationalization Act Passage Day, 1795.** On this day in 1795 Congress passed the Nationalization Act, requiring a five-year residence in this country before a person could become a citizen of the United States. More importantly, the act also required renunciation of all national allegiances and titles of nobility.

This January day celebrates America as the "land of no lords or ladies." Even after more than two hundred years, however, the renunciation of royal titles dies hard. Many are those who diet and exercise as they dream of becoming homecoming queens and kings. In a few brief days, Valentine kings and queens of hearts will sprout up all over the land, mirroring the countless fraternal orders and mystical women's organizations that abound with noble titles. Also, many are those who swear allegiance to multinational corporations whose reign is greater than any earthly kingdom.

✠

The spirit of equality among all, regardless of race, religion and bank accounts, comes slowly. Perhaps we can look forward to the year 2095 with the hope that finally we will have lost our medieval taste for royal titles. On this anniversary of the passage of the Nationalization Act in 1795, you might consider applying for international citizenship as a cosmopolite, a citizen of the cosmos. Being a cosmopolite might inspire you to treat all peoples as neighbors and equals, regardless of their national or regional citizenship.

✦

The Unorthodox Feast of the Magi's Return Home. 30

Reread the Almanac entry for January 18th on the Lost Magi. Today celebrates the miracle that all three Magi arrived at their home city on the same day, and at the same time. To their delight and awe, while each came from a different direction, on a different road, they met one another on a hill outside their home city. To their wonderment, they discovered they each had been following the same star, only seeing it from a different angle.

✠

Today's feast celebrates the richness of unity in life that seems to be disguised as diversity — whether in politics, religions or matters of belief. While beginning in different directions, various roads lead to the same place; what is important is to find your road. Once you discover the best road for you, follow it with confidence and joy.

⚜

Today is also the anniversary of the **Birthday of Franklin Delano Roosevelt** in 1882. His life-road led to being the thirty-second President of the United States and to leading his country in times of great crisis and war — and he traveled that road in a wheelchair!

---

31 Cope with the Problem in a Nonviolent Way Day.

This last day of January honors the American paleontologist Edward Cope, who lived from 1840 to 1897. His large collection of fossil mammals (you might reread the entry in this Almanac for January 24) is at the American Museum of Natural History in New York. Cope was a Quaker and so refused to carry a gun during his fossil-hunting expeditions in the West, despite the great danger of being killed by unfriendly Native American Indians.

Once, when surrounded by a band of hostile warriors, he astounded his would-be attackers by removing his false teeth and putting them back into his mouth again and again. The surprised Indians let him go without harm, overwhelmed either with astonishment or humor.

⚜

As we close the cover on this first month of the new year, spend a few moments reflecting on how you can "Cope" with your problems when you feel surrounded by hostile attackers — or even by the devil. Nonviolence does not mean rolling over and playing dead, but perhaps simply playing, making yourself look silly and so entertaining your enemy. With or without false teeth, ponder on Cope's method of playing with peace today when you are confronted with a need to cope.

✳

THE

MONTH

OF

FEBRUARY

This second month is named for Febura, a Roman festival of purification once celebrated on February 15th. In Latin the name means "I purify by sacrifice." It is fitting that Lent begins in this second month, for this spiritual season provides an excellent opportunity to be purified by sacrifice and prayer. It was once said that if the weather is fine and frosty at the end of January and the beginning of February, it is wise not to put away one's warm winter clothes, for there is more winter ahead than behind. The Anglo-Saxons named this second month *Sprout-Kale*, for the time of the sprouting of kale or cabbage. They also called February *Fill-Dyke*, since it is the season when the snow melts and rains fall, causing the ditches to fill to overflowing. An old proverb says,

February fill dyke, be it black or be it white.
But if it be white, it's the better to like.

Feast of Holy and Humorous St. Brigid of Ireland, the Patroness of Nuns, Milkmaids and Fugitives.

1

Known as the "Mary of Ireland," this woman saint was a powerful force in Gaelic Christianity, known for her holiness and for performing miracles. Legend holds that a holy but slightly drunk Saint Mel consecrated her a bishop, and so she can be the patroness of women priests and bishops. Blessed Brigid, hasten the ordination of women in our day — for that will surely be a miracle.

Today, pray for bishops, or a new Church Council, drunk with the same wine as the apostles on the first Pentecost, the wine of the Holy Spirit. So intoxicated by the divine, they might see clearly that nothing other than prejudice prevents women from being ordained priests and bishops. After all, early Christian home churches had leaders who were women, and it was the tradition for those community leaders to preside at the Eucharistic Meal. Even if no basis for such equality in all things could be found in Scripture or tradition, Jesus told his disciples, "I have much more to tell you, but you cannot bear to hear it now" (Jn. 16: 12), that the Spirit of God would continue to guide us. Surely the Spirit can lead us to this Godly reality of equality and the full use of all God's gifts. On this feast day of St. Brigid, regardless of your church or religious faith, pray that in the new millennium women may be given full, rightful and equal status.

St. Brigid was also known for her good humor. A touch of Irish wit is only proper on her feast. There's a story of a family from Kerry that was delighted when an Irish matchmaker found a wife for their handsome but poor eldest son. The matchmaker's choice was the daughter of a very rich Waterford farmer. But when the eldest son saw the bride-to-be, he turned her down. His father asked, "Lad, what's wrong with her? She's from a rich family!"

"Begob," said the son, "she's lame!"

"And what's that to it?" asked the father. "Surely you're not wanting her for racing?"

�֍

---

2 **Groundhog Day and the Feast of the Purification, or Candlemas, the End of Traditional Christmas.** Forty days after Christmas, this feast celebrates Jesus being presented in the temple, where the rites of purification were performed for Mary, his mother. Since the liturgy for this feast of the Purification refers to Jesus as the Light of the world, it became the custom to bless candles on this day — thus the name Candle Mass or Candlemas. In former ages, this day marked the conclusion of the celebration of Christmas, and only then were home decorations removed. One tradition called for cutting down the tree from which would come the yule log to be used the next Christmas. Such ancient customs seem quaint to us today — for our customs are dictated more by the business market and its power-gospel of advertising.

~~✵~~

Today also marks the midpoint in the season of winter and is by tradition a day for forecasting weather and the arrival of spring. Yet this highly anticipated forecast is made not by computers or radar but by a groundhog. Coming out of his hole, if the groundhog sees his shadow, he returns for six more weeks of hibernation. If there is no shadow, he climbs out of bed to greet the early arrival of spring.

Hibernation is practiced by more than just groundhogs. In nature its purpose is for the survival of life in the midst of hostile winter. Humans, however, also hibernate to escape from the harsh realities of life. Many are those who retreat into their holes from hostile forces, real or imagined, only occasionally peeking out to test the emotional weather. On this second day of February, ask yourself if you are hibernating from some threat, problem or difficult issue instead of coming out of your hole. Like the groundhog, when we hibernate we become sluggish of spirit, our gifts remain dormant and our lives are lived only half-awake.

✵

Spiritual Weather Forecast Day. The shadow of the clouds of doom and gloom have hung over humanity since time began. Armageddon, the day of doom, seems to be an elastic day. The battle of Armageddon was forecast in the book of the Apocalypse (Rev. 16: 16) as the great battle between good and evil, the Devil's "Last Stand." Many spiritual forecasters are predicting one or another year around the millennium crossing as the terrible time of Armageddon. They look for signs in society and in nature as the overture to this final day of destruction.

The signs used to forecast this approach of the End Times are many, ranging from the way the stars are constellated in the sky to the proposed common currencies in North America and Europe.

✦

Noah is the patron saint of weather forecasters, and also the patron of those who ride out the storm. Today, when stormy weather predictions of destruction are common, let Noah and his wife be inspirations that you can ride out the storm if you are willing to build an ark.

No wood is needed for this ark, only the lumber of love soaked in hope. Fasten together the planks with prayerful devotion and secure them with an iron trust in God's abounding love. Bring aboard your ark not simply your family but all of creation as your companions. Then live in your ark; make it your home, rain or shine. I solemnly assure you that regardless of how terrible and long is the storm, you will see God's rainbow when the clouds clear.

✷

---

4 **Birthday of Rosa Louise Parks, 1913.** Today's festival honors the birth of the brave African-American woman who refused to give up her seat in the front of a bus to a white man on December 1, 1955. Her courage in refusing to acknowledge the validity of Montgomery, Alabama's segregated seating laws led to her arrest by the police. Her brave defiance of the injustice and ugly evils of racial segregation initiated the Montgomery bus boycott by African-Americans, beginning the Civil Rights Movement in the United States.

✦

Rosa Parks broke a law so that laws could be made forbidding segregation. This day offers an opportunity to examine how each of us responds to injustice in words or by actions. Rejoice, today, in the birth of this heroine whose quiet determination to resist evil began a revolution for the civil rights of all Americans that continues to ripple throughout the world.

✷

Feast of St. Agatha, Patroness of Buns and Bells. This Sicilian saint is invoked in the face of danger from breast diseases, fires and volcanic eruptions. In 251 she rejected the advances of a pagan Roman senator, who thereupon had her breasts cut off. In art she is typically shown holding them on a plate. People who didn't know her story easily mistook these artistic representations for bells or buns, and so she became the patroness of bell makers and bun bakers. On this day, round buns or breads were once blessed in churches and were called Agatha's buns. The rest of her patronage is explained by the fact that she was sentenced to be burned at the stake but her execution was interrupted by a Sicilian volcanic eruption. Eventually she was beheaded.

5

❧⚕☙

Consider calling on St. Agatha the next time you are caught in a sudden volcanic eruption — whether it happens at a mountain on the Pacific Rim or in your home, your office or on the street. As the pace of life grows ever more hectic, such volcanic explosions are becoming commonplace.

Contemporary advertising uses women's breasts to attract customers to products that range from spark plugs to spare parts. This feast that views Agatha's breasts as blessed offers an opportunity to restore women's breasts to their bodies rather than being perceived as objects for commercialization.

Perhaps instead of churches blessing buns as symbols of Agatha's breasts on this day, the coming years will see a new ritual of blessing breasts on her feast. Such a blessing might assist the respectful viewing of a woman's entire body as good and beautiful. And the present threat of breast cancer makes Agatha's feast a powerful holy day for women.

✠

The Birthday of Babe Ruth, 1895. George Herman, the Babe, was born on this day in 1895 in Baltimore, Maryland. His baseball career began in 1914; after pitching for the Boston Red Sox, he was sold in 1920 to the New York Yankees where he

6

played in the outfield. He set many records, and was called the greatest slugger in baseball because of the 714 home runs he hit in regular season games. Yet what is often overlooked is that the great Babe Ruth struck out over 1,000 times!

⚜

This February day provides a tonic for you if it seems that you are constantly "striking out," missing the mark and making mistakes. Do not feel dejected by your string of errors; rather, find encouragement in Babe Ruth who was remembered not for his records in striking out but for his home runs.

Fear of striking out, whether in business or romance, in prayer or politics, should never prevent you from stepping up to the plate and taking a swing at whatever life next pitches at you. Don't hide in the dugout of life, protesting that you only make errors, but with the swagger of the Babe walk up to bat with confidence.

God loves losers, as was clearly shown by Jesus of Nazareth, whose death on the cross was the ultimate strikeout — for it appeared that the devil and evil had won the game and defeated not only all that is good and right but even God. God does more with strikeouts than with home runs, or so it seems in the message of the Gospels. The Good News lived out by Jesus was that everything is upside down, the reversal of society's status structure, the world's way of winning. By his parables and by his life, Jesus taught God's lesson that often what is out is in, defeat is victory and those who are up are really down.

✶

---

7 **Pedestrian Prophecy Day, 1899.** "Everything that can be invented has been invented" — Charles H. Duell, Commissioner of the U.S. Office of Patents, speaking in 1899. Reflect, today, on all that has awed the world since 1899 and you will have a snapshot of what awaits us in the twenty-first century. As someone once said, "The future ain't what it use to be."

⚜

This Almanac acts as a bridge between millenniums. The

supersonic speed at which new discoveries and inventions will appear in this new millennium will be awesome. Each new advance in technology and science, however, requires a corresponding advance in our thinking. Albert Einstein once said, "Since the breaking of the atom, everything in the world has changed but our thinking."

Look about your life and reflect on how some commonplace twentieth century invention has changed the way you think, the way you see the world and yourself. See if it has expanded your vision and your heart. A test case for this reflection could be to ask yourself whether television, as a window on the world, has made you more compassionate toward the sufferings of the peoples of other nations? Has television been an instrument of entertainment or of expanding your heart to include your neighbors in need on the other side of the globe?

Consider applying this experiment to other twentieth century inventions.

⚜

February Pentecost Vigil. The annual celebration of the Holy Spirit, the feast of Pentecost, comes fifty days after Easter. In the prayer and worship year, today celebrates the second feast of the Spirit. This February feast of God's Holy Wind initiates the coming Lenten Season, forty windblown days on the way to Easter.

The Gospels tell us that it was the Spirit of God that drove Jesus into the desert for his forty days of prayer and fasting. We, likewise, need to have God's Holy Wind at our backs if we wish to celebrate a productive and prayerful Lenten season.

⁂

Today is a good day to begin to prepare for Lent by praying for the gift of God's Wind to fill your sails. Woe to those who leave port on Ash Wednesday with no wind behind them, for they face the curse of being stalled, as if they had never raised anchor. Don't be caught off guard by the sudden appearance of Ash Wednesday; begin today to pray for God's Wind. This prayer could be part of your daily pre-Lenten devotions:

Come, Holy Spirit, and inspire me to renewal and reform,
   challenge me to prepare for days
   of reinvention and recreation.

✵

---

9 Feast of St. Apollonia, Martyr and Patroness of Dentists and Those Afflicted with Toothaches.

Apollonia was an unmarried woman of Alexandria in Egypt in the third century. For providing a safe house for Christians, a mob of pagans tortured her, breaking and removing her teeth in the process of trying to kill her. Fearing that she would deny her faith as a result of her great pain, Apollonia leapt into a fire and died.

Apollonia's martyrdom made her the patroness of those who suffer from toothaches as well as the patroness of professionals who attempt to remove the pain. Be grateful today if your religion does not forbid your seeking relief from painful tooth problems.

⚜

The feast of Apollonia provides an occasion to reflect on the pain experienced at the termination of life. Like a root canal or the removal of a wisdom tooth, dying can hardly be painless. This feast also raises the question of the right to anticipate your death, since saintly Apollonia apparently thought she had this right. Anticipation is a legal and musical term with spiritual implications. In law, *anticipation* refers to the use of an inheritance before it is available for use. In music it means introducing a note of a new cord before the previous chord is resolved.

On this feast of Apollonia, consider discussing anticipated death with friends or family. Death is the doorway to a new song of life and the reward of our inheritance Jesus promised to those who believe in him. If you can legally and musically anticipate, can you not also morally anticipate your death — and your promised inheritance? Before making a quick judgement on this moral problem, consider today's lack of universal medical care, especially for the poor and certain terminally ill persons, and the scarcity of hospice care. These issues, along with making medicines for controlling and removing pain easily available to all who are in need of them, are all significant aspects of this moral question. Pray, today, to Apollonia, as the patroness of those who contemplate anticipating their deaths, for guidance and faith.

⚜

Today in 1870 also marked the **Establishment of the U.S. Weather Bureau.** If you are brave enough to have an open, free discussion of the issue of anticipated death, I can predict without much risk of error that you will experience stormy weather today.

✵

The Second Coming of the Groundhog. On this day, according to some old legends, the groundhog again comes out of his hole to check on whether winter is about over. Regardless of his previous prediction on February 2, today he makes a new prediction based on the facts and events of the past eight days. Learn a lesson from the groundhog, especially about those things that may have frightened you earlier in life.

⚜

Whenever you have had a few days to ponder — have gained new insights or advice — consider acting like the groundhog and do not hesitate to make a new judgment. Blessed are those who, when they recognize a deeper truth, frequently change their minds — and by doing so, change their lives.

✵

Nelson Mandela Released from Prison Day, 1990. This South African president was an ex-con. Use this day to examine your prejudices and fears about those who have been imprisoned and released. Nelson Mandela is not unique in being an innocent man who's been imprisoned unjustly for years. What are your feelings regarding those who have served their sentence in prison and are now released into society? Without God's vision as to their innocence or guilt, how should you treat them now that they are released from prison?

As a second reflection for this day of Mandela's release from prison, ponder his friendly, generous and non-vengeful attitude toward those who imprisoned him. By his humane treatment of those who "stole" a good part of his life, he has provided a powerful model for how to respond to mistreatment and pain. Mandela did not require "justice" for those who had taken away precious freedom and the prime years of his life. Instead, he practiced heroic forgiveness and love for the common good.

※290%※

This is a day to reflect on how we should respond to those who are responsible for offenses against us and our families. The common good of the world and everyone in it requires that we become heroic in the style of Nelson Mandela.

✳

---

12 Birthday of President Abraham Lincoln, 1809.

Lincoln was the last president to be elected who did not belong to a particular Christian denomination. He was, however, deeply religious; he kept a Bible on his desk and would read it often for comfort and guidance. We might wonder if Lincoln could be elected today; not only was he not a member of any church, Lincoln was also convinced that he was illegitimate, like his mother. He once observed, however, that "bastards are generally smarter, shrewder, and more intelligent than others." Only after his assassination on April 14, 1865, and his death on April 15, was it proven that Abraham Lincoln was not illegitimate.

※290%※

When young Lincoln was fourteen, his parents joined the Pigeon Creek Baptist Church. At that time there were bitter feelings and fierce competition among Baptists, Methodists, Presbyterians and members of other Christian denominations.

Lincoln disliked the animosity he saw in churches, and this fact is proposed as the reason why he never joined a church as an adult.

This would be a good day to reflect on what makes any church or religion legitimate. Does not being a true child of God imply having a real respect for all God's children? Perhaps, then, illegitimate religions and "bastard" churches can be recognized when their members do not love and respect those of other faiths. Instead of seeing other religious people as sons and daughters of God, illegitimate believers attack others and their beliefs. As this day honors one of the greatest American presidents, look with new eyes upon any friends or family who, like Lincoln, live compassionate lives and are concerned about justice for all but do not go to church.

13

Birthday of the Million, 1300. Cathedral church bells must have rung out loudly and canons boomed their salutes to accompany the joyful shouts of clergy, nobles and peasants at the birth of the *Million*. With the narrow medieval streets filled with drunken celebrators, university scholars must have pondered the rapidly expanding world that now required the ability to count things to the staggering sum of one million. Prior to this awesome event, the largest number used was the Greek *myriad*, which meant 10,000. When asked how many poppy seeds existed in the entire universe, the mathematician Archimedes (200 B.C.) is reported to have said, "myriads of myriads of myriads."

In only seven hundred years we have come to counting in not only hundreds of millions, but billions and trillions, if not zillions of trillions. Numbers beyond those we can count on our fingers are easily lost in the whirl of such staggering figures. As you prepare for tomorrow's feast of lovers and friends, recall the line of an old hit song: "I found my million dollar baby in a five and ten cent store." While your beloved may be worth a million dollars, love can only embrace numbers like one or two, or for those with extra-large hearts perhaps as many as five to ten. Reflect, today, on the fact that God does not love a million people, God loves one at a time. Rejoice on this eve of Valentine's Day that to God you are Number One. On this birthday of the Million, rejoice if you are loved by someone, because to that person you are also Number One.

✳

---

14 St. Valentine's Day, Feast of Friendship and Love.

This is the second largest feast for sending greeting cards, with over one million sold annually, about half that of Christmas cards. In fact, this is the birthday of the greeting card. On this day in 1445 the first known card, a love note, was smuggled out of the Tower of London. For centuries, men have proposed marriage in handwritten, decorated Valentine's Day messages. In the 1840s Esther Howland became the first commercial publisher of valentines. Until that time all cards were hand colored — and even thereafter many cards were created by hand and heart. This artistic love affair with greeting cards, along with Esther Howland's initiative, led to the pre-Civil War days of 1840-1860 becoming the grand age of valentines.

While this is a festival for friends and lovers, it is interesting to note that three out of four valentines are sent to relatives. Men continue to purchase valentines more than any other kind of card.

Today honors Saint Valentio, who died in prison on this day in 269. Legend has it that this saintly man enjoyed playing Cupid, that before he was imprisoned he secretly married couples who had been banned from marriage by the Roman emperor Claudius II. February 14 is also an example of a baptized pagan feast; it incorporated Lupercalia, which was celebrated at the same time of year. On this Roman festival young men drew the names of women they would court that year.

❧❀❧

While greeting card companies produce beautiful full-color cards, why not consider making an "old-fashioned 1445-1840" valentine for that special person in your life. First, become hearing-impaired to the voice of your inner-critic who harps that you can't even draw a straight line. As you create your own original, one-of-a-kind work of art, remind yourself that it's the passion and love with which you create your love card, and not the artistic execution or design, that will make it a masterpiece. Not only will it be the work of a master lover, but a treasure to keep.

✳

Non-Spectator Day. A principle of Zen states, "Being a spectator while one is also a participant spoils one's performance." Today, beware of *watching* yourself instead of *being* yourself. Early in life we take on the habit of self-observation to monitor our behavior. Yet trying to be both the audience and the performer at the same time leads to being stilted and unnatural. While frequent self-supervision is helpful to remove habits and behavior that are unloving or irritating to others, like all good things self-monitoring should be done in moderation.

15

⚜

As the Zen masters say, "When you eat, eat; when you walk, walk." Living in the present moment as fully as possible helps satisfy the itch to monitor yourself and still be yourself. As in theater, so in life — the true artists are those who are so fully possessed by what they are doing that they have no time to watch themselves. When they forget to be possessed in this way and give into the temptation to observe their wonderful performance, then they usually stumble.

Practice today the virtue of self-forgetfulness, which is at the heart of making love — being totally engaged in what you are doing or in another person. Those who make love daily by self-forgetfulness find ecstasy in celebrating the love they have been making day by day.

✳

The Invention of Monkey Business, 5,000,000 B.C. Today celebrates the primate's "best kept secret." Usually

16

inventions and discoveries are front-page news, but not so with Monkey Business. The French philosopher, Rene Descartes, is said to have speculated that monkeys and apes have the ability to speak but that they keep it a secret. Descartes said they keep silent to avoid being put to work. While the name of their craft, Monkey Business, did not appear until 1828, monkeys have made having a good time their business for over five million years. Learn a lesson from your ancestors high in the branches of your family tree and learn to keep quiet.

⚜

The next time you feel like criticizing someone or "telling it the way it is," think twice. You may have to spend four times the time and work repairing the damage done by your quick temper. As with monkeys, not speaking will help you to avoid unnecessary work.

Also, if you have to attend a meeting or are selected to be on some committee, consider practicing a little Monkey Business. Those who freely speak out are often the first to be placed on committees or given assignments to perform. If you want more playtime in your life, practice this brief Monkey Business ritual as you enter a meeting: Moving your hands to match your words, say to yourself, "See nothing, hear nothing and *speak nothing*." Protect your playtime; it is essential for creativity and for making love. Friendship and love without play quickly evolve into dull duties, into simply obligations to be kept.

✳

---

17 **The Discovery of the Planet Pluto, 1930.** On this day in 1930, Clyde Tombaugh discovered the planet Pluto at 3,690 million miles from the sun. Percival Lowell had begun the search in the first decade of the twentieth century. He was seeking a planet named "X," whose existence was based on the irregular motions in the orbits of Uranus and Neptune.

The smallest of our sun-star planets, Pluto is not like its sister planets but is more a methane snowball. Some astronomers think Pluto should be called a distant asteroid rather than a real planet. From Pluto, our blinding sun would seem no larger than Jupiter appears from Earth!

⚜

Spend a few seconds today to reflect on the fact that this planet, which existed from the birth of our solar family, was not discovered by earthlings until 1930. This discovery is within the lifetime of some of you reading this Almanac. In the coming fifty years of the new century, also within the lifetime of some who are reading this Almanac, will come a fantastic parade of such discoveries. Blessed are those with elastic minds and hearts which can easily expand with wonder. Woe to those who are inflexible in heart and mind, for they shall snap under the strain of the twenty-first century.

✳

Be Salt Day. Jesus told his followers, "You are the salt of the earth." That image is as rich in opportunities for holiness as there are varieties of uses for salt. It has been estimated that salt has over 14,000 specific industrial applications: food seasoning, curing of animal hides, use in the manufacture of plastics, dyes, insecticides, explosives, rayon, chlorine gas and cosmetics, to list just a few. Salt is a natural preservative for foods, as in the curing of meats. It is also necessary in making bread, cheese and other foods. Furthermore, salt hinders the growth of bacteria and yeast.

18

⚜

If you're a follower of Jesus, today's a good day to experiment with new and different ways to be salt to your world. You can, in fact, try as many ways as the number of uses for salt. Consider, today, being "salt" by preserving tradition or by hindering the growth of the bacteria of prejudice and revenge. Embody the salt necessary to make insecticides for those things that "bug" you, or to develop explosives to awaken the living dead, or to whip up some cosmetics to put a happy face on a sad experience.

✳

19 **Clean Your Coffee and Tea Cup Day.** The practical life and the spiritual life are one, and the wise remove any seeming lines between them. So, today, mix equal amounts of table salt and white vinegar and use the mixture to clean your stained china.

In 1914, Sterling Morton II, son of the "Old Salt" himself, the founder of the Morton Salt Company, suggested the slogan, "When it rains, it pours." This was not meant to be a glib commentary about the negative side of life but to convey that Morton Salt would pour easily even in the negative weather of life.

⚜

Yes, the spiritual life and the practical life are one. Take a little time today to reflect on whether, like the salt of the earth, you pour out good humor, kindness and love as easily on your "rainy" days as you do on your sunny days. If not, examine yourself for the reasons why you are only sunny-day salt. It's on stormy days, when computers break down, marriages break up, business deals break apart and depression breaks out, that the good old salt of humor and compassion most need to flow — just like Morton salt.

✻

20 **The February Blahs Day.** *Blah* is American slang for bland or unexciting. These gray February days are the Blah Days, difficult days to get up in the morning, difficult to maintain focussed attention, difficult for teachers trying to inspire their students. Teaching, like parenting, requires great faith in the future and great patience with the present. It is said that all truly good education is the construction of a *time*-delayed-action-*bomb*; it is assembled carefully in the classroom for explosion at a later date.

⚜

If you find yourself impatient today with any work whose harvest is in the far distant future, take heart. Take care as you daily fill the bombs of your projects or relationships with beauty and truth, creativity and confidence, joy and excitement, hope and freedom. Then set the timer for...later. It is also said, "A school is a building that has four walls with tomorrow inside." The same is true of a home with small children, or of any good church!

✳

Death Day of Malcolm X, 1965. Born in Omaha, Nebraska, in 1925 with the name Malcolm Little, he was sent to prison for burglary in 1946. There he embraced the Black Muslim faith and upon his release from prison in 1952 became a Muslim minister and a charismatic advocate of African-American separatism. He split with Elijah Muhammad of the Black Muslim religion and while on a pilgrimage to Mecca was converted to Orthodox Islam. In 1964 he founded the Organization of Afro-American Unity, which while promoting Black Nationalism also was open to interracial unity. He was assassinated in Harlem on this day in 1965 by gunmen who were purported to be Black Muslims.

21

❧❀❧

Malcolm X's death day is an occasion to remember the ugly racial segregation that existed at the time of his death and that still persists. Black Americans were not allowed to attend schools with white Americans, to swim in the same pools, eat in the same restaurants, ride together on public transportation or even to vote, to mention but a few of the shameful segregation laws that existed in America. As citizens of this land which boasts of equal rights, we should never forget, never let eclipse from our memory, this time of shameful, hate-filled segregation of other citizens. Perhaps someday, one of our presidents will make a public confession for the long years of the national sin of segregation, asking forgiveness of those who because of their race had this social sin inflicted upon them by individuals, society and their government.

Today, take a good look at your life and consider if there are any present sins of segregation of which you, our society or our government are guilty.

✦

---

22 **Birthday of President George Washington, 1732.**
Our first president proposed that he receive no salary, but only be reimbursed for his expenses. This had been his practice while a general in the revolutionary army, and he wished to continue it. So, although Congress had fixed the salary for the president at $25,000 a year, Washington refused to take it. However, his expenses amounted to almost exactly what his salary would have been. His detailed expense account recorded even the most insignificant of needs, including a ball of string!

Washington was a Virginia planter who owned slaves. Yet, unlike Patrick Henry and Thomas Jefferson, Washington's will granted his slaves freedom at his death. Especially since he was frequently in debt and could have used the money, Washington's generous parting deed is far more significant than his having served as President of the United States for only room and board.

❧

Heroic acts are often overshadowed both in history and private life by lesser ones. Living by the words you profess, whether words of the Declaration of Independence or your religious creed, require greater heroic conviction than the seemingly bold deeds applauded by crowds. Examine your life on this day of George Washington's birth and consider how authentic you are to your beliefs.

✦

---

23 **Lenten Satellite Day.** This is a Lenten celebration not to see if you are like a moon orbiting around a planet or some NASA object orbiting the earth, but to see if you are an original satellite. The word *satellite* was first used for a person who attended, or was a follower of, some prince or person of great importance. The satellite was a parasite, who praised the prince and curried favor for personal gain.

∗⊚∗

Today, pause and ponder whether you are a disciple-follower of Jesus or only a satellite. A true disciple is called not to flatter or fawn over the master with pious songs and prayers, but to follow the master. As Jesus himself said, "It is not those who say, 'Lord, Lord,' who shall enter God's domain but those who daily do the will of God" (Mt. 7: 21).

In the prayer of Jesus, we say with one breath, "your kingdom come, your will be done on earth as in heaven." To follow Jesus is to strive constantly to make God's time-reign-kingdom come wherever you work, live or even visit. No better definition for a disciple of Jesus could be found than one who makes God's time his or her time. The prophets spoke of God's reign as coming at some distant time, and Jesus announced that this long-awaited time had come with him. So it must be for all who dare call themselves his followers. If our lives announce only the old time of injustice, inequality and religious, racial and sexual division, regardless of how many times we have been *baptized*, we should find another name for ourselves besides Christian.

✸

Walpurgisnacht, Night of the Witches. If you go out after dark tonight, keep an eye in the sky not for shooting stars but for flying witches. On the eve of the feast of Saint Walpurgis, who later became known as Saint Walburga, it was the legend in Northern Germany that witches gathered to hold their secret rituals in the Hartz Mountains. While Saint Walburga was a holy nun, her name was perhaps confused with that of the Teutonic goddess Walburg, accounting for the odd connection of a holy woman with witches.

∗⊚∗

This Walpurgisnacht, consider how easily old pagan or pre-Christian symbols are married to Christian ones, and rejoice.

The principles of Celtic evangelization, or conversion a la Saint Patrick, were: Take people as you find them, build on what you find already present, change only what is absolutely necessary and graft the message of Jesus onto the sturdy stock of whatever people you encounter. Do not be scandalized if you scratch the skin of any Christian practice, holiday or ritual and find a pagan skeleton. Rather, reverence this relic of religious childhood with the conviction that its seeds were God-planted.

Add some frosting to this reflection by asking yourself these questions: What present secular celebrations should be made into religious holy days? And what songs, rituals and sacred signs would be appropriate to them?

✹

25 Feast of St. Walburga of Germany, Healer and Abbess, and the Birthday of Showman Buffalo Bill Cody, 1846.

This English nun was a forerunner of woman's equality. In 761 she broke with church policy and became both the abbess and abbot of an order of nuns and monks. As an herbalist, she is a patron of crops. Since she was skilled in medicine, she is a protector against frenzy and coughs. In this season of colds and coughs, consider praying this blessing for those afflicted with colds: May St. Walburga, woman of power, cure your cough.

⚜

Today, don't forget Buffalo Bill, who is more famous for his showmanship than for the number of buffaloes he killed. When we have to attend to a duty we prefer not doing, we often are tempted to revert to childhood patterns and use a minor illness to stay home from "school." If you're tempted to stay home from work, to miss some boring meeting or other obligation, using the excuse that you've got a cold, consider praying this blessing: "Old Buffalo Bill, great showman, remind me that 'the show must go on'!"

✹

Lenten Fast Day. Moslems, Jews and Christians all have religious days of ritual fasting. Abstaining from food has an ancient history as an act of purification, a sign of mourning for both personal and national afflictions. At one time for Catholics, Lent was a fast of forty days and is still an encouraged religious action today for this season of renewal.

26

We could use more fasting in our country if Harper's Index is correct. It states that, at the current rate of increase, by the year 2059 *all* Americans will be overweight!

While religious fasting from food has significant value as an act of discipline — and nothing of value can be achieved without discipline — the question is: fasting from what? On this Lenten day, regardless of your religious denomination, instead of controlling what goes into your mouth, consider fasting from what comes out! Practice the discipline of not allowing any negative words, harsh judgments or opinions of others to leave your mouth.

※❀❀❀※

Given a choice, we should always seek the greater good. Far greater good would come to the world by abstaining from what exits your mouth than reducing the food or drink that goes into your mouth. As a penance, such fasting from foul talk is much more difficult than fasting from food. As today's food for thought, reflect on these words of Jesus, "What comes out of the mouth has its source in the heart; and that is what defiles a person" (Mt. 15: 18). "For the words that the mouth speaks come from the overflowing of the heart" (Lk. 6: 45).

✵

Heart Home X-Ray Day. A healthy heart requires a good diet, proper exercise and frequent medical examinations. Now a new home examination makes it possible for you to see clearly into your heart and to know precisely the condition of its health.

27

※❀❀❀※

This day's reflection is a home health care examination. To

take the examination, sit still for a few minutes and reflect on your conversations in the past few days. The basis of this test is found in yesterday's words of Jesus that what we say is from the overflowing of our hearts. If your speech is full of negative comments about others, then your heart is overflowing with toxic acid. If your speech is tainted with the venom of cynicism and criticism, then your heart is full of poison. If you find your words green with envy and jealousy, even if they are disguised as humor, then you have a crystal clear x-ray of your heart filled with puss. Throughout this day, take frequent mini heart tests, even in the midst of a conversation, as you monitor your speech.

✷

---

28 International Day of Reinvention.

Consider, today, how to reinvent yourself as part of being a follower of Jesus. His primal call was for us to reform, or reinvent, ourselves in order to live in God's kingdom. Reinvention is essential — since each of us enters life as an original, why should we leave it as a copy? Most of us have been invented by family, friends, obligations, social expectations and customs.

◄❧❦❧►

If you have a few minutes today, draw a blueprint or outline for how you might like to redesign yourself. You can also list those overused parts of yourself that could stand to be removed, or draw up a list of your undeveloped talents and the parts of yourself that to date have been neglected.

✷

Leap Year

29 Feast of the Leaping St. Oswald of Worcester.

From his death in 992 until the early twentieth century the feast of this English monk of Danish descent was celebrated only in leap years. Then in the 1930s Oswald's feast was moved to February 28. (In case you're asked, a leap year is every year whose number is divisible by four. However, centennial years become leap years only when they can be divided by 400.)

Today's saint could be called St. Oswald the Unemployed since he seems to have been forgotten when patron assignments were given out. While a holy monk-bishop, he wasn't surrounded by any of the grand legends of wondrous exploits necessary to become a patron saint. Perhaps it is time as we cross over into a new millennium to correct this omission and make him the patron of those who leapfrog their holy days and holy duties.

Blessed St. Oswald,
> patron of those who only attend church
> once every four, or fourteen, years
> and whose spiritual life is frequently abandoned
> as they leap from week to week
> without praying on bended knee,
> pray for us.

On the other hand, leapfrogging over certain obligations can have a recreative effect, serving to renew and refresh our spirits. Furthermore, if you have a moment to spare, consider what life might be like if Oswald's old feast day wasn't the only one celebrated just in leap years. What if Christmas, Easter, Valentine's Day, the World Series, the Super Bowl or the Academy Awards were celebrated only every four years? If this Old Oswald factor were introduced, perhaps these religious and secular holy days might be entered into with greater zest and joy and we would begin to truly appreciate them for what they are.

THE
MONTH
OF
MARCH

This third month is named after Mars, the Roman god
of war and patron protector of crops. The Dutch name
for March was *Lentmaand*, which, of course, is a source
word for Lent; the Old Saxon name for this month was
Hreth-monath, which meant "rough month," because of
the cold, boisterous winds at this time of year.
The French Republican calendar renamed this month
Ventose, meaning "windy month." A once popular
old adage said, "A bushel of March dust is worth
a King's ransom." If dry, the wind of this month
has long been considered good for plowing and tilling
the soil. May the Lenten Winds of March
dust off your spiritual life.

March Weather Forecasting Day. This first day of March
is another opportunity to predict the weather. Tradition says
that if it is mild and gentle like a lamb, then the last day of the
month will be as fierce as a lion. If, however, today is harsh and
the wind is howling like a lion, then the 31st will be as fair and
mild as a lamb.

1

If you're in a foul-weather mood today and leave home
roaring like a lion, then take time on the way to work to ponder
your departure from those you love. Tame the lion while you're
away and return home gentle, like a lamb. This transformation
from lion to lamb will be enhanced and deepened if you strive
during the day to be a sacrificial lamb and take upon yourself
the mistakes, sins and errors of others with whom you work.

If you leave home gentle as a lamb, however, come home a
lion of a lover, and not some angry beast of prey because of

your bad day at work.

✳

---

2 **Birthday of Dr. Seuss, 1904.** Not only was he creative, Theodor Geisel, who later became known as Dr. Seuss, was patiently determined, for he weathered the rejection of his first book, *And to Think That I Saw It on Mulberry Street,* by twenty-seven different publishers. Children loved what publishers thought was not worth printing, which is a lesson in and of itself. Seuss persisted in his style of creativity, which he called "logical insanity," until almost fifty of his books had been published and over 100 million copies had been sold by the late 1980s.

✦

Inside each of us is a hidden cave where an important part of us lives, that part of us that never really grew up and became an adult. For many, this hidden self is starved for some "logical insanity," such crazy impossibilities as Seuss' elephant who sat in a tree in order to hatch an egg. Too logical sanity — or too logical sanctity — drives humans insane. Abuse of the hidden child within, treating that child too practically and realistically, is the source of such insanities as overwork, aggressive competition, hairsplitting definitions, angry outbursts and most of the evils that cause early aging.

Take a pinch of time today to select some logical insanity to entertain your hidden, cave-dwelling child — and to save your soul. A few possibilities: Sing aloud on the way to work; buy a toy or borrow one for your desk to remind you to play more; have an imaginary companion with whom to carry on a conversation; when you pray today, consider doing so as would a small child, perhaps drawing a picture of God and the saints as your prayer.

✳

---

3 **Birthday of Alexander Graham Bell, 1847.** On this day, in the midst of the United States' aggressive landgrab called the Mexican War, was born the inventor of the telephone.

Also on this day, Congress authorized the issue of the first official U.S. postage stamps. Within a hundred years Bell's invention would compete with the postage system as the primary means of communication. The birthday of the patent for the "harmonic telegraph," Bell's instrument for sending the human voice over a wire, is March 7, 1876. The first message he transmitted over his telegraph was to his assistant: As he accidentally spilled acid on his clothes, Bell said, "Mr. Watson, come here. I want you."

Bell's interests as an inventor were many. He experimented with electric probes to be used in surgery several years before the x-ray was discovered, with devices for locating icebergs by the use of sound echoes, with breeding sheep, and with early airplanes in the form of man-lifting kites. The story is told — which most creative people will affirm — that Bell personally disliked his own telephone because it interrupted his experiments.

Today, Alexander Bell would rejoice that telephones can be turned off or switched over to answering machines so as to allow time for experiments, for family life, for loving, for addressing a crowded desktop, for prayer or for reflective living. Consider on this Lenten day the fruits of a regular discipline of fasting from responding to your telephone.

Commemoration of the Divine Ding Dong. In the lives of many, "ding dong," the sound of a telephone ring, has the same summoning godly force as if it were Archangel Gabriel's trumpet. A story told about the French painter Edgar Degas illustrates the message of this feast day.

A friend of Degas had just installed a modern telephone in his home and was extremely proud of it. He invited Degas to dinner and also arranged for another friend to call him in the middle of the visit. When the telephone rang, the man jumped up and ran to the other room to answer it. He came back to the table beaming with pride. "Well, so that's a telephone," said Degas. "It rings and you run."

As children we were taught that it is rude to interrupt others while they are talking. Yet we allow the telephone to interrupt conversations and dinners as if it were the voice of God calling us.

～⁂～

Remembering how in yesterday's entry Alexander Bell considered the telephone to be a disturbance to his creativity, if you feel addicted to answering the telephone, regardless of what you are doing, consider performing this little ritual as a way to help you avoid being controlled by the telephone: The next time it rings while you are in the midst of something important, turn toward the instrument and bow before it three times, saying, "O Master, Divine Ding Dong, I worship you and usually run whenever you call me. This time, however, I declare my independence — may your ringing be the sound of my Liberty Bell."

✵

---

5 **Lenten Lost and Found Day.** The British poet, T.S. Eliot, said, "Where is the life we have lost in living? Where is the wisdom we have lost in knowledge? Where is the knowledge we have lost in information?" One can also ask, "Where is the spirituality we have lost in religion?"

～⁂～

This is a Lenten day to seek sincerely what you may have lost — the life lost in the business of living, wisdom lost in the acquiring of facts and education, and your spirituality lost in the rituals and rules of your religion. Playing Lenten hide-and-seek is a spiritual activity in which we seek what we have lost in the business of living, learning and religion — especially religion.

Spirituality is not something one does on "special" occasions like Sunday morning or at prayer times. Nor does it need to be an elaborate system or a strict schedule of religious activities. Spirituality is simply another name for a whole life lived according to one's beliefs. In such a "seamless" spirituality, our beliefs give a vision of reality that is illuminated from within by the perpetual presence of God. If you've lost some life in living and are seeking this kind of vision-based spirituality, there's no better place to look for a model than the life of Jesus. For his words and work showed how he saw everything as aflame with the divine. His whole life showed a vision of a God whose love is so seamless that no one or no thing is excluded. To be able to live that vision out in your daily life in the world is the purpose of whatever religious activities, rituals or prayers that form your daily spiritual practice. So, on this Lenten day, seek out that vision that may be hiding in the heart of your spirituality.

✴

Kything Day. The Scottish word *kything* means to be spiritually present to another person. Today, experiment with the practice of being spiritually in communion with someone. As you connect with a friend, a family member or someone you know who is in need, do so by recalling memories of that person, perhaps an image, a common thought or emotion or a scent. In your kything prayer you might strive to picture that person in his or her environment. Then add to your kything a blessing prayer for whatever needs that person might have on this sixth day of March. On any day, whenever the thought of someone enters your mind, practice the prayer of kything. Blessed are those who do not only go to Communion but *live* in Communion.

6

＊＊＊

We need each other. By consciously connecting yourself with those who share the same vision as yours, those with whom you are joined by love and friendship, is to be for them a source of graceful energy. While invisible to the eye, even the eye of a microscope, love is as real a source of energy as electricity. Perhaps someday we will have the technology to see love. For now, we can only see its powerful effects all around us. Even when we love others at a distance, we see those effects by eyes of faith, for love knows no limits or boundaries.

✴

7 The Birthday of Ebenezer Scrooge, 1842.

Scrooge was born in the Delivery Room of Charles Dickens' study, as he wrote the manuscript for *A Christmas Carol*. It would become a book in the following year, 1843, but on this day the famous Ebenezer took real form as he flowed from Dickens' pen. He is perhaps history's most infamous miser; to this day his very name means stingy, tight-fisted and miserly. Dickens gave birth to Scrooge's soul with the words, "Nobody ever stopped him in the street to say with gladsome looks, 'My dear Scrooge, how are you? When will you come to see me?' No beggars implored him to bestow a trifle, no children asked him what it was o'clock, no man or woman ever once in all his life inquired the way to such and such a place, of Scrooge."

Scrooge's famous phrase, "Bah Humbug," his response to the Christmas spirit, to any celebration and fun that isn't fund-raising points to a deep-seated temptation in each of us. "Waste not, want not" is the old adage that many of us have taken to heart. Today's birthday challenges our creeds of "constructive" use of time and money and asks, "Am I a Scrooge?"

⁂

While you may think this entry should be placed in December just before Christmas, Scrooge's birthday should be celebrated every day! Happiness and love are not found in bank deposit boxes or in stocks and bonds. Rather, we are truly enriched by kindness and gratitude, by expressions of love. Expressing gratitude, even for little things, causes flowers, rainbows and fireworks to inwardly flood us with joy. Yet most of us are Scrooges when it comes to being generous in giving away gratitude, praise and congratulations.

Bah Humbug — if I praise someone, he or she will only get a big head, and remember, "Pride goes before the fall." It's better to point out someone's shortcomings and mistakes; it helps a person to be humble. Besides, it makes me feel better, more superior, and, therefore, richer. *Bah Humbug* about thanking others for minor acts of kindness. It makes them think I didn't deserve whatever they did for me. Gratitude only robs me of my high-interest-paying investment in myself. *Bah Humbug*, this book is a waste of time.

The purpose of Lent is to "rend our hearts," to rip open and extend their capacity to hold the riches of love. Use this Lenten birthday to release your littleness of heart, your Scroogeness, and practice a little kindness and gratitude.

✠

Birthday of the Camel, 4,500,000 B.C. Contrary to the common wit that the camel is a prime example of the work of a committee, this animal is magnificently designed for its environment. Camels can go without drinking water for eight days in the summer and eight *weeks* in winter. This is because the water a camel drinks enters its entire system and because they sweat and urinate very little. The camel is a classic living example of recycled water.

8

⚜

The strange and odd shape of the camel gave birth to the old joke that it was designed by a committee. Today, reflect on the fact that you can't judge a book, a person or a camel by its shape and look. What is unseen beneath the surface truly may be magnificently created.

Each of God's creations is a masterpiece, even the bizarre (which in French originally meant "handsome"). In ancient China they said it takes two to create a masterpiece. First, it takes a master artist who produces the wondrous work of art. Second, it takes someone who is able to appreciate the masterpiece. Today, you and I share in the great honor of being an essential partner in God's ongoing creation. As one of your spiritual exercises today, notice with wondrous awe at least five masterpieces of God. The Divine Creator will be thrilled that you wanted to be part of those masterpieces. And if you like the experience of awe, you might also do this exercise tomorrow — and even the day after.

✠

9   **Grin and Bear It Day, 1775.** These early days in March often hold surprise attacks of Old Winter, which is reluctant to surrender to Spring, only eleven days away on March 21. Determined to die with his boots on, Winter pelts those in the northern part of the northern hemisphere with snow, sleet and icy rain. Perhaps the only realistic response to the long gray days of winter is that old expression sailors liked to use after long days of bad weather: "Grin and bear it." Not only does that saying apply to the weather outside, but also to bad weather inside, for we all know what it means to make the best of a difficult or painful situation.

⚜

Today's expression first appeared in print just before the American Revolution in *Memoirs* by William Hickey. Perhaps "Grin and bear it" was the literal response of many of the colonists to the harsh rule, heavy taxes and oppression of the British Crown. In effect, one-third of the colonists said, "Grin and bear it, for we wish to remain English subjects under the rule of good King George III." Another third said, "Grin and bear it, just leave things as they are. We don't want to get involved unless we personally, or our businesses, are negatively affected by English rule." The remaining third said, "We will not bear it any longer, and we will not grin until we're free."

The weather is beyond our control, so bearing up under it with a smile makes sense. However, other aspects of life which are painful and difficult – like the English rule in early America – are not always to be borne with a grin.

Pray today, if you are suffering, to have the wisdom to know which of these to say, "Grin and bear it" or "I will not bear it any longer, and will grin only when I am free of it."

✳

10   **The Feast of Saint Adam of Eden.** Today we celebrate the birthday of our primal great-grandfather, Adam, whom God made from the clay of the earth, breathing into him the breath of life. While we keep the first birthday in history, we might recall a line from *The Adventures of the Copper Beeches*, in which Sherlock Holmes cries out, "Data, Data, Data! I can't make bricks without clay."

On this feast of St. Adam reflect with Sherlock Holmes on this perennial problem: While information and ideas are important in any work, what is really needed is clay, the raw stuff of creation. What is the clay Holmes wants? Perhaps it's imagination — fertile images of untried possibilities — or the *raw earth* of common sense; both of which can bring data to life. Intellectual data is clean, sterile and static, while clay is slippery, dirty and messy. Both slippery imagination and static data are required for good decisions.

≈❧◆☙≈

Regardless of what projects you will work on today, be sure to use both elements: mix sterile data with a generous measure of the earthy clay of creativity and common sense. At Adam's birth, Genesis tells us that God breathed life into the limp clay doll God had formed, and much more than a simple life-form came into being. Adam became clay standing up and clay thinking up the names of the animals, fish and birds that God created as companions for him. God breathed into Adam a complex intelligence, a free will, a conscience by which to reflect upon his behavior and the wondrous divine gift of creativity.

While our bodies are clay — and shall return to dry, dusty clay — the divine breath that makes us alive will at our deaths also return from where it came. Meanwhile, God does not expect us to create solutions for problems, to make love or to bring our prayers to life without clay.

Note: The Orthodox Church celebrates the Feast of Saints Adam and Eve on December 24, Christmas Eve.

✡

A New Lenten Sweet and Sour Dish Day. As you try to come up with creative dishes to deal with the traditional fasting from food and abstaining from eating meat during Lent, consider this new dish for the Purple Forty Days: Daily eat your own words. Eat them before they are spoken, and find in this

11

hidden meal a unique penance. Instead of savoring those sweet tasting words of criticism, sarcasm or complaint – or those deliciously rich words of rudeness – swallow them. While healthy for the soul, you may find this meal sour and difficult to swallow.

This is a Lenten dish that will advance the Age of God faster and create more good than any dishes devoid of meat. Criticism and sarcasm are not limited to any age group, but they seem to flourish in mid-life and the senior years. Perhaps by that time hope in a better world and the goodness of all people has run out of gas. Frequently those mature in years fear they will not live to see their youthful dreams come true. With age there often comes impatience, not so much with oneself, but with others and with institutions and churches known for their high ideals.

The prophets of old who railed against the injustices of their day were not teenagers, and it's true that we do not admonish them for their sour words. Yet, it's too easy to claim the license of a social or religious prophet. If you think you are such a prophet, test with careful prayer the critical words you want to speak to see if they are truly from God. If you're not sure, it is far better to eat your words of criticism and sarcasm than to speak them. You will help make the world more beautiful and a better place by not adding any potentially toxic waste.

---

12 **Chinook Wind Day.** March is known as the windy month, and today celebrates a special March wind. In these days of late winter a warm, moist wind begins to blow off the Pacific Ocean from the direction of the Chinook Indian villages along the coast of the Northwest. As the Chinook Wind crosses the Rocky Mountains, it heats and dries. This causes sudden dramatic changes in temperature: In only fifteen minutes, it can rise as much as 44° Fahrenheit or 24° Celsius. Since the Chinook can melt the snow on the ground as it passes over, it is also called the Snow Eater.

As a way to celebrate this day, consider being a Chinook Snow Eater when you walk into some icy situation at work, at home or when visiting a neighbor. The cold may not be caused by anger or resentment but by the bleak chill created in rushing around trying to do too much. Sweep over the room with a smile and the good snow-melting humor of a Chinook, and make a difference. Helping to raise the temperature of even one or two persons by the warmth of affection can begin a global warming, for they in turn can do the same for one or two others.

Even the Chinook doesn't expect to melt every glacier it passes, nor should you. Today reminds us to use the warm wind-gift of the Spirit, which the Risen Jesus promised would be ours. If today you know in advance that you will enter the chilly landscape of a business meeting or a potential conflict at the office, before you leave home say this prayer:

> Come, Chinook of Christ,
>> fill me with the warmth of your love
>> so I can change,
>> like your northwestern cousin Chinook,
>> every icy terrain that I come upon today.

✳

Pedestrian Prophecy Day, 1876. "This 'telephone' has too many shortcomings to be seriously considered as a means of communication. The device is inherently of no value to us" — Western Union internal memo from 1876.

13

❧

Cast a glance at your home or office telephone and give thanks that it is not just a telegraph. Be grateful that its early problems were resolved so that by this wonderful invention you can hear the voices of those you love. Then cast a glance at some new inventions and don't be too quick to judge them of no value to society.

Also cast a prayerful glance at some people you believe have too many shortcomings to really be considered as valuable.

It might be someone seeking employment from you who is presently on welfare, someone who has served time in prison and bears the "X" of an ex-convict or someone eager to work but lacking credentials or experience.

While the Western Union memo of 1876 is worth two dozen personal reflections because it is so humorous an error in judgment, we should be aware that Western Union has no corner on the market of shortsightedness.

14 **Birthday of Albert Einstein, 1879.** The famous father of $E=MC^2$, when asked for his telephone number on one occasion, went and looked it up in a telephone directory. The surprised questioner asked, "A man as brilliant as you does not know his own telephone number?" To which Einstein replied, "I have far more important things to keep in my mind than something I can look up in a book!"

His response can be a wake-up call for us concerning the sort of things with which we fill our minds. Today, examine the kind of things that fill up your mind. In 1930 in *What I Believe,* Einstein said, "The most beautiful thing we can experience is the mysterious. It is the source of all true art and science."

The mysterious is also the source of all great religions. Do not be ashamed if your beliefs are beyond scientific or rational explanations but are truly mysterious. For true science, as Einstein and other great scientists have shown, is a cooperation with the Divine Creator in bringing understanding to what was once not understood. At the same time, Einstein understood the profound truth that some things are beyond scientific explanations: such realities as God, prayer, grace, love, faith and hope.

As you celebrate the birthday of one of the greatest giants of the twentieth century, reverence the *mysterious* in your life.

Ides of March — a Day to Beware. On this day in 44 **15**
B.C., Julius Caesar was assassinated, and so began its history as
a day to lay low. As Shakespeare's Julius Caesar warned, "Beware
the ides of March."

However, March 15 is also a day to celebrate. It was the
glorious day when Columbus returned as a hero after his first
voyage to the New World. The State of Maine celebrates this
day when in 1820 it became part of the union of the United
States. If you are a member of the American Legion, then you
can celebrate the Legion's founding in Paris on this day in 1919.
If you are an African-American or a citizen of any racial or
ethnic background, you can rejoice that today in 1965 President
Johnson proposed the Voting Rights Act. And if you are a musical
lover, celebrate today the 1956 Broadway opening of the musical
My Fair Lady.

Today's seed thought is that bad days for some may be
good days for others. At the end of a particularly bad day, when
your heart is full of misery, pause and remember the many
good things that have happened on March 15. In your prayers,
give thanks for all those who like Columbus have returned home
jubilant, those who on your bad day have found hope in the
future. Then feel a sense of communion with all on earth — the
joyful and the sorrowful.

Such a reflection can be liberating, for it has the power to
place both successes and failures, pains and joys in the larger
framework of the entire human family — with whom we are
mysteriously united by our incorporation in the body of the
Risen Christ.

✴

Bathing in the Shannon Day. An old Irish expression **16**
suggests how you can make your shower or bath today an occasion
to be specially gifted — if you've a mind to do so. "To be dipped
in the Shannon (River)" is said to free one of all bashfulness.
For most people shyness is a learned behavior — or learned

affliction — that appears in the self-conscious teenage years. But to bathe as a blessedly bold baptism, whether you are "dipped" in a tub or "sprinkled" in the shower, defeats the devil of shyness.

※⚜※

So even if you lack the holy water of the Shannon River, any water will do for this washing away of shyness. Wash off your shyness and see beneath the wondrous unique image of God that is you, and generously share that beautiful gift with others.

Also on this day, take seriously any sightings of green icebergs! This is not the work of the wee folk or of some wild Irishman who is dyeing the icebergs green for tomorrow's feast. For years travelers in the Antarctic have reported seeing green icebergs instead of the usual bluish-white ones. Historically, scientists have either disregarded the sightings or said they were optical illusions. Now, however, most agree that there are green icebergs!

Hundreds of feet below the surface, the seawater of the Antarctic region freezes. In the process, some icebergs incorporate the dissolved remains of plankton, the ocean's floating minute plant life. When these icebergs become top-heavy and capsize, they reveal their green-colored undersides. The more organic plankton matter, the greener the iceberg will be. It is presently estimated that fewer than one in a hundred Antarctic icebergs are green. So? Perhaps the confirming of green icebergs is a sign that we should be prepared for new scientific discoveries in the next millennium of other things once considered only optical illusions — like proof of the existence of leprechauns or wee folk!

✗

---

17 **Feast of St. Patrick, Patron of Ireland and Parades.** Today's "wearing of the green" in honor of Saint Patrick, along with all the green parades with their bagpipes and blarney, is part of a folk ritual that announces the death of winter and the coming of green spring. On this day, Irish and wanna-be Irish

all toast the saint of Welsh birth who became the missionary to the isle of saints and scholars. He is the patron saint of Ireland, of parades and of all things green. His love and incorporation of pre-Christian lore and customs also makes Patrick the patron saint of the *shee*, or wee folk, who were the old gods driven from mortal sight.

Even if you are not Irish or Catholic, this is a day to celebrate, and so to enjoy that God is not the God of the sad or mad. No other saint's feast day is so associated with play and make-believe — leprechauns dance on your roof and the *shee* abound. Pubs overflow and parades defy bad weather as good friends party and good times abound. If holiness is properly understood as sharing in the divine nature, then joy in God's mystical mirth needs be included. Every saint's day and every religious holy day should be an occasion for fun and joyful celebration. Woe to those who practice a drab religion, for the road to heaven is made for parades. And if you're not Irish, determine to celebrate the feast of your ethnic or racial patron saint with all the fun and color of this Irish holiday of Saint Patrick.

The Feast of Blessed Blarney. To be Irish is more a state of mind than of birth, so today's holiday is for those of any and all nationalities. In 1602, Cormac McCarthy was responsible for surrendering Blarney Castle, near Cork, to the English as part of an armistice. While the English waited daily for the surrender in fulfillment of the terms, instead all they got from the castle's caretaker were soft and long speeches. According to tradition, which is also blarney, to kiss a stone high in Blarney Castle gives one the gift of gab to win over others.

Ponder for a moment the wisdom of Cormac McCarthy and confront your obstacles today by the use of blessed blarney, humor and soft speech instead of resorting to bitter resentment and anger.

✳

19

Feast of Saint Joseph, the Husband of Mary and Father-Protector of Jesus, and Swallow Return Day at the California Mission of San Juan Capistrano.

What St. Patrick's Day is for the Irish, today is for Italians. As the Irish celebrate with parades and partying, Italians celebrate the feast of their patron with the St. Joseph Table. This tradition began centuries ago in Sicily at the time of a long famine. The starving families turned to prayer, asking the help of the patron of families, especially Italian families, St. Joseph. Their prayers were answered, and the famine came to an end. As an act of gratitude, the people decided to make offerings in his honor of what was most precious after a famine: food.

Today's Italian St. Joseph Tables continue that tradition by displaying favorite dishes of food that are works of art, both in taste and beauty. By custom, since this feast comes in Lent, no meat dishes are served among the glorious masterpieces of St. Joseph Tables. At the end of the celebration — which for some includes giving the *fava*, a lucky bean — all the food at these altar-tables is given away to the poor.

These altars are erected in church halls and also in private homes. The home tables of St. Joseph are usually in response to some favor or request having been granted.

❧✦❧

Join today with Italians celebrating their heritage by sharing a meal at a sacred table or by having a special home meal which is prepared in thanksgiving for some past favor from God. Also seriously consider making some donation of food, or a gift of money, to a Food Kitchen to assist the poor and needy. Gather ideas for your acts of gratitude from your Italian friends, whose thanksgiving involves preparing beautiful food, which is a gift for the eyes and nose and then becomes a gift for the poor. The best acts of gratitude are those you can give away with pride.

Rejoice today too in the swallows' return to the old mission of San Juan, a sign that spring is close at hand. Look for signs of spring's return into the area where you live.

✻

Construction of the Church of St. Basil, Moscow, 1555. 20

The beautiful golden onion domes of the Church of St. Basil are renowned images of Moscow's Kremlin, the citadel of the Russian czars. The two architects, Postnik and Barma, so pleased Ivan the Terrible with their masterpiece that he had their eyes blinded so they would never be able to design anything more beautiful.

⚜

That success can be fatal is a thought upon which to chew on this March day. Czar Ivan's reward to Postnik and Barma is symbolic of how easily we can be blinded by success, a blindness that is usually self-inflicted. Like opium, success is addictive, and those who achieve it want more and more. As with all addictions, success usually comes at the price of life, family and self.

Whether or not you have scored a great success, created a masterpiece or only a modestpiece, ask yourself today if your achievement is blinding you to the enjoyment of a life filled with simple pleasures. This is a good day for such an "I" examination.

✻

Spring Equinox. 21

The Earth in her circle journey around the sun reaches that point where the hours of day and night are equal — and the earth begins to tilt eagerly toward the sun. In the glory of our earthen globe, while we in the northern half of our planet are celebrating spring's arrival, today is the beginning of autumn for those in Australia and Peru, in the southern hemisphere. Today as they, perhaps with nostalgia, see summer end, those in the northern hemisphere rejoice to see winter over, at least officially.

⚜

Today or in the coming days, celebrate your own spring rites, joining with creation in an Easter-rising from the tomb of winter. This could be the occasion for a party, a special dinner or a ritual to assist you in being in communion with creation. It is the custom in some Japanese homes to have four different sets of tableware, one for each season. Today in Japan, winter plates are boxed up and bright spring dishes appear to take their place. While you might consider it a luxury to have four sets of dishes, pause before making a judgment. A luxury to one can be a necessity to another.

A luxury, which is usually something that is beautiful, can awaken us to live at a deeper level of life. For some it might be a piano, for others it might be a collection of classical recordings, a water garden, or an evening out for a fine dinner. All these can be luxuries that are really necessities for the soul. To know what luxuries feed you on an essential level is to know how to balance the spirituality of a simple lifestyle with the nourishment that gives richness to your soul.

✳

---

22 **End of the Forty Years War, 1014.** Basil II of Constantinople grew tired of the war with the hated Bulgarians that had gone on for forty years. He sent word to Samuel, the ruler in the Bulgarian capital of Ohrid, that he was returning 15,000 of his prisoners of war. Then Basil had all but 150 of the 15,000 soldiers totally blinded. The fortunate 150 were blinded in only one eye so they could be single-eyed guides, each leading a hundred men home. When Samuel heard his army was returning, he hurried out to meet them, only to find thousands of helplessly blinded men. At this shocking, horrible sight, Samuel suffered a stroke and died two days later.

❧

Jesus warned that when a blind person leads another blind person, they both fall into the ditch. One-eyed leaders, like those chosen by Basil II in 1014, along with totally blind leaders, exist today in all levels of society. While many prefer to be like blind followers and leave their life direction to others, each of us is a leader. Parents and politicians, coaches and clergy, disciples and masters are all called to lead others by word and example. In family, business, education, religion, as well as politics, there are those whose vision is single-eyed: They can only see today's stretch of life's road.

If you recognize that you are seeing only with the eye of today, practice opening the other eye that looks, and then plans, ahead. If you find that you still see with only one eye, you might pray this prayer:

> Lord, you who opened the eyes of the blind,
>> giving sight to the sightless who longed to see,
>> grant me the gift to look ahead.
> As the future races toward us at supersonic speed,
>> open my eye on tomorrow
>> so I will be able to respond with grace
>> not just to this day,
>> but to all that is coming.

✴

The Feast of Sour Wine, Vinegar. Perhaps as long ago as 5,000 years before the Christian Era (B.C.), the Babylonians discovered the various uses of fermented vinegar made from date palms. The name comes from two French words, *vin* meaning "wine" and *aigre* meaning "sour." The Carthaginian general Hannibal used vinegar to clear the path for his elephants to cross the alps to invade Italy. His soldiers, the Roman writer Titus Livius said, heated the rocks that blocked their path and poured vinegar on them, causing them to split.

On this second full day after winter, when colds are still about, consider this old remedy for a cough: Mix one-half cup of apple cider vinegar with one-half cup of water, add one teaspoon cayenne pepper and four teaspoons of honey. Take this mixture whenever you need to "crack" the hard rocks of coughing and at bedtime.

※⁂※

As we have seen, the practical life and the spiritual life are one, and the wise do not draw a line between them. So when your path is blocked by the large boulders of life's problems, place four times four teaspoons of honeyed humor on them as you secretly sip the sour wine of difficulties. As you do, like Hannibal, you may find your way cleared of difficulties.

✶

24 Eve of the Feast of St. Dismas, the Good Criminal.
The Feast of St. Dismas on March 25 is usually eclipsed by the feast of the Annunciation. The name Dismas has been given by tradition to the condemned criminal who died on the cross next to Jesus. The dying Jesus overreached his pain and extended compassion to Dismas along with a guarantee of paradise that very day. Though tomorrow is the actual feast day of Dismas, the events and commemorations that crowd that day easily can overshadow this saint's feast.

❦

Today, pray for all who are imprisoned, especially those who will experience the same fate as Dismas: capital punishment. This feast is an excellent occasion to examine your personal beliefs concerning our contemporary justice system. Since a majority of those presently in American prisons are guilty of nonviolent crimes, we might ask: What is the proper place of prisons in our society? Is the present approach of imprisonment as punishment for wrongdoing — instead of rehabilitation — what citizens should desire from the penal system?

This is also a day to examine our attitudes toward those imprisoned. In his parable of the Last Judgment found in Matthew's Gospel, Jesus said, "I was in prison and you visited me" (Mt. 25: 36). And those judged by him worthy of reward in the next life responded, "Lord, when did we see you in prison?" (Mt. 25: 39). Today's feast of the saintly ex-convict Dismas asks the question: Have you ever visited Jesus in prison? If your answer is no, you might ask yourself why you have neglected this Christian duty.

✶

Feast of the Annunciation and of Jesus' Conception. 25

Nine months from Christmas, this feastday celebrates Mary's response to the Archangel Gabriel about being overshadowed by the Holy Spirit. Once known, logically, as the day of the conception of Jesus, this fact has long taken a back seat to the announcement of the birth. A feast of the early sixth century, it was a public holiday in the Middle Ages. Truly this was a high holy day, marking the beginning of the legal year, a practice that continued in England even after the Reformation, until 1752. According to some traditions, it was also the day of the crucifixion and death of Jesus, the day the world was created, the fall of Adam and Eve, the sacrifice of Isaac, the day of the Exodus from Egypt and the future day of the Last Judgment. On this Smorgasbord Feast day, you can pick buffet-style which one or ones of the many feasts you wish to remember.

❧✦❧

Aware of the many predictions of the approaching End of the World that are part of Millennialism, take care today. Since it was once believed to be the day of the Last Judgment, this day would be much more serious than the Ides of March. To live today as if the world would end — making it the day on which you stand before the Divine Judge — would make this a feast of significant days: Reconciliation Day, Pardon Your Enemies Day, Prayer Day, Love Your Neighbors Day and Abstain from Sin Day. If even only a handful of people celebrated March 25th in one of these ways, it would indeed be a high holy day.

✴

Fire Drill Day. 26

In order to insure the safe and orderly evacuation of schools in case of a fire, frequent fire drills are held to teach the children how to behave in a disaster. Since these fire drills do not follow a schedule, those who respond to the fire alarms do not know if it is a drill or a real fire. Today is the celebration of the invention of the fire drill — a practice that has protected countless lives.

❧✦❧

Blessed are those who hold regular fire-disaster drills in their personal spiritual lives. These exercises could be called Calvary fire drills, for they are exercises to prepare you for a cross, so that when your cross comes you will respond in an appropriate way. Instead of fire, these drills are practice for such personal disasters as physical or sexual assault, robbery by pickpockets, the violation of your home by thieves, the loss of your spouse, being informed you have cancer or losing your employment or your good name by public accusation.

To respond to one or all of them in the way of one who believes in God's abiding care and love, to embrace a disaster without self-pity or anger, requires frequent practice drills. While the Gospels do not tell us if Jesus practiced such Calvary fire drills, his behavior when he was stripped of honor and inflicted with great pain and suffering shows that he was prepared.

Take a few minutes today to reflect on how you would like to respond to one or several of the disasters that are listed, perhaps adding one or two of your own. By such fire drills you keep one eye open for the possibilities of tomorrow.

⚜

Today is also the **Birthday of the American Poet, Robert Frost**, in 1874 in San Francisco. He attended both Dartmouth and Harvard, but did not earn a degree. A Frost-bite thought for this day could be: It isn't necessary to get a college degree to make the world more beautiful by your life and work.

✷

27 **The Feast Day of Your Conception.** Two days ago on March 25 we celebrated the Conception of Jesus, whose birth will be celebrated nine months hence on Christmas. Today is a feast to remember the day you were conceived in your mother's womb. As a symbolic gesture, count down nine months from the date of your birth and turn to that day in this Almanac. As one of your ✷ Star-Date entries, inscribe it as *Conception Day*. When we come to that day, remember your father and mother prayerfully and with gratitude. Then reflect on how, along with their love, the Holy Spirit was also involved as the Spirit of

Love in the holy act of your conception.

If you believe that life begins at conception, then consider measuring your years from that date instead of your birth date. When asked your age, you can playfully give two numbers.

Or you can count six months from your birth date and inscribe that day in this Almanac as your half-birthday. Consider throwing half-a-party for yourself on that day. On your half-birthday you might reverse the usual birthday custom and give gifts to those you love to celebrate the occasion.

Life is a celebration, and the more personal feast days we enjoy the more life can be lived as a joy instead of a duty.

28

Birthday of Your Surname, 1100 A.D. While first names have been with us for millenniums, the last name is an invention of the first part of the Second Millennium. The oldest recorded first name is *En-lil-ti,* which was found on a Sumerian clay tablet from about 3300 B.C. Scholars believe it may not be an individual's name but that of a Sumerian god. If that's true, then the oldest recorded human first name is *N'armer,* who was an Egyptian pharaoh shortly before 3000 B.C.

Early in the Second Millennium in Venice, wealthy families began to give their children a last name, or surname. Previously, the name of a person's clan or village served as the second name, as in Jesus of Nazareth. While family names were used briefly in ancient Rome, after the fall of the Empire this custom was abandoned. As late as the fifteenth century, many English and all Irish had only a first name. King Edward decreed in 1465 that every Irishman should take a surname based on the name of his town, occupation or craft.

The common custom among the Irish was to take the name of one's father, placing an "O" or "Mc" before it to indicate "a descendant." O'Brien or McBrien, then, was the son of Brien. Scots similarly used "Mac." Italians frequently placed "di" as a preface, as in di Giovani, son of Giovani. In Poland and Russia it was indicated with a "ski" or "sky" at the end of a name.

Klansinski, then, was a descendant of Klansin.

In the Middle Ages, German princes forced Jews to adopt Germanic names, which had to be bought from the prince. Expensive names were those like Goldberg, "mountain of Gold," and moderately priced names described trades, as in Schneider, which means "tailor." Poor Jewish peasants were forced to have cheap names, such as Schmutz, meaning "dirt," or even Eselkopf, which means "ass head." Naturally, Jews with such names changed them at the first opportunity.

⚜

Today, in the mail that comes addressed to you, when you are greeted or are asked to give your name in a business transaction, you can appreciate having a last name. In one of these situations, or even before the day begins, give thanks for your family name. Be especially grateful that you do not have to buy your name like those poor Jewish peasants in the Middle Ages. Spend a few moments looking at your family name and prayerfully remember your parents, grandparents, great-grandparents and all those who for some five hundred years have passed that name from generation to generation.

Each time you either see or write your family name, also look for your other family name, written with invisible ink. It too is a Jewish name, but one more beautiful and precious than Goldberg. Once, when Jesus was teaching a small circle of his disciples in a house in Galilee, a message came to him that his family was outside, that his mother, brothers and sisters wanted to speak to him. Opening his arms as wide as the circle of disciples, he said, "These are my mother, brothers and sisters. All who do the will of God are family to me" (see Mk. 3: 31-35). Belonging to the family of Jesus, having God's family name, cannot be obtained by paying any price. It does not even require Baptism, but only doing the will of God. Is Jesus saying that those other than Christians might belong to his family? Jesus, after all, came not to begin a new religion but rather a new way of living, living as a global family.

What greater honor is there than being a brother or sister of Jesus, for think of how God must look upon you and how God must listen to your prayers. Yet honor requires responsibilities.

So on this day of family names, strive to treat your brothers and sisters as you would a cherished member of your own blood family. Make your love concrete by caring for their needs in crisis as well as their needs for comfort, consolation and compassion.

In 1997, the *Xinhua* news agency declared the family name of Li, used by eighty-seven million Chinese mainlanders, to be the most widely used surname. How many of the world's over one billion Christians behave as if they had a second surname such as O'Jesus, di Jesus or Jesuski? In these March Lenten days, pray about how you treat your family, your real family.

✳

Bobo Masquerade, Creating Order Out of Disorder Day. 29

The Bobo people of Sudan, Africa, south of the Sahara and north of the equator, celebrate the divine gift of order today. According to their religious legends, the god Wuro created a perfectly balanced cosmos, with the earth, rain, the sun and humans living in perfect equilibrium. By farming, people threw everything out of balance, so the god Wuro created the god Dwo to bring back balance and natural order to life. The Bobo people on this feast parade with giant painted masks covered with long dark streamers to represent Dwo. By this ritual reenactment, the god Dwo helps them to chase away any evil present and to restore order, bringing the necessary rain for their crops.

❦

Bring order into disorder and clean house today! In the book of Genesis, God brings order out of chaos at the beginning of creation. To bring order to your desk, closet, room or garage is a divine feeling since you are acting as God did in creation, and as Dwo did in the Sudan. No wonder it feels so good, so heavenly, to bring a sense of order to your work or life.

On this day when the Sudan Bobo people masquerade, perhaps you could masquerade too, especially if you have children, by wearing a wastebasket as a hat and with a broom as your baton. Launch into cleaning up your office, room, house and life. As you rejoice in the divine feeling of seeing your space pleasant and harmonious, remember that order by its very nature reverts to disorder, and disorder quickly turns into chaos.

Mindful of this cosmic law, enjoy feeling divine by frequently restoring order out of disorder and chaos — perhaps even reenacting a brief Bobo ritual by bringing order to your desk or kitchen at the end of the day.

✵

30 The Purchase of the Polar Bear Garden, Alaska, 1867.

This is a good day to practice what appears to be folly but is really great wisdom. At 4 A.M. on this day in 1867, William Seward, the Secretary of State for President Andrew Johnson, purchased Alaska from Russia for the super sale price of only seven million dollars. Seward sealed the sale by signing a treaty with Baron de Stoecle, Czar Alexander II's minister to the United States. Most Americans, seeing with only one eye (see again the entry for March 22), unable to perceive the vast hidden resources contained in Alaska, called this treaty purchase "Seward's Folly" or "Seward's Icebox" and "Johnson's Polar Bear Garden."

❦

The next time you're tempted to view something with only one eye, able to see only today's use or only what is on the surface, remember Johnson's Polar Bear Garden purchase. While instant judgments and evaluations are commonplace responses to anything new, the practice of Alaskan Delay could prove prudent for you. When asked what you think of this new discovery or that new thought or course of action, you could answer, "Remembering Johnson's 1867 Polar Bear Garden, I would prefer waiting a few years before making a judgment." If you are asked about the "Polar Bear Garden," you can retell the wondrous tale of the multibillion dollar investment that cost a mere seven million dollars.

✵

The Feast of the Non-Saint Etgall. The Irish saint Etgall is the patron of anonymous saints. After centuries of harsh monastic asceticism at Skellig Michael, a cluster of hermitages on a barren island off the coast of Ireland, all the monks but one had left the island. Etgall, the hermit-anchorite, lived there alone until 823 when Vikings came to the island searching for treasure. Not finding anything of worth, in anger, or perhaps hoping for a ransom for the holy man, the raiders carried off Etgall as their prisoner. Legend says he died of starvation, yet the hermit had lived on hardly more than bread and water for years! More likely, he grieved the loss of his beloved sea birds' cries, the loss of the crash of the waves and the awesome grand silence of his island retreat, until death rescued him.

⁂

His feast is in no calendar, save this one. He converted no heathens, worked no miracles, wrote no poetic prayers nor illuminated a single manuscript. His sole claim to holiness was akin to yours and millions of others: Etgall struggled daily to respond creatively to whatever life sent his way with a passionate love of God. Blessed are all the anonymous but powerful saints of today, whose prayers and lives move both heaven and earth.

⁂

Also check the weather today to see if March, whether lion or lamb, has gone out, as the old adage goes, the opposite of how it arrived thirty-one days ago. Test old adages without necessarily abandoning them.

✳

THE
MONTH
OF
APRIL

Appropriately, the Saxon name for this month is *Easter-monath*. It is also the time when trees and plants begin to open their buds and the earth's womb opens with new green life. The Latin *aperire*, the root word for the name of this fourth month, means "to open." Were a new universal calendar to be created in the twenty-first century as humans venture out into Space Stations, perhaps the opening month of the year could be April. The method for numbering the years in this new calendar might also be changed to be more inclusive. Such a Space Calendar might be a compromise resolution with other existing calendars, including those of Islamic, Jewish and Eastern religions. Would you be *aperire* to a new calendar?

***

April Fools' Day. Today is an important festival for the age of Millennialism since it celebrates how the future can make fools out of us. Recall the March 25 entry and how it celebrated the feast of the Annunciation, which was the Conception of Jesus, and also New Year's Day. This trinity of feasts was an eight-day celebration which ended on April 1. However, by the middle of the sixteenth century the dates of the old calendar of Julius Caesar no longer corresponded to the times of the seasons. Pope Gregory XIII reformed the existing calendar in March of 1582. His new Gregorian Calendar corrected the error and made the beginning of the new year not March 25 but January 1. Nevertheless, countless people refused to embrace this radical change and continued to celebrate their new year on the first day of April.

The reform also required creating a leap year and removing ten days; so in the first year of the reform October 15 became October 5. Although the new calendar decreed by the pope was received by most Catholic countries, numerous nations refused to follow it and continued to celebrate today as New Year's.

1

Those who did not embrace the change were called "April Fools."

⚜

Today's folly, and there should be large doses of it in your life, echoes the ancient spring celebrations of fun at the way Mother Nature fools us with the weather. Refuse to react like an old-fashioned April Fool when you find you have been robbed of time, be it ten days, ten hours or ten minutes. Time is not stolen from you today by a pope in order to bring order to time, but rather is pickpocketed by canceled air flights, traffic jams, unexpected extra work, visiting relatives or needing to return phone calls. Instead of responding to your lost hours with fury, do so with fun, especially on this All Fools' Day.

How can you have fun when you are frustrated or even angry over the loss of time? If you are forced to wait, try playing a game of hide-and-seek with your frustration. Tell your fury to close its eyes and count to ten, then go and hide in your imagination or slip into dreaming about something you'd like to do that your busy schedule has forbidden. If you have lost time due to the arrival of the unexpected, then try playing a game of "Knock, Knock, Who's There?" Ask yourself a riddle like, "Who stole your time — or did you generously give it away?" Knock, knock, who's there? "Who really took away that precious hour, Mr. So-and-so or the one who said, 'I was hungry for your time and you fed me: Enter now into paradise'?"

Whenever your TIP (Time Is Precious) schedule is interrupted and you are on the edge, use the occasion as an opportunity to work with God. When we choose the human way over the divine way, God must constantly rearrange and readapt, finding new ways to lead us to harmony and holiness. Those who make their schedules flexible find it easier to follow God's lead. Blessed are those who are not TIPped over, who do not worship the clock, their daily schedules or their lists of must-do-today things.

✺

---

2 **The Cart Before the Horse Day, 1785.** While this could be an encore of yesterday's feast, the absence of horses from daily life makes the old expression more a puzzle than a playful

image. Only a fool would put his horse behind his cart, yet consider the ingenious case of Jean Pierre Francois Blanchard. Today celebrates his invention of the parachute in 1785 — yes, 1785, over a century before airplanes. Three cheers for Jean Blanchard, who is a patron secular saint of those who create inventions before they are needed, and who must only wait till their day comes. Blanchard was a French balloonist who tested his creation fit for the next century by attaching a parachute to a basket containing a dog, which he dropped from his balloon.

⚜

The next time you have an idea for something without an immediate purpose, rejoice and shout, "Viva, Jean Blanchard!" Then begin to design your idea. It need not be an invention; it might only be a better way to do some routine task or a way to reconstruct a potentially sagging vocation. Regardless of its nature, play with the idea, for while necessity is the mother of invention, the grandmother of inventiveness is play.

✴

It's Raining Cats and Dogs Day. Today's festival comes from the old expression for an unusually heavy rainfall, perhaps like the record breaking one in Unionville, Maryland, on July 4, 1956, when 1.23 inches fell in one minute! The record rainfall for a year belongs to Cherrapunji, India, where from August 1860 to August 1861 it rained 1,042 inches! Dogs and cats falling from the sky could have been the theme of yesterday's celebration of the unknown hero of the first parachute drop in 1785. While history recalled the inventor, Jean Blanchard, who knows what honor was given to his unnamed test pilot, Monsieur Mutt?

On this dog and cat day, we also honor a dog whose name we do know, Bobby, a homeless Skye terrier. As a pup he attached himself to an elderly shepherd named Auld Jock. In 1858, old Jock died, but for fourteen years, day and night, Bobby guarded his master's grave. He only left the grave to go to the restaurant where Jock used to go, there he was daily given food which he carried away to eat at the grave. Touched by his devotion, Edinburgh's citizens erected a shelter at the grave to protect

Bobby from the harsh cold of winters. In 1872 Bobby too died and was buried next to Auld Jock.

As for cats falling like rain, and landing on their feet, the record seems to go to an unnamed heroine in 1973. This feline fell from the twentieth floor of a tall building in Montreal, Canada, and suffered only a pelvic fracture.

⚜

As a moral for today's pet feast, choose one from these possibilities: Before going outside without wearing a hard hat, be sure and check the sky for brave skydiving, parachuting dogs. Scan the skies overhead for dive-bombing, bold cats trying to prove their ability to always land on their feet. Or, pattern your friendships on the faithful terrier of Edinburgh, Scotland, Bobby, whose loyalty lasted long beyond death and whose fidelity withstood frigid weather and isolation. Bobby, be a model for us today in our faithfulness to friends, to those we love and to God.

✡

---

4 Futurama Fun Day.

Futurama Fun Day. In this month that begins with April Fools' Day, we celebrate how the future can fool us. At the New York World's Fair of 1939-1940 the General Motors' exhibit was the most popular. It was called Futurama and contained these predictions for America in the 1960s: "Federal laws forbid wanton cutting of wooded hillsides. People do not care much for possessions. Two-months paid vacations will be common. Cars will be air-conditioned and cost only $200, and the happiest people will live in one-factory villages."

⚜

Daily we travel from the past to the future over the Bridge of Today. Some of us are forever looking backwards from where we have come, and some of us are attempting to camp out on the Bridge. Like those in 1939's Futurama, some try to foresee the future. This "future" is not so much what will happen as what we attempt to cause to happen. As you cross the Bridge of

Today, consider creating your own future, which is like making Irish stew.

Understand as you begin your "Future Stew" that into the Pot of Tomorrow will have been thrown large chucks of global and social changes over which you have little or no control. Many of these will be radical and difficult to swallow, so add large pieces of sweet dreams, mixed with spices of idealism and vision that can flavor those large chunks of social changes. Add handfuls of the spices of the vision of God's tomorrow, which includes the divine perpetual presence in every aspect of the world, a vision which Jesus lived out daily as he crossed the Bridge of Today. Next, add those spices of dreams of a life rich with personal time for self and family along with time for service to others, the vision of loving deeply and being loved, as well as a wish to be ever-flexible, strong and faithful without being rigid. Then add the potatoes of pals, good friends who will be companions willing to join you in high adventure, which is surely the "name" of tomorrow.

Finally, add any other ingredients to suit your personal taste. Allow this pot to simmer daily on a back burner, and remember to stir it frequently. Occasionally taste your stew from the spoon of stolen moments of dreaming, both for your pleasure and to see if some new ingredient needs to be added to your tomorrow.

✳

Feast of St. Vincent Ferrer, Patron of Builders. This noble-born fourteenth century Spaniard was known for his preaching eloquence. While he spent hours preparing his sermons, his outstanding good looks and deep baritone voice caused women to swoon. On one occasion he preached that Judas Iscariot had repented before his death and was now with Christ in heaven. While Jesus himself would have delighted in such a last-minute conversion, especially of one of his trusted friends of the inner-circle, the Inquisition did not delight in Vincent's wishful theory. He was barely spared the "honor" of being made the patron of scaffold builders or those burned at the stake when his friend, Benedict XIII, one of three contending claimants to be bishop of Rome, had his Inquisition file with its condemning evidence burned.

⚜

April is Easter Month, and a good opportunity to consider if Vincent Ferrer was guilty of heresy by saying that Judas had repented before his death and so would be among the Easter People of heaven. In the court of human justice, it is heresy to suggest that villains and notorious criminals might escape punishment, be their names Ivan the Terrible, Hitler or Judas. Even though Scripture has God saying, "Vengeance is mine," humans prefer jumping the gun and taking their own revenge on criminals. While we do not know how God takes vengeance, its quality or style, we *are* held accountable for our deeds and thoughts of evil and harm to others. Jesus was the picture of God in human flesh, and on the cross he granted a last-minute pardon to St. Dismas, the criminal dying on the cross next to him.

Reflect on this question today: If you were asked for forgiveness by one who had betrayed you and caused you great pain, would you grant it? The Risen Jesus used an Easter Eraser to remove the failings of his friends; consider using it yourself.
�֎

---

6 **Futurama II Day.** Enjoy, or regret, this day as you have the rare pleasure of experiencing not Futurama but the future-all-around-you. This is a feast for imagining that it is ten or twenty years from the stew you created two days ago in your Pot of Tomorrow. Now that the future is here, how does it fit your vision of what it would be like? Does the future you slip into today fit comfortably? Does it measure up to your dreams, or is it a bad fit? Do you find it too tight, with not enough freedom of movement? If you find it more beautiful than you could have dreamed, know that you helped to make it so. If, however, today isn't beautiful, then wear it as best you can, but take out your design board. On this Futurama II Day, redesign the future that you will be wearing five years from now.

⚜

Today is also the **Chinese Feast of *Qing Ming***, a festival in which people visit graveyards to remember their ancestors. *Qing Ming* means "bright and clear" and is a happy rather than somber festival. At the tombs of their ancestors, the Chinese clean away weeds and burn incense sticks and red candles. They also leave wine and rice gifts for the spirits of the dead. A good way to passionately prepare your future would be to celebrate your own *Qing Ming*. However, rather than going to your ancestors' graves, go to your own! Clear the weeds that choke off your dreams. Light again the pleasing incense sticks and candles of hope blown out by the winds of *what is* rather than *what can be*. The past is dead — leave token gifts to honor your past. Then, generously sow the seeds of the future that you wish, God willing, to be your final legacy. Visiting the cemetery where someday you will be buried, even if only in your mind, can provide you with a "bright and clear" passion to do all you can today to create a beautiful future for yourself.

⚜

Life on the Moon and Other Hoaxes Day, 1835. The circulation of the *New York Sun* reached a record peak in 1835 after a week-long series of articles by Richard Locke stating that Sir John Herschel had discovered life on the moon. Using the world's largest telescope, Herschel was said to have seen fur-covered bat-like creatures which "were evidently engaged in conversation; they appeared impassioned and emphatic...and were given to producing works of art and contrivance." This scientific study, however, was soon revealed as a hoax.

Of course, it's not only newspapers that create hoaxes and fraud. For example, Sir Cyril Burt, a British psychologist, deliberately made up scientific data for three decades from the mid-1940s to 1960. The data was contrived to support his theory about the relationship between heredity (good breeding) and intelligence. His fraudulent claim was that intelligence is over seventy-five percent inherited. The aim of his research was to support the ongoing practice of the British class system.

Even the great scientist Isaac Newton (1642-1727), it is now shown, tinkered with the numbers to add weight to his theory of universal gravitation. Then there's the story of the historic Piltdown Man, who was discovered in 1908 in Piltdown Common in Sussex, England, and was hailed as the missing link between apes and humans. In 1950, using modern equipment, researches discovered the skull was a hoax made up of an ape's jaw and part of a human skull which had been stained to give the appearance of great age.

Naturally, there are more examples, but these are enough for today's reflection on how easily we believe and how readily we create evidence for our beliefs. Who among us is immaculately free of tinkering with the facts or adjusting the figures to prove a fact or position. Because of our deep prejudices, we are willing to believe lies, exaggerations, gossip and hearsay if they support our personal theories.

April Fools' Day was a day for playing pranks and innocent hoaxes and shouting, "April Fool." Today is a good opportunity to ponder on how fudging with the truth and exaggerating the facts can make us the fool, and a not-so-funny hoaxer.

8

The Birthday of the Rainbow – the Dawn of Creation. Today the rainbow is at least five million years old, having appeared with the first rains that fell on a hot, steaming earth at the time of creation.

Then, one day eons and eons ago, a prehistoric shower that was more than an April shower began to fall. It quickly turned into a downpour that didn't stop for forty days (read: many, many moons). Rivers, lakes and oceans joined in holy wetlock. Not only do the Hebrew Scriptures of Genesis record this rainy season, it is found in numerous other scriptures of early peoples.

After forty days the rains stopped, and one vast lake covered the earth on which floated the ark of Noah. On April 8, Noah came out of his great boat, along with his family and all the creatures he had taken aboard his floating zoo. In gratitude he made an altar of stones and offered sacrifice to God. God was pleased, promising never again to drown the world with water.

As a pledge of this promise, God painted a brilliant rainbow that arched across the blue cloudless sky.

━━◦◉◦━━

Whenever you see a rainbow during this spring season of rain, reflect on God's promise made to Noah, the promise to be a companion forever with him and all his descendants, and with all the creatures he had taken on the ark. This Covenant of Noah has profound consequences, for it unites God with all humanity and all creation, thus uniting us with all pre-Jewish, pre-Christian peoples and with all the natural world, including forests, marshes, mountains, cows, dogs and cats, birds and fish. Today, rainbow or not, celebrate the Covenant of Noah with the same enthusiasm as when we commemorate the Covenants of Abraham, Moses and Jesus.

If you have a garden or favorite plants or a cat, dog, bird or other pet, find a memorable way today to celebrate with them this Covenant of Noah that makes them special and beloved of God.

✤

Hallelujah Replacement Day. "Alleluia," the Easter season victory shout, has its source in the Hebrew "Hallelujah," meaning, "Praise Yahweh." While today it is a Christian proclamation of victory over death, it originally was a liturgical directive given at the beginning and end of the recitation of a psalm. Today it is still a prayer word whose meaning is not understood by many. While not restricted to prayer and worship, among more religious people it can be heard as an exclamation in praise of God's work or of something wonderful.

In or out of the Easter Season, consider a new replacement exclamation for those magical and wondrous moments in life, those times that call for more than a liturgical directive, but rather for a shout of Good News. The next time you feel God's presence or power, experience a personal minor miracle, a stroke of good luck or hear someone speak electric words that inspire you, consider shouting "Immanuel!" Also Hebrew in origin (even in its spelling, which is usually transposed as Emmanuel), it is

9

the name the angel gave for Jesus, as the prophet Isaiah had predicted. Immanuel means "God is with us" and therefore carries profound implications. The use of this one word, even spoken quietly to yourself, is an affirmation that God is here — that the reign of God, as Jesus said, is among us.

⚜

If you wish a daily reminder of the Good News of Jesus that God's kingdom, God's time, has arrived, cultivate a use of Immanuel as a one-word prayer to awaken you to that reality. You might ask: What about other times not so wonderful, times of suffering, accidents and even disasters? As with other ancient languages, Hebrew can have shaded differences of meaning in the same word. So it is with Immanuel, which can also mean "*May* God be with us." As such, this one-word prayer becomes a plea for God to appear and help us resolve whatever problem must be faced. Since Jesus promised to be with us always, calling upon his ancient name can bring the power of the Risen Christ to our side.

Such a use of Immanuel isn't original, for today's scholars say that Isaiah did not use it as a proper name! It was more an ejaculation or religious slogan that evoked a faith-filled response to life.

What's in a name? Far, far more than we can ever guess!

✴

---

10 Celebration of the First Human Cannonball, 1877.

On this day in London in 1877, the first human cannonball was shot out of a canon. Today this unidentified hero is the patron saint of all those who leave home as if shot out of a canon, with hardly a kiss or a hug.

⚜

This is also No Accident Day: It's no accident that it's also the **Feast of the Birthday of SSt. General William Booth**, founder of the Salvation Army, in Nottingham, England, in 1829. If he were a Catholic, he would have been canonized, so let's make him a saint for founding — in the face of great opposition

— this outstanding religious community of men and women who care for the poor and needy. SSt. William Booth is like a holy cannonball shot by the Holy Spirit to arouse in the churches such creative innovations for the Gospel as brass bands and street-corner preaching.

※⊛⊱

Pray today, regardless of your denomination, for a new William Booth to bring some enthusiasm, joy and excitement into your church. Pray today that Booth will inspire you to inject into your faith life a large dose of his spirit of both joyfulness and care for the poor. Today his Salvation Army is among the most respected of charitable organizations. Consider celebrating his feast day by sending a donation to your local Salvation Army to care for the poor whom SSt. William loved.

✦

Pointing at a Rainbow Brings Bad Luck Day. It was an old English belief that if you pointed up to a beautiful rainbow dreadful bad luck would fall out of the skies upon you. While you may draw another's attention to a rainbow, by all means, in this month of showers, don't *point* at the beautiful bow. Also, guard against ever stepping on a rainbow. It is believed that even if you walk across an oil patch on the road with its rainbowed colors, you will fall victim to foul luck. Instead, stop and chant, "Rainbow, rainbow, bring me luck. If you don't, I'll break you up."

※⊛⊱

As children we were taught that it is impolite to point at a person. Today's reflection awakens us to the fact that this is also true for any rainbow, bird or bug. Treat with great reverence all you encounter today, for according to the Rainbow Covenant of God with Noah, the Divine One is with all humans and all creatures, large and small.

✦

12

Alleluia Replacement Day. While a respectable religious word, Alleluia, like a hothouse plant, is restricted to a sheltered life inside a church building. To hear it spoken in daily speech today is rare. Recall the April 9 entry on Hallelujah, which spoke of it being a liturgical directive that became a prayer in itself. Consider today the liberating effect in worship and prayer if Alleluia were to be translated not into proper English but into American slang as "Whoopee!"

Whoopee began as a proper Middle English word, "whoop," which was used to arouse enthusiasm and as a call to have a good time, as in "whoop it up." Consider the consequences if "Whoop it Up" were placed as a liturgical-worship directive before a prayer or at the top of a worship program. As slang, to "make whoopee" means to make love. Now there's a liturgical directive to write in red ink on every page of your prayer book, and to be shouted loudly at the beginning of every Mass or worship service: "Whoopee! Let's make love — with God, and one another!"

13

The Birthday of President Thomas Jefferson, 1743. Today's celebration provides an opportunity to honor a great man and a genius and to personally ponder a presidential paradox. The same man who penned those famous words of 1776 that everyone had equal rights to "life, liberty and the pursuit of happiness" had at the time 175 humans enslaved for his personal profit and pleasure. The human ability to believe one thing and live another, to be unmoved by your belief or to rationalize exceptions to your principles is further revealed by the fact that by 1822 Jefferson had increased his ownership to 267 slaves. During his lifetime he only freed three, and an additional five more at his death — each of whom were blood relatives. The Jefferson Memorial in Washington has his words carved in its white marble walls, "I have sworn eternal hostility against every form of tyranny over the mind of men."

Today, reflect on what beliefs you firmly hold but fail to extend to others. Take time to examine those things you've sworn hostility towards but still tolerate in your own life.

✳

Noah Webster Copyrights His Dictionary Day. On this day in 1828, Webster applied for a copyright on his famous book of books. Yet this was a period when few were terribly interested in the correct spelling of words. Those who could write were more concerned about the style and content of their words. George Washington and many of the founders of our country were celebrated bad spellers. If you find yourself among their ranks today, rejoice, for you are in good company.

14

❧❀❧

While computer programs today provide the writer with the gift of a spell-check and even proper replacement words for an incorrectly spelled word, they do not provide the adventurer's feast of getting lost in Webster's Wonderland of Words. I refer to that electric experience of going on a dictionary quest to find the correct spelling of a word, and in this expedition to have a Columbus Experience! Like Christopher Columbus, who found something other than what he set out looking for, you will discover new and wondrous words for the first time. Like Columbus, you will not be the first one to discover them, but the joy and excitement, I assure you, will be as fresh as if you were.

✳

"Women and Children First" Day. On this day in 1912 the "unsinkable" Titanic sank, taking a terrible toll of human life. Part of the myth of that sea disaster is that the women and children passengers escaped death to board lifeboats as the ship's stewards called out, "Women and children first." In reality the unspoken call was, "All first-class women and children first." According to authors Hollingshead and Redich, only 4 of 143 first-class passengers and 15 of 93 second-class passengers

15

drowned. All the while the crew was holding third-class women and children below deck, some at gunpoint, as the lifeboats were being loaded.

⚜

Ponder your personal responsibility as wealth and social class continues to determine who are survivors and who are not. The poor, especially those of color, and immigrants, like the poor aboard the Titanic, are kept below deck, out of reach of good health care, quality education or equal treatment under the law.

On this Income Tax Due Day, as you grumble about all the taxes you pay, consider for a moment that some of your tax money does go to help those who would have been held below deck by gunpoint on the Titanic. While no one likes to pay taxes, they are a way that we all share in the support of our country and its many social programs for the poor, elderly and needy. That the government could be run more efficiently is another issue, perhaps to appear on a later date in this Almanac. For today, kiss your tax envelope as you place it in the mail and say, "May the poor get more of my money than others who have less need of it."

✳

---

16 **The Birthday of Holy Mother Eve of Eden.** This is the celebration of the birthday of Eve, the primal great-grandmother of all humans. Saint Mother Eve's actual birth date is lost in the mist of time almost immortal, but is too important not to be celebrated. Today we acknowledge that we are all related, even if this awareness is buried deep within us. We are not strangers but family who simply fail to recognize each other as sisters and brothers. Scientific evidence has recently confirmed the Biblical position of a primal mother from whom the human race arose.

While this reality of being related is usually unconscious, at times of disaster we *feel* a desire to reach out and assist those who are involved. Also in times of great joy, like the end of a world war or the victory of the hometown team, crowds of thousands respond to one another like long-lost sisters and brothers.

⚜

"We are all related" is a prayer of faith and communion that could well be repeated over and over in the midst of a crowd, a traffic jam or checkout line. The ritual of Holy Communion is intended to awaken us to this deeply buried and unspoken truth. The Native American Plains Indians, at the conclusion of their pipe ceremony, would all murmur: "We are all related." This ritual of smoking was communion not simply with those who participated but with every single person and with everything in creation. We could say this ritual prayer, "We are all related," at Holy Communion or any time in our daily lives when we find ourselves at the crossroads of communion. And each time we pray it today, we can remember all the way back to our mother, Eve, and beyond.

✳

"Good to the Last Drop" Day. Legend attributes those words to President Theodore Roosevelt. Once, while a guest, he was asked if he wanted another cup of coffee. Teddy is said to have replied, "Will I have another? Delighted! It's good to the last drop!" First used by Coca-Cola in 1908, that slogan became famous when adopted by Maxwell House Coffee. Coffee is good to the last drop, and good for countless other uses besides being a morning wake-up drink. **17**

Hair needs a tint? Rinse it with coffee to highlight brown or red hair. Spots on your black suede? Sponge on a little black Maxwell House. Head hurts? Drink a couple cups of coffee, since it acts as a vasoconstrictor and will reduce the swelling of blood vessels which is the cause of hangover headaches. Your plants need a perk-up? Gently work coffee grounds into the topsoil. Ants causing you trouble? Sprinkle dried coffee grounds outside doors and cracks. Coffee will deter ants from entering your home. Finally, if you want an added zing to your spaghetti sauce, add one-quarter to one-half teaspoon of instant Maxwell House to the sauce and it will give your store-bought spaghetti a brown tinting and reduce the dish's acidic flavor. While Americans now drink about 1.75 cups of coffee a day, that is about half of what was consumed in 1962. Even if you personally drink less, consider having a can of good, rich coffee in your home for the above uses and more. And the can — well, it's got countless uses too.

⚜

Yes, the practical life and the spiritual life are one, and wise are those who view them as joined at the hip. Not only is coffee good to the last drop, so is all of life. In a hurry to rush on to life's next experience, we frequently leave lots of life untasted and unsavored. Consider using Teddy Roosevelt's fabled response as a daily reply when questioned about whether you enjoyed something. Returning from a party, you might respond, "It was good to the last drop, to the final moment — I was the last one to leave." When watching a sunset, you might say, "It was good to the last drop — as the fading light blended into purple, I couldn't take my eyes off it." In your last days or even on your deathbed when asked about the quality of your life, you might respond, "Delightful! It was and is good to the last drop!"
✳

---

18 Inspection of Pandora's Box Day. The first woman created by the gods in early Greek theology, or mythology, was named Pandora. They gave her countless gifts — which accounts for her name, *Pan,* for "many," *dora,* for "gifts." The Graces, three sister goddesses who were givers of charm and beauty, clothed the first woman with knowledge, beauty, cunning and flattery, and the gods gave her a box or vase with the instructions never to open it. Pandora couldn't resist the call of curiosity, however, and opened the lid. At once all the world's evils, vices, sins and diseases, along with every possible trouble, flew out and into the world! Fearful at what she had done, Pandora slammed the lid shut and fled. Thus did early Greek theology explain the presence of evil in the world.

"Opening a can of worms," as an expression for letting all sort of evils loose, is only a contemporary way of saying, "opening

Pandora's box." While the massive escape of evils from Pandora's box is what is remembered from mythology, what is often forgotten is the gift the gods had left in the box. In her great haste to escape from what she had done, Pandora failed to see what remained in the bottom of her box — hope!

❦

Regardless of the culture, almost all the ancient scriptures have a story about how evil entered God's creation. Regardless of how powerful and numerous the evil forces might be, none of these ancient scriptures end without hope. So even though every age of transition abounds in predictions of gloom and doom and prophecies of the destruction of the world — and this new millennium is no exception — there is good reason to hope.

We long to hear predictions of hope for a better future along with prophecies of promise for a better world. Reflecting on the twentieth century reveals a massive growth of evil, with great worldwide wars, atomic destruction, genocide of millions and an ever-escalating ability of humans to use science and technology to destroy one another. Anyone who studies the twentieth century cannot be an optimist about the twenty-first century. Yet hope is not optimism. It is rather a gift of God which is the flower of love. Where there is love, there also will be hope. The best way to make tomorrow full of hope is to fill today with love.

❦

To this day is also attributed the legendary **Midnight Ride of Paul Revere, 1776**. He rode forth to announce, "Be prepared. The British are coming." Consider, today, being a Millennium Sentinel to rouse the people. In honor of Paul Revere, by your actions and words of love, announce, "Be hopeful! The Millennium is coming (has come)!"

✦

First Use of Chemical Warfare in America Day. In 1623, the British invited the Native American Indians who lived along the Potomac River to a treaty. The delegation was headed

19

by their chief, Chiskiack. To celebrate the treaty, the British proposed a toast, "symbolizing eternal friendship," after which Chief Chiskiack, his family, tribal elders and two hundred companions dropped dead from poison.

⚜

Consider two other common forms of chemical warfare. The first is the concealed malice hidden in sarcasm. Sarcasm comes from the Greek word that means "to tear flesh." It's a form of speech intended to hurt others through mocking ridicule or searing humor (a poisoned reminder like, "I won't hold my breath until you...).

Teasing is another form of chemical warfare in which the poison is disguised as humor. What is meant to smell funny is designed to inflict deadly pain and embarrassment. This chemical is used in childhood on playgrounds and at school to attack the weak. Children's radar for another's weaknesses and personality faults is keen. Adulthood has perfected the use of this cruel chemical to the point where it even defies being called warfare. When challenged after an attack of tease gas, the aggressor says, "I was only kidding. What's the matter, can't you take a joke?"

Today, sign a chemical weapons treaty with yourself, pledging never to use sarcasm, ridicule or teasing as weapons against others.

✡

---

20 **The Birthday of Hijacking, Chicago, 1926.** In the midst of the prohibition era in Chicago, rival gangs stole bootleg liquor from one another as another way to destroy the opposition. A member of one gang would jump on the running board of another gang's bootlegging truck and with a disarming smile would say, "Hi, Jack," before sticking the muzzle of his gun in the face of the unfortunate driver.

Today's airline hijackers usually are not that friendly as they commandeer an airplane, but the results are the same.

⚜

You can be hijacked today even if you never step aboard an airplane, so beware. Hijacking is the act of robbing a plane, train or armored truck while it is in transit, but it also means forcing or coercing someone to do something. Being "in transit," on the move, makes the target an easier one to hit. Children are expert hijackers who target you as you are hurrying out the door to work, with a disarming "Daddy, dear, can I...?" Or as you are busy fixing dinner: "Mommy, dear, is it all right if I...?" Adults bearing an agenda and a big smile also target you while you are "on the move," while busy with some task, to coerce you to serve on some committee or take on some duty. Being busy, "in transit," as on an airplane, your defenses are down.

The telephone is a favorite tool of lurking hijackers. The next time you feel you are being "hijacked," regardless of how noble or worthy the cause, resist! Ask your friendly hijacker to put the request in writing, so you can pray and reflect on it. After some quiet time and prayer, you can freely decide if you should respond to the request, and so never have to suffer from negative after-feelings of having been exploited.

✡

Death Day of Baron von Richthofen. 21

The famous German ace of World War I, the "Red Baron," was shot down over France and killed on this day in 1918. Few if any enemies have achieved such hero status as Manfred von Richthofen. His dead body was escorted to the grave by a British honor guard to be buried with full military honors, with Allied aviator officers serving as his pallbearers. A large wreath from British headquarters was hung on his grave, with the inscription "Our gallant and worthy foe."

᠅

Reflection for today: Do you respect those who are opposed to your views and positions, or do you treat them as "enemies"? Do you respond to those who challenge your beliefs, and even act against you, as gallant and worthy foes or as enemies to be hated and defeated?

Jesus calls upon us to perform a miracle — with the hidden

implication that such a miracle is possible to perform – when he says, "Love your enemies." The miracle created by such love is making enemies into friends, even if these friends have agendas totally at odds with yours.

Once, long ago, it would have been considered a miracle to fly, as did Baron von Richthofen. Greater than the marvel of human air flight, greater than the miracle of transforming water into wine is the miracle of transforming enemies into lovers. Consider working a miracle or two today.

---

22 **Dan Hartman's Electronic Jumpsuit Day.** This festival would be better called "Jump-Out-of-Your-Suit Day." Jumpsuits, originally used by paratroopers, are one-piece garments, a type of coveralls similar to those worn by garage mechanics. The rock star, Dan Hartman, performs wearing a $5,000 silverized guitar suit. His electric guitar fits into a pelvic pouch equipped with electrodes that transmit signals through wires sewn into the suit's lining and connected to a small, powerful transmitter in the thigh of the suit. He adjusts the tone and volume by pressing a button on the left sleeve. "Dynamite way to perform!" Hartman says. "I can feel the vibrations in my body. I know what my expectant mother must have felt. I *am* the music."

The writer of Galatians says, "For all of you...have clothed yourselves with Christ..." (Gal. 3: 27). To have put on the Risen Jesus is to wear an electric jumpsuit like Dan Hartman's, only one that is wired to the rest of verse 27 of Galatians: "...in you are neither Jew nor Greek, slave or free, female or male, for all are one in Christ." And similar to Hartman, you can say, "I don't hear the Good News; I *am* its music." Instead of letting your brain be the location of your belief that you are one in Christ, let your entire body be wired with that dynamic message. Your whole body, not just your mind, was baptized into the Risen Jesus. So let your entire body ring out that tingling new song. Today, wherever you go and whatever you do, *be* the mystical music.

If you happen to find yourself in some place filled with the loud music of division, hate or prejudice for those of another race, religion or group, remember Dan Hartman. Find a button on your left sleeve and tune up the clarity and volume of your mystically wired jumpsuit of Christ. You don't have to say a word – I assure you, you will *be* the good news music that will drown out the evil music of mischief and malice.

The Feast of St. George, the Patron of England, Horse Lovers, Knights and Defenders of the Weak. 23

George was a Palestinian soldier who died for his faith during the persecution of Christians by the Roman Emperor Diocletian (284-305). The Crusades carried back his fame and name to England, where Edward III made him that island's patron saint. Legendary is his story of victory in battle over an evil dragon which made him the ideal for knighthood's struggle against evil in its various forms. St. George is usually shown slaying the dragon while dressed in a knight's armor with a white banner on which is a red cross. The British flag is a form of the red cross of St. George, with the cross of St. Andrew, an X, behind it. For centuries the English would cry, "Saint George" as they charged into battle.

While not all dragons are evil and need slaying, evil dragons cry out for St. George and St. Georgette to challenge them in combat. Dragons are huge, fire-breathing reptilian monsters that prey upon the weak both in legend and in legions of places today: sweatshops, multinational corporate businesses and the "city halls" of countless organizations. Mindful that "You can't fight city hall," dragons are usually left alone. However, armed with the cross, consider going forth today to meet some local dragon in combat. The main weapon of a dragon is not its size – while it is indeed large – or its considerable flamethrowing ability, but fear!

Today's hero, St. George, was victorious against the dragon of evil because he rode into combat under the sign of the cross.

If today you should find your path blocked by some fire-breathing dragon — at home, at the office or at a school board meeting — you can flee in fear or engage the terrible dragon in combat. If your choice is the latter, mindful of St. George's Cross, first make the sign of the cross upon yourself, then trace it over the dragon! For as Jesus might have said, "Love your dragons and you will not destroy them, but will convert them — especially when you find a fire-breathing monster staring at you from your mirror."

✵

---

24 National Promote Saint Elvis Day.

Recently newspapers carried the story of David Sprite of St. Louis, Missouri, who has begun a vigorous campaign to have Elvis Presley canonized. Born in 1935 in Tupelo, Mississippi, Elvis died in 1977, or so some claimed. Recent history has seen few persons with more look-alikes and imitations — not to mention reported apparitions — than Elvis Presley. Sprite is collecting 10,000 testimonials which he wants to send to the Vatican's congregation for the canonization of saints. While the "King" undeniably was blessed with talent and a personal charism that moved millions with his music, his lusty personal life marked by drugs and overindulgence may be a big drawback. Traditionally, to be canonized a saint requires three proven miracles. That, of course, would not be difficult. If David Sprite's search for Elvis miracles joins forces with the *National Enquirer*, he will have three times three thousand miraculous testimonies to send to Rome.

꙰

Recall the April 22 entry on Dan Hartman. If you find "*being* the music" of the Good News difficult, consider calling upon the assistance of (St.) Elvis. If ever he is made a saint, his statue surely wouldn't be stiff and static on some pedestal; it would be vibrantly alive. Today, may Elvis inspire you to "*be* the music" of the Good News with his captivating style that employed his whole body.

✵

Feast of St. Mark, Arbor Day and Baptism Day. The season of Easter, which continues for fifty days after the feast of the Resurrection, is a time to celebrate your baptismal day, whether or not you know the actual date of your baptism. This April day allows you to celebrate that significant event in your life. By that bath in the river of the Holy Spirit and of Christ's death and resurrection, you became a new person, a person with the power to respond to life in new ways. One striking example of this newness comes from the archives of the Ford Motor Company.

In the early days of the Detroit Ford Motor Company there was a story of a machinist who for years had "borrowed" various tools and parts from the company shop and had somehow always conveniently "forgotten" to return them. It seems that in time the machinist had a conversion and was baptized as he joined a church. He took his baptismal conversion in Christ seriously, and the next morning he loaded up his pickup truck full with all his "borrowed" tools and parts and drove to work. He begged the plant manager to forgive him as he had not intended to steal them. The plant manager was so impressed with all this that he sent a long cable with the entire story in detail to Henry Ford, who at that time was touring Europe. Ford cabled back a message containing only two sentences: "Dam up the Detroit River. Have entire plant baptized!"

⚜

Take a bath or shower today and renew your baptism of radical conversion. While Baptism is a sacrament which needs to be received only once in a lifetime, on this day we consider the need for a plunge that produces real results. Today honors that unnamed saintly Ford machinist whose reformed post-baptismal life should not so much inspire us as shame us.

⚜

Saint Mark, patron of Venice and Gospel writer who shares this feast day, was a convert of St. Peter. His baptism radically changed his life as it did many early Christians and the Detroit machinist. In his Gospel, St. Mark could have given Jesus these words: "Know that it's never too late to be awakened to what happened to you when you were baptized."

⚜

This day also celebrates **Arbor Day**, a secular festival initiated by J. Sterling Norton in Nebraska in 1872 for the purpose of enriching the land by planting trees. Plant a tree today or find one to caress. As you do, recall that any tree takes years to grow from a sapling into a mighty tree that enriches all creation. Let a tree be an awakening lesson for you about how it seems necessary to "grow into" your baptism. Be patient with your reluctance to be new — but be impatient in your passion to make your baptism bear a great and rich harvest.

✸

---

26 **"Now, It's Perfect!" Day, 11,941 A.D.** This April day marks a long-awaited event at the Mt. Rushmore Memorial of four great American presidents, George Washington, Thomas Jefferson, Abraham Lincoln and Theodore Roosevelt. The massive memorial was carved out of the side of a mountain in the Black Hills of South Dakota by Gutzon Borglum. Paradoxically, there was no rush at Mount Rushmore, for Borglum began his work in 1927, and it was unfinished when he died in 1941. His son Lincoln eventually completed the giant sculpture.

One day Gutzon Borglum was asked if he thought his artwork was perfect in every detail. He looked up at the towering face of George Washington which measures sixty feet high, the height of a five-story building, and studied it. Then, Borglum replied, "Not today. Washington's nose is an inch too long! But the weather and wind will erode the stone away, and Washington's nose will be exactly right in 10,000 years."

⚜

Today could be named April Patience Day, for the secular saint Gutzon Borglum is surely the patron saint of the patient. He challenges anyone eager to "get it right," or have it perfect the first time, to let go of the sweet taste of perfection today. In many aspects of our lives, other elements, like Borglum's calculation of the wind and weather, will bring our labors to the point where they will be "exactly right."

On this feast day pray the Lord's Prayer and pause after the phrase "Your kingdom come...." In that pause, reflect on how God and Borglum are alike: They are willing to wait a very, very long time to see their dream complete. On this festival to be celebrated 10,000 years, or ten millenniums, from now, don't be sad or disappointed about going to your grave with your labors incomplete.

�֎

Feast of "Tomorrow Should Look Like Yesterday." 27

Today marks a contest in the early days of the 1900s, the dawn of the last century of the Second Millennium, which can be a guide to the dawn of first century of the Third Millennium. H.H. Kohisaat who was the owner of the *Chicago Times Herald* offered a prize of $500 to anyone who could create a new name for what people were calling "the horseless carriage." The new invention that would soon replace the horse-drawn carriage looked like a carriage without a horse, which accounts for how it was being called. The winning name for this new invention was "motorcycle," which was defined as a wagon driven by steam or a self-contained motor.

While the winner got his $500, the public didn't take to this name and it was abandoned. Instead, they began using a new word which was a combination of two Latin words meaning *self* and *moving*. The people of Chicago began calling the horseless carriage an *automobile*.

❧⦿❧

Congratulations to the inventive people of Chicago for creating a new name for a new invention, even though it continued for years to look like an open horseless carriage. This April day has two reflections for consideration. Is it natural to want tomorrow to come dressed up like yesterday? Or perhaps that expectation reflects a failure to use our creative imagination and is therefore *unnatural*. Newness, by its nature, should be shocking, or surprisingly delightful, as in surprise gifts and surprise parties. Yet religion seems to be always looking backwards to yesteryear, in love with routine or ritual. Christianity, which celebrates Jesus – who said, "Behold, I make all things new" – should be the world's teacher of newness in all things, but seemingly it fears the new and different.

If you want your religious expression to be new and fresh, consider being an "automobile," being self-moving instead of waiting patiently for your church to be all dressed in new clothing for a new millennium. Automobiling in your prayer, your home rituals and your service will make you not only a follower but a living companion of the Risen Jesus, who gave us his life-renewing Spirit and said, "Behold, I make all things new!"

---

28 Discovery of the Best Known Cure Day, 159 B.C.

Much like America before Columbus, this remarkable medicine was known as a cure-all long before its official discovery in 159 B.C. It had been successfully used as a medicine by the ancient Egyptians, Chinese, Persians and others for at least two millenniums before being recorded by Publius Terentius Afer. Terence, as he is known, however, was not a medical doctor but a great Roman comedy playwright! His famous and ancient cure-all drug has a traditional Latin medical name, *Diem adimere aegritudinem hominibus*, or DAAH for short. That name-phrase first came to light in his play *The Self-Tormentor*, in which one character says, "Time removes distress," or as it's more commonly translated, "Time heals all wounds."

DAAH is an over-the-counter drug requiring no prescription and is famous for having absolutely no side effects. This cure-all is also remarkable for being free of charge – well, almost free – since nothing in life is free. The cost of this miraculous medicine of Time is giving up the need for an instant cure, whether it be the healing of heartaches and heartbreaks, the fractures of friendships and marriages, the failures of life, the deaths of the people and things we love or the oozing wounds of childhood abuse and ridicule.

If you have a recent wound or perhaps an old one that is still draining, rub it gently today with Time, confident of its healing power. Those who use this cure-all drug need to take it with large doses of patience and never on a stomach full of hurry-hurry. If you find that you are suffering from impatience in your healing, remember where the great cure-all was first recorded — in a Roman Comedy. Humor, especially self-humor, cures impatience and speeds up the effectiveness of the medicine of Time. Humor also requires no prescription and is as free as sunlight for those who prefer to see life on the sunny side.

✳

Ptahhotpe's Incurable Disease Day, Egypt, 2350 B.C. 29

While cures have been found for most of the diseases that plagued the ancient world, no cure has been found for the disease first diagnosed by Ptahhotpe in the twenty-fourth century B.C. While not a medical doctor, but rather a royal governor and vizier under King Izezi, his words are as true today as when they were first spoken over four millenniums ago: "Beware any act of avarice; it is a bad and incurable disease."

※◎※

Every act of greed, regardless of how small or seemingly insignificant, is a deadly virus of the world's oldest incurable disease. While avarice is usually associated with the accumulation of wealth, this disease is not just restricted to money. One can be greedy about "private" time, talents or knowledge and can horde spiritual treasures as easily as gold. You can be stingy about expressions of gratitude and praise, (see the entry for March 7, the **Birthday of Ebenezer Scrooge**) and miserly as you withhold your congratulations from those who surpass you in achievement.

While both the medical and religious establishments have yet to announce a cure for greed and avarice, you can experiment with home cures. One such cure is to do the very opposite of what your disease prompts you to do; instead of taking or hoarding, give. This home cure can work wonders, especially if as you give away some of your wealth or talent to others you do so cheerfully and with great generosity.

⚜

Today is also the **Feast of St. Catherine of Siena,** who didn't hesitate to be generous in giving her advice and criticism to the popes of her day. She thus became the patron saint of papal critics.

⚜

And, if you live in the area of the United States west of the Mississippi River to the Rockies, this is a day to rejoice and be grateful to President Thomas Jefferson. On this day in 1803, he made the famous Louisiana Purchase from the French Emperor Napoleon, acquiring the abundant land where you are presently living.

✳

---

30 Dictator Day: the Death of Adolf Hitler, 1945.

On this day in 1945, one of the world's most notorious dictators kept his word and committed suicide in Berlin. He had promised that if he failed in his determination to achieve total victory for Germany he would kill himself. Certainly not the first dictator, he also will not be the last.

Today provides an occasion to mark the world's first official dictator, who appeared 500 years before the birth of Jesus. The Roman republic provided for the need of rapid reaction in emergency times by allowing for the creation of a temporary ruler, or a Caesar. The Roman Senate could appoint someone who would have supreme control for a specified time period. Legend says that in 458 B.C. the Roman general Cincinnatus was appointed to this office to meet the threat of an advancing army. He defeated the enemy and resigned immediately, having been a dictator for only sixteen days. The temporary ruler's power was such that his word automatically became law, hence the Latin name *dictator,* meaning, "I have spoken."

⚜

While dictators come in both sexes and in all ages, what they have in common is that when they speak their word is final! While today we recall the death of a famous dictator, perhaps you know some less famous ones — or those who act like dictators, one of whom may even have your name! Ask yourself today if you are inclined to be a dictator by reflecting on questions like these: When I speak on an issue, am I open to discussion about it? Do I suggest or propose solutions, or do I state them as absolutes? How often do I use phrases like "You should..." or "You must..." or "You have to..."?

✳

THE
MONTH
OF
MAY

Francofúrti ad
Mænum

While the Anglo-Saxons named this month *thrimilce* because their cows could be milked three times a day at this time of year, we do not know it as "Three-Milking" because prior myths prevailed. From ancient times the Romans used this fifth month as an opportunity to honor their Elders, or *Maiores*. Some, however, believe this month is named after Maia, the Roman goddess of growth and increase. You can choose which of these you prefer, but remember, "Cast not a clout till May is out." This old wise warning advises not shedding your winter clothing too quickly (clout being a rag or a piece of clothing). Superstition once held May to be unlucky for weddings since it was the month of the festival of Bona Dea, Roman goddess of chastity. Yet that might make it an ideal month for a wedding, since chastity is not the absence of sex but a pure, love-filled sexuality.

May Day, Ancient Feast of Springtime and Flowers. From April 28 to May 3, the ancient Romans held a festival in honor of the goddess of spring, Flora. The spread of the Roman Empire throughout Europe carried with it this springtime celebration. In the Middle Ages in England it was the custom of people to begin this first day of May by getting up early to "bring in the May." Homes were decorated with flowers and green tree branches, while in the village square people erected a maypole, which sometimes was over 100 feet tall. A woman chosen as the May Queen ruled over the festival which featured dancers who held streamers tied to the maypole while circling it with dance.

In 1889 the Second Internationale, a group of French socialists, dedicated this first day of May to common working people. Similarly in the Catholic Church today, it is a second feast of Saint Joseph, who is honored as the patron of the laborer. At one time the Soviet Union marked this as a socialist worker day but used it primarily as an excuse to have a giant military parade in Red Square in Moscow.

⚜

As with many old festivals and their rituals, the maypole is no longer the joy of adults but is simply a relic preserved by children. While the maypole was originally a male fertility symbol, it has been now desymbolized and deposited in the Museum of Kindergartens. Those of previous ages enjoyed and celebrated sexuality not as isolated from life, but as the companion of fertility and creativity. Symbols hold the power to speak to the depths of the mysteries of creation and are essential for living a fully human life. Perhaps the Third Millennium will see a renaissance of such symbolism. For now, recalling the flower customs of Medieval Europe, this would be an ideal day to bring flowers to work or to decorate your home with them as a way to "bring in the May."

✯

2

Feast of St. Zoe. A slave and a Christian of the early church, Zoe and her husband Hesperus were not outstanding in their faith life. However, in 135 when they witnessed their two sons being viciously tortured for refusing to deny their religious beliefs, they were inspired to take a stand for their faith. Zoe's martyrdom was to be hung by her hair from a tree, after which the entire family was roasted to death.

⚜

St. Zoe has been a patroness without a cause, until now. She has been neglected for almost two millenniums as a saint to be invoked for some affliction or the patroness of a particular profession. Today we celebrate St. Zoe as the patroness of those being tortured by hairsplitters. Having been hung by her hair, she knows the pain of those who are hung up by people who love to split hairs, who love to argue over petty points of contention and quibble over insignificant trifles. Those who must deal with such nitpickers are often overwhelmed with the desire to tear out their hair in extreme vexation and anguish. If today you encounter such precise hairsplitting perfectionists, pray to St. Zoe to give you the courage to be patient with their obsession. Being a martyr is witnessing to your beliefs, and it can be done in myriad ways. Loving your enemies can be witnessed in your hair being made to stand on end, not out of fright but in being pulled taut by patience.

✡

3

Write a Letter Day. This day is celebrated by taking time to write a letter instead of using e-mail or making a telephone call. Letter writing takes time since it is a form of making love. In an age of instant electric correspondence and faxing facilities, letters are for love. You say you don't have time? Then open a bottle of fine wine today to toast Lewis Carroll, whose real name was Charles Lutwidge Dodgson (1832-1892). This English mathematician and author of the timeless fantasies *Alice in Wonderland* and *Through the Looking Glass,* by his own account, wrote 98,721 letters in the last thirty-seven years of his life!

Secular saint Lewis Carroll should become the patron saint of scribes and letter writers. While the wizards of technology always promise more free time for leisure, the reality is highway or homeway robbery. The magic of technology, while making it possible to do many things faster, only casts an enchanting spell that makes us do more and more. To find time for thc luxury of leisure in which to love yourself and others in old-fashioned ways requires defending yourself from the wizards of technology. Just as you secure your home and workplace with security systems, locks and alarms, guard yourself from the array of home machines you own that itch to pickpocket your clock and calendar.

Write a letter today to someone you love, and perhaps consider sending a card of kindness to someone you don't love!

✡

4 **Give What You Have Day.** Emotions were at a high pitch in Berlin in the early days of the famous Berlin Wall. Hostilities flared when truckloads of stinking garbage were dumped over the wall into West Berlin by those living in the eastern sector of the city. Mayor Willie Brandt was flooded with demands for revenge at this offense, but he responded in a unique way. Mayor Brandt requested that every flower in West Berlin be brought to a specific place at the wall. Then as a great avalanche of fragrant and beautiful flowers was poured over the wall into East Berlin, a large banner was raised. Written on the banner were the words, "We each give what we have."

Today, you may be dumped on with the garbage of angry words, offensive and stinking sarcasm. Over your wall others may hurl the old, rotten refuse of your past slights and mistakes that they have gunnysacked for weeks, months or years. Consider how you should respond. You can cast back garbage for garbage — or, like the citizens of West Berlin, you can give back beauty. Jesus calls his disciples to return kindness for rudeness, love for hate and flowers for garbage. Take a few moments now to create as vividly as possible in your mind a picture of yourself being made into a garbage dump. Imagine yourself sending back beautiful flowers of love and kindness and rejoicing that "We each give what we have." This May feast is a perfect day for a garbage "fire" drill (See the entry for March 26 — **Fire Drill Day**).

5 **Disappointment into Design Department Day.** Elvis Presley's eleventh birthday was a great disappointment. He had asked for a bicycle as his birthday gift but instead was given the "surprise" gift of a guitar. Instead of going into depression, Elvis went into his design department to be inventive with his disappointment. Elvis made the most with what he had been given and found that it was a great treasure!

SSt. (secular saint) Elvis Presley is today's patron saint for those who find themselves with a surprise disappointment. We all need a design department where we can experiment with life's constant flow of disappointments.

⁂

Consider experimenting on this day with some disappointment. Remove the *dis* and turn it into an *appointment* with destiny. Regardless of what you have been given in life, like SSt. Elvis, make the most of it. May 5th is a good day to review life's disappointments and to remember it is never too late to make the most of them.

✸

Instantaneous Communication Day. As a measurement of time, an instant is only a fleeting moment, or to say it scientifically, one-one-thousandth of a minute. An instant is the present moment in which you are standing, from the Latin *instare*, "to stand upon." In the good old days, communication was slower, resulting in life being lived at a slower pace. The time required for Queen Isabella to learn of the voyage of Columbus was five months. Almost 400 years later, the time for the news of President Lincoln's assassination to reach Europe was two weeks. Then, the time for Neil Armstrong's news that humans can walk on the moon was 1.3 seconds. Near the end of the Second Millennium, fiber-optic wires could conduct 800 million pieces of information in one second, with these glass wires being cheaper and more efficient than copper cables. As we move further into the Third Millennium, we can expect information to travel faster, perhaps instantaneously.

6

⁂

While instant communication opens great possibilities, in our private lives it requires instant responses. While our brains can process information with the speed of light, responding in a way that is spiritually sound corresponds more to the speed of lilac buds blooming. The ancient Chinese liked to place messages under their pillows in order to sleep on them for a night before sending a response. Harry Truman responded to hostile messages by sitting down and writing an angry letter. He never mailed any of them, however, always tearing them up the next day.

Practice the discipline of waiting when you are unable to reach someone by one of today's instant means of communication. When leaving a message to have your call returned, remember Queen Isabella and be at peace even if you have to wait five months. Tempted to instantaneously give someone a piece of your mind, remember Harry Truman and write a letter that you will never mail. Not purity, but patience, may be the greatest virtue of the Third Millennium.

Although the communication about another event on this date in history was not instantaneous, the global impact was significant. Today marks the 1915 sinking of the passenger ocean liner, the Lusitania, by a German submarine. While Germany had warned Americans not to travel on this British ship, since it was reported to be carrying military arms, many did, and 120 Americans were among the 1,195 lost. The news of this disaster greatly contributed to America's desire to join with the Allies against Germany in World War I.

---

7 **Birthday of Vinegar, 5000 B.C.** As we saw on March 23, three millenniums after the invention of wine the Babylonians stumbled onto vinegar, the result of spoiled wine. On this day in 1880, Heinz vinegars, still familiar to us today, were first bottled. The main ingredient in vinegar continues to be alcohol, which in high-quality vinegars comes from corn or apples and water.

Among vinegar's many uses are killing grass in sidewalk cracks, removing stains from upholstery and clothing, kissing bathroom germs good-bye by using one part vinegar to one part water, eliminating odors from used jars and spraying as a room air deodorizer.

Vinegar also has healing powers: It relieves itching bug and mosquito bites and the pain of sunburns; it cures hiccups with one teaspoon of apple cider vinegar in one cup of warm water; it relieves arthritis by drinking a glass of water with two teaspoons of vinegar before each meal; the same measure can also be used as a cure for an upset stomach.

⚜

Again, the spiritual life and the practical life are one, and blessed by God are those who marry the two. Vinegar is a sour drink, and many are the afflictions cured by a good dose of sour wine. Criticism stings us worse than a mosquito bite, and swallowing it without trying to justify yourself can be as sour as vinegar — but good for the soul. Swallow the criticism slowly as you savor what part of it speaks to the truth, separating out what doesn't will help you to grow. Rare is criticism that is totally without foundation in reality. Just as important, removing stains from your soul and heart instead of your upholstery is done by applying the sour vinegar of asking forgiveness. Unlike the sweet wine of simply expressing regret ("Excuse me, I'm sorry") for some offense, asking for forgiveness leaves you vulnerable, in a sour place, since the other person can refuse to pardon you.

Perhaps you can create some of your own sour vinegar soul cures.

✺

Feast of Julian of Norwich. A great mystic who was never canonized as a saint, Julian can be the patroness of millions of Monday mystics — those who experience God in the mundane and commonplace events and activities of daily life and who are never rewarded with a halo. An old saying sums up this feast of a non-saint but holy woman, "Pigs and saints are not honored until after they are dead." In the case of holy mystics, even death does not always elevate them to the acknowledged ranks of the saints.

8

⚜

Once mystics were considered to be akin to geniuses, as having some rare gift not given others. In reality a mystic is simply someone who experiences God and views life through that experience. Everyone who is born into this life comes with the equipment necessary to be a mystic, since we were all created for communion with God. This communing talent that mystics possess is often lost in the passage from childhood (where all is awesome and mystical) into adulthood. Today, 99% of the population has been successfully demystified by education, religious institutions and the grind of daily life and so is unable to truly wonder. But mystics, the one percent who hold out — or those who return to childhood — enjoy the prayer of wonder, of being awestruck by the sensation of the Divine Mystery in creation and throughout life. Contrary to popular belief, mystics are not those who have otherworldly visions but rather those who have visions inside this world.

The Native Americans were fond of saying that if you wish to see life, you must look at it twice. Experiment today on this feast of a future haloed saint, Julian, and try to look twice at as many things and persons as you can. According to the Native Americans, if you do, you will be gifted with a vision. It is worth a try, especially if you believe the radical Christian dogma that God is everywhere.

�֍

---

9 **Joseph Gayetty's Toilet Paper Day, 1857.** The festival that marks this ninth day of May could also be called Recycled Junk Mail Day. While recycling was the downfall of Gayetty's invention of toilet paper, today's commemoration could make a strong statement about recycling. Gayetty introduced toilet paper in grocery stores in packages of individual sheets, but they failed to sell and soon disappeared. In 1857 Americans could not understand why they should waste money for new clean paper when they could use old department store catalogs, newspapers and advertisements in their outhouses and bathrooms. Besides, Gayetty's perfectly clean sheets of paper were uninteresting, since they offered no reading material for "the world's most private library." Those who are militant advocates of recycling paper and catalogues might consider going back to the 1857 form of recycling.

In 1879, looking like the Smith Cough Drop brothers, Edward

and Clarence Scott successfully offered their "recycled, reinvented" Gayetty paper in small rolls with perforated sheets. This latter innovation was the idea of the British inventor Walter Alcock, who had failed in his ten-year struggle to overcome Victorian rejection of such an unmentionable product being marketed.

✦✦✦

While today's junk mail would provide time-killing reading material if Americans were to then use it as toilet paper, it would be a killer on contemporary plumbing. Using junk mail in your bathroom would be a prophetic statement, however, for it would say that conservation isn't soft and squeezable. Today's festival provides you with an opportunity to reflect on one daily product which you consider to be absolutely necessary in your life, but which for the majority of the world's peoples is a real luxury item. Such a reflection could lead to prayer:

Blessed are you, Our God,
who gives us wondrous luxuries like toilet paper,
which once were unknown to kings and queens.

✦

The Feast of Saint Job. Today is one of those rare Old Testament feast days that frames the history of discrimination in the Church, which usually only makes saints out of Christians. Even holy ones like Moses and Isaiah do not have feast days in the Calendar of Saints. To give your child an Old Testament baptismal name in the days of the Inquisition would prompt an immediate and often serious investigation. But today celebrates Old Job the Afflicted, who in the Middle Ages escaped the anti-Semitic bias to become the patron saint invoked against depression and ulcers. Job was the patient, long-suffering hero who in the Old Testament story was the pawn in a bet between God and Satan. His many sufferings, physical and mental, included being "comforted" by bedside friends.

✦✦✦

Lord, I know it's a work of mercy to visit the sick, but protect me, please, from friends who come to comfort me in my suffering and pain — and only add to it. With Old Job, I personally pray that on my hospital door will hang a sign *No Visitors Allowed* so I can suffer with patience in solitude.

Before rushing off to visit someone who is sick in the hospital, you might pray a prayer to St. Job and ask for wisdom. Ask this suffering saint to inspire you to know if your proposed visit is to cure your guilt for not having visited that person when he or she wasn't sick or if your presence will truly assist that person in this time of bedridden suffering?

✳♋♋✳

Today is also **Golden Spike Day**. In 1869, a golden spike was driven into place to complete the first transcontinental railroad in the U.S. The tracks of the Union Pacific and the Central Pacific were joined at a point called Promontory, north of the Great Salt Lake in Utah. As there is no real separation between the sacred and the secular, the spiritual and the practical, today is a good day to unite your prayer and your work, to join the *patience of Job* and the *patience of your job*. Patience on the job often requires the patience of long-suffering, but it also requires the long-loving faithfulness of Job.

✳

---

11 **Mother's Day, the Second Sunday in May.** Read this entry on the Sunday in May on which it is celebrated, or think about your mother as you read it today. Anna Jarvis is the acknowledged founder of this beautiful festival honoring mothers. In 1914 Woodrow Wilson signed a joint resolution of Congress recommending its observance. As a day for sending greeting cards, Mother's Day ranks fourth, behind only Christmas, Valentine's Day and Easter.

Consider making your own Mother's Day card, especially if you are an adult. Famous physician, Jonas Salk, gives us an idea for a perfect verse for such a Mother's Day card. He once said, "Good parents give their children roots and wings. Roots to know where home is, wings to fly away and exercise what's been taught them." And so your Mother's Day verse might read, "Thanks, Mom, for giving me deep roots and good wings."

✳♋♋✳

In the last years of the Second Millennium many parents seemed more intent on giving their children wings instead of roots, eager for them to fly away from the nest. Parents who wish to reverse this trend will be zealous to give their children a strong sense of unique family traditions and history, strong religious customs and memorable household rituals as roots for future growth. Such roots are essential to withstand the violent storms of change that are brewing just over the horizon of the Third Millennium.

While both roots and wings are necessary, roots are particularly important in an era of radical change and upheaval. Moreover, history abounds with examples of adult children growing their own wings, but how often do we see any growing their own roots?

✵

Remember Gerard de Nerval Day. Understanding what was said in yesterday's reflection on Mother's Day, it is often easier for a mother to give deep roots than to give good wings with which to fly away from the nest. This is poignantly seen in the case of the French writer, Gerard de Nerval, who in 1855 hanged himself from a lamppost with apron strings! **12**

≈≈✦≈≈

Today's reflection calls you to check your wings for their size and strength. If you are a mother, look today at your children's wings. If they are undeveloped, consider possible exercises to help them grow stronger.

For example, you may want to develop rituals of departure for a daughter or son about to leave home. Because our contemporary society tends to be weak on homespun rituals, you may need to create your own ritual. Good rituals need few if any words, as a good-bye kiss demonstrates. So too, this ritual of giving wings needs few words. Either alone or with the family, you might take a kitchen apron and a pair of scissors and pray silently. Then slowly and with reverence cut the strings off the apron and place them in the hands of your adult child with a kiss, saying, "You are free, my beloved. May God and my blessing go with you as you fly away from here to fulfill your destiny with glory."

Even those who are not mothers need to create rituals of giving wings. If you are in any way a teacher, mentor, coach or guide for others, be sure to always give those entrusted to you a strong pair of wings.

✯

---

13 Birthday of the Farm Tractor, 1890s and 1916.

The World War I battle of the Somme saw the first military tank, made by the British. The genius Leonardo da Vinci had designed a rather close resemblance of the first enclosed protected military vehicle as early as the fifteenth century, but it was never built. About thirty years before the British tank of 1916, large four-wheeled, steam-driven "tractor engines" appeared in the north-western United States. Used by large wheat farmers, they could pull forty plows across a field. Thus the army tank of 1916 was the son of a farm tractor driven by an internal-combustion engine.

Often the order is reversed, with things created for military use finding their way into peacetime society. War is hell, but also the source of many useful products of daily life. Children of war include Kleenex Tissues, designed as air-filters for World War I gas masks and battlefield surgical bandages. Wristwatches were created for use by pilots in the same war, since pocket watches were too difficult to use in those first military airplanes. World War II gave us the T-shirt, which stands for training undershirt, and, of course, the jeep and its cousin, the all-purpose, four-wheel recreation vehicle.

❧❀❧

These are but a few of the by-products of war and are examples of how God, whose vision does not include war, but whose creativity is unbounded, can indeed write straight with crooked lines.

In your private wars, domestic or occupational, consider the peaceful use of some of your weapons. For example, take the weapon of gossip today and use it to spread the good deeds, achievements and hidden deeds of charity done by those you dislike. Consider the peaceful conversion of other favorite verbal weapons, like the sticks and stones that don't break bones but do inflict great pain. Such swords of speech turned into plowshares of peace can be signs of hope for a Peaceful Millennium, the first one without war.

✳

The Festival of the Birth of the Countdown. Today is a good day to start the countdown for students — and teachers — beginning at midnight tonight. In this age of frequent spacecraft launchings, countdowns are familiar to all of us. It's easy to inwardly hear that classic cadence: "five, four, three, two, one...zero." It's interesting to note that this technical procedure originated with a motion-picture director, Fritz Lang, in his late 1920s science fiction movie, *The Girl in the Moon.* Lang's creative idea of counting backwards heightened the suspense of a key moment in his film. It created growing anticipation at the launching of a great rocket. His principle of reversing what was normal not only achieved his desired dramatic effect, it also gifted aeronautical science with an idea that helped involve and gain the support of the public.

14

❧❦❧

As a delayed May Day folly, play with a bit of foolishness today by practicing Lang's principal of reverse ordering. Just for fun, eat your desert at the beginning of a meal, or, if eating out, you can give your tip to the server at the beginning of the meal instead of when paying the bill. (Who knows, this might give you better service!) Also, consider the possibility of praying in the middle of a meal or an activity instead of at the beginning to help you be awakened to the presence of God in the midst of what you're doing. Take a few moments this May day to create a variety of your own reverse-behaviors that might heighten your anticipation and your involvement in life, and in so doing continue your playful celebration of May Day.

✳

15 **Festival of the First Recorded Traffic Violation, 1769**. The arrested offender, N.J. Cugnot, earned a jail sentence for reckless driving when he propelled his speeding vehicle into a wall. A captain in the French army, Cugnot had invented the first mechanical road vehicle, a three-wheeled, steam-driven tractor carriage used to pull a cannon. Cugnot was traveling at his carriage's top speed of four miles an hour when he drove into a wall. Those who saw the incident described this first on-the-road vehicle as "a whisky still on a wheelbarrow."

As you get in your personal mobile miracle today, realize how it can become an instrument of destruction. Hold the ignition key in your hand and pause for a moment. Reflect on how your car is the great, great grandson of a military vehicle designed to pull a cannon before the time of our American Revolution. Then remember how God, speaking through the prophet Isaiah, urged a transformation of instruments of war: "They shall beat their swords into plowshares and their spears into pruning-knives" (Is. 2: 4). This brief prayer ignited by Isaiah's vision of an age of justice and peace can be said while your car is warming up to help the oil flow efficiently in the engine:

> May that Great Age you promised us, O God,
>   come quickly to our war-weary world.
> O patient God of peace and harmony,
>   your servant, Isaiah, foretold
>   of a conversion of weapons into useful tools,
>   quoting your very words:
> "Nation will not lift sword against nation
>   nor ever again be trained for war."

✳

16 **Feast of St. Brendan of Ireland.** Brendan, who founded many monasteries in Ireland, was a seafaring monk of the sixth century who sailed to Scotland, Wales and, it is believed, even to North America. It is debated whether Brendan's journal of his crossing of the Atlantic in a *curragh,* a boat made of animal skins, is fact or fiction. To test its viability, author Tim Severin built a boat in 1976 according to Brendan's description and successfully sailed it from Ireland to America. Whether or not St. Brendan actually made the journey, he called the land to the west across the Atlantic "the Promised Land of the Saints."

⚜

For innumerable poor, uneducated, oppressed European immigrants, and countless others from all parts of the world, America has been and still is the land of promise. May St. Brendan and all the saints inspire us to fulfill the other half of his name for America and make it also a land of saints. This is not a call for you to make an appointment to be fitted for a halo but simply to embrace more fully the vocation to which everyone is called, the vocation to be holy. Some four millenniums ago, God told Moses to tell the people, "Make yourselves holy...because I am holy." (Lv. 13: 44).

One household test for holiness is to ask yourself if you are zealous in making your native country a place of real promise for everyone. Do you support legislation, projects and initiatives that provide aliens, immigrants and those citizens in poverty with a promise for a better life. Do you strongly oppose all forms of racial, religious, social and sexual discrimination? Do you volunteer to assist those who are less fortunate? Do you pray that — and act in a way that — St. Brendan's vision of America might be fulfilled?

✮

Jewish Holocaust Memorial Day. This is a movable Jewish memorial day, which you are invited to keep today since no one should ever forget the six million Jews systematically murdered in Hitler's "final solution of the Jewish question." The years 1933-1945 span what is commonly called the Holocaust, which includes the persecution and the outright extermination of European Jews by Nazi Germany.

Not only do Germans bear the guilt of the Holocaust, we Americans also share in it! The fires of anti-Semitism raged in the United States in the 1930s, fueled by the Klan and over a hundred Jew-hating organizations. A 1939 *Fortune Magazine* poll reported that 83% of Americans were opposed to allowing escaping European Jews to enter the United States! Many help-wanted ads read, "Christians Only!" This anti-Semitic prejudice was even spread by the radio broadcasts of a Catholic priest, Father Coughlin.

Sensing the intense American hatred of Jews and fearing that his New Deal would be labeled the "Jew Deal," President Franklin D. Roosevelt wrote "File, No Action" on a bill to admit 20,000 German Jewish children.

⚜

In this month of remembering our dead, remember the Holocaust victims today as you ask God for forgiveness over America's refusal to help save some of the victims. Pray also for all American Jews who suffered from persecution and prejudice here in the United States at the same time as the Holocaust was happening in Europe. Like African-Americans, Jews have known — and still do know — the pain of segregation laws that exclude them from clubs and organizations. Take time now to examine your own Jewish prejudice and pray for the grace to be cleansed of it. Holy saints of the Holocaust, both Jewish and Christian, pray for all who practice the sins of discrimination.
✴

---

18 **Third Millennium Monster Day.** On either side of the great millennium crossing, give or take twenty years, doom sayers and disaster predictors scan the heavens and the news for omens that predict the approaching End of the World. One place usually overlooked, the nursery of a hospital, was once the best place to find omens. In ancient Rome, those responsible for divining the future considered a freak birth to be an ominous warning of approaching doom. From the Latin *monere*, "to warn," they derived the word *monstrum*, "the divine warning of an ill omen." Monstrum, in turn, is the mother of our word "monster."

⚜

In 1995, the then U.S. Ambassador to the United Nations, Madeleine Albright, told Congress, "The amount of biological warfare agents Iraq admitted producing is more than enough to kill every man, woman and child on Earth." Some religious prophets of the approaching Armageddon End of the World have quoted both the Bible and Madeleine Albright as warning signs of the total annihilation of all humans near or shortly after the year 2000. They hold out the theory that AIDS, the Ebola virus and the Gulf War Illness (GWI) are the beginning of The End.

In 1883 the volcanic island of Krakatoa exploded, causing 50-to-100 foot tidal waves that killed 36,000 people. Dust from the volcanic explosion covered much of the surface of the globe. This disaster was viewed by some as a warning of the End of the World.

Similarly, the world's worst earthquake killed an estimated 830,000 people in the Chinese provinces of Shensi, Shansi and Honan in January of 1556. When news of this terrible disaster reached the rest of the world, it too was announced as one of the prophetic warning signs of the nearness of the End of the World.

In the seventeenth century the End of the World was likewise predicted when a smallpox plague killed over sixty million people in Europe from the years 1618 to 1648.

In every age, and guaranteed to appear in every major crisis of the coming centuries, the ugly Frankenstein monster of fear is perpetually birthed in the nurseries of the minds of those whose sole diet is disaster.

✳

Pioneer Flight Day: Amelia Earhart Becomes the First Woman to Fly Solo Across the Atlantic, 1932. 19

Today and tomorrow are twin feasts of heroic feats that show how both women and men can rise to great heights of courage. Tomorrow is the anniversary of Lindbergh's solo flight over the Atlantic and today remembers the same feat by Amelia Earhart (1897-1937). This native of Atchison, Kansas, was a pioneer in the efforts of women to be granted equal rights in all fields of endeavor.

While not everyone can fly solo across some vast ocean, you can set out solo and take a stand for the equal rights of all people. Many such solo and also communal efforts remain on the horizon, for much needs to be done to achieve full equality in today's prejudiced world.

⚜

Look at your life and see if there is some "solo" activity you find a bit frightening and set out today to accept its challenge. So often fear grounds us, preventing us from flying high. So honor SSt. Amelia today by "taking off."

Possibilities for solo flights for those interested might be listed under "Undesirable and Unpopular Causes for Their Time." In the mid-nineteenth century, "Anti-Slavery" would have been found on that list, as would "Women's Right to Vote." In 1919 when the Eighteenth Amendment to the Constitution established prohibition, those who flew solo by saying that "drinking alcohol in moderation is socially acceptable and good" would have been shot down by a battery of the antiaircraft guns manned by "dry" religious and social reformers. In 1941, because of the war with Japan, Japanese-American citizens were herded against their will into concentration-style camps. It would have been a nearly solo flight to voice opposition to this injustice, for only the NAACP and ACLU spoke out against this imprisonment of American citizens. Silent, safe and well grounded were all national Catholic and Protestant church organizations, as well as all the other supposed guardians of justice. In the 1950s, speaking out or demonstrating for the civil rights of people of color would likewise have made one a companion of Amelia Earhart and Charles Lindbergh.

These social causes are no longer unpopular today, but that doesn't mean that the long list of those suffering from injustice and inequality has been eliminated. Take a few moments today to muse on present-day unpopular causes — such as seeking the end of capital punishment — that await the brave souls willing to fly solo against a storm of loud social support. Blessed are those who are willing to take solo stands in the pattern of the prophets of old.

✹

Feast of the Soaring, Heroic Spirit: Charles Lindbergh Begins His Solo Atlantic Flight, 1927. **20**

On this day in 1927, a quiet-spoken twenty-five-year-old aviator took off in his monoplane, the *Spirit of St. Louis,* from Roosevelt Field in Long Island, New York. More than thirty hours later Lindbergh landed in Paris at Orly Airfield, completing the first nonstop solo flight across the Atlantic Ocean. As he landed, this modest hero was greeted by a crowd of 100,000 Parisians; he soon returned to New York for a ticker tape parade with an estimated crowd of over 4,000,000.

❧✿❧

Every age has a hunger to be inspired by men and women of courage. Today, it's not so much a hunger as a *starvation* for heroes and heroines as that need is now met mostly by self-serving athletic and entertainment stars.

Yet in every community there are men and women who quietly — without ticker tape parades — serve others in hidden heroic ways. Many are volunteers, others are simple workaday professionals who never consider themselves to be heroes or heroines. On this day of a great and famous hero, reflect on some of the hidden heroes and heroines you know, and have known, in your life. Also, consider the possibility of satisfying your hunger for a hero by becoming one yourself!

Finally, rejoice today, for our society is filled with millions of heroines and heroes whose private lives of service crisscross like stars in the night sky. For all these heroic stars are bright beacons of the vocation of being the Light of the World.

✻

Birthday of Pulse Taking, Ancient China. **21**

Tens of centuries ago, the Chinese invented the medical technique of taking one's pulse, a procedure still done whenever we visit a doctor. Your pulse is the alternate expansion and contraction of artery walls as your heart action varies the volume of blood within the arteries. The Chinese cultivated the skill of diagnosing illnesses simply by taking a patient's pulse. They said that fifty-one different types of pulse beats were to be identified at eleven different locations on the body, with each pulse type being linked to a different health problem.

When we are excited, our heartbeat is accelerated. Anger awakens primitive messages to fight or flee, and so the heart is jump-started to prepare us to do one or the other. While "blowing off steam" – causing the pulse to beat faster than a jackhammer – was once believed to be healthy, today it is not. This is especially true if the cause of your anger is something beyond your control. Among the common folk cures for being angry are to count to ten or to breathe deeply. You might like to try combining these practices with the Chinese cure of taking your pulse. This could become a frequent prayer form, for if you cataloged all those things that cause your pulse to race wildly with anger, they might add up to the classic Chinese count of fifty-one different types.

Instead of folding your hands in the traditional prayer position, this prayer has the fingers of one hand holding the wrist of the other. Also nontraditional is the fact that no words are involved in this prayer form, for your attention is totally focused on counting your pulse beats. Remain quiet in this pulse prayer, opening simply to God's presence, until after the anger attack has passed. Practice this prayer-cure each time you have an anger attack and you will be healthier and holier as a result.

---

22 **Metal Detectors Replace Holy Water Fonts Day, 2031.** The National Conference of American Catholic Bishops today announced that all holy water fonts at the entrances of parish churches were to be replaced with airport metal detector doorways. The bishops stated that these new security measures were necessary due to the recent spread of random attacks at Mass, together with the potential danger created by laws allowing all American citizens to carry concealed handguns. While many Catholics regretted the loss of holy water at the entrances of their churches, they stated that they prefer knowing that they and their children would be safe from harm while at church.

This action was taken jointly by the National Council of Catholic, Protestant, Islamic and Jewish Faiths, though in the case of the non-Catholic religions it did not include the removal of holy water fonts. This National Council of All Religions further legislated that as of today, to insure prayerful silence in churches, mosques and synagogues, the following would be forbidden in all worship spaces: pagers, beepers, cellular phones, laptop computers and a popular Third Millennium fad, wristwatch-telephones.

At first glance the reflection for this day may appear comical, but it may actually be prophetic. Consider that it was only in the last decades of the twentieth century that weapon and bomb detectors first appeared in airports, then courthouses, government buildings and even schools. The presence of these detectors and the searching of luggage and your person for weapons has become so commonplace as to almost be routine. The resulting effect is a state of perpetual anxiety and fear.

Recently the newspapers reported a thriving new business in a Brooklyn housing project, a gun rental company. According to the police, one could rent a nine-millimeter gun to protect oneself for $20 a night. If you intended to shoot someone with one of the rental guns, the price rose to $100. Chain gun rental stores, like video rental stores, could soon be commonplace in your city.

Pray today that the twenty-first century will see an American revolution against the tyranny of firearms. Add power to your prayer by promoting efforts to limit and control handguns and automatic weapons.

23

The Worthless Radio Day, 1921. The associates of David Sarnoff responded to his urgings that they invest in the radio by saying, "The wireless music box has no imaginable commercial value. Who would pay for a message sent to nobody in particular?" Their prediction is a classic example of miscalculation about the future. Take heed, all who make dire predictions about tomorrow.

꧁꧂

If today's celebration were to be given another name, it could be "Don't Listen to Your Associates Day" or "Trust Your Intuition Day and Light the Match of Enthusiasm Day." The Russian immigrant and radio pioneer, David Sarnoff (1891-1971), went on to become general manager of RCA, the Radio Corporation of America, and then its president. He also played a major role in the development of television. While his associates saw no value in the wireless music box, his enthusiasm for it was well rewarded.

Henry Ford once said, "You can do anything if you have enthusiasm...the irresistible surge of your will and your energy to execute your ideas.... Enthusiasm is at the bottom of all progress...without it there are only alibis." It seems that David Sarnoff also applied the advice of Thomas Edison, who once said, "Touch the match of enthusiasm to the fuse of energy and let yourself explode."

✺

---

24 **Knowing Whelm is Enough Day.** While *whelm* is not *when*, it should be a clear signal for knowing when enough is enough. Whelm is a good English word that is seldom if ever used, except when proceeded by the word "over," to make *overwhelm*. Today honors this forgotten word, whelm, which means "to cover with water, to submerge or bury."

In 1997 it was estimated that the average worker in a large corporation receives or sends some 177 messages a day by the vast array of memos, e-mail, cellular phones and other forms of instant communications. According to a Gallup poll in that same year, about a third of the executives surveyed said they feel "almost always or usually overwhelmed."

꧁꧂

As the speed limit of life increases, not only high-level executives but ordinary people experience being more than whelmed. You may not send out or receive 177 messages daily, but a common feeling is not simply being submerged, up to your head, but being overwhelmed by demands and expectations placed upon you. Drowning persons use all their strength trying to get their heads above water, and so they have no energy left for anything else.

Begin today to take frequent whelm tests to check whether you are keeping your head above water. If you find you are exhausting yourself and are sinking deeper instead of rising, take some action. Life and water are to be enjoyed, and swimming is a prehistoric pleasure that takes us back to the time when all life was in the oceans. Good swimmers know their limits, just as those who wish to enjoy life — and not drown in it — know theirs. Blessed are those who know how to unplug, depage, turn-off, not answer and enjoy floating in the Sea of Life.

✦

Feast of the First Cataract Surgery, Babylon, 1000 B.C. 25

Three millenniums ago eye physicians were performing cataract operations in India and Babylon — and were subject to medical malpractice! The price of these operations was set by law and so was the cost of malpractice. If the surgeon caused the loss of a wealthy person's eye, the physician's hands were cut off. If the operation was performed on a slave and the slave was blinded, the surgeon had to compensate the owner with another slave.

≈❦≈

Eyesight, then and now, is precious. So be grateful on this feast for that great gift which you usually take for granted until you lose it. In a normal life span, the human eye will bring into focus some twenty-four billion images. Sadly, the average human is blinded by those billions of images, and so only rarely remarks about the beauty of a particular image. Yet every scene is awesome, breathtaking in its beauty, for those who are cured of the cataracts of the commonplace. Familiarity breeds not so much contempt as blindness to life's beauty.

Today is Cataract Self-Surgery Day. It's no accident that this optical affliction which clouds the lens of the eye has the same name as a large waterfall or floodgate. The blindness caused by contemporary life's flood of images is cured by stopping the waterfall, by the practice of closing your eyes for five to ten seconds. When you open them, you can see what is before you as if you were looking at it for the very first time. Look upon that image with the same love, intensity and gratitude as if it were about to disappear forever. Then, close your eyes a second time for twenty seconds of blindness and say, "Gone forever, gone is the wondrous image I beheld." When you open your eyes, deeply drink in the view before you.

This do-it-yourself cataract treatment should be repeated as frequently as necessary to insure your freedom from blindness.

✳

---

26 **Feast of St. Augustine of Canterbury.** In 597 Pope Gregory the Great sent the Benedictine abbot-bishop Augustine to convert and civilize the Anglo-Saxons on the island of England. It has been said that each age is only one-to-two generations away from reverting to barbarism, and so parents have roughly the same task as St. Augustine.

❧✦❧

Civilization and conversion are the twin tasks of parents. They would thus be well served to pray to Augustine of Canterbury for assistance in this daunting task. Making children civilized requires more than teaching table manners or how to treat guests in their home or how to dress appropriately for an occasion. It also includes instruction in values and morals, which is extremely difficult, if not impossible, without a strong basis in a religious code of behavior. Not lying or stealing and respecting the rights of others requires a supporting spiritual foundation. Even adults need to be continuously converted and civilized since contemporary society is inclined toward casual behavior as well as casual dress.

You can also celebrate the feast of Augustine of Canterbury by taking a healthy canter, a medium-paced walk. Originally, a "canter" referred to the gait of a horse between a trot and a gallop, which at one time was called a Canterbury gallop. It was so named because it was thought to be the pace of pilgrims riding to the shrine at the Cathedral of Canterbury in England. Since few people ride horses today, you can observe this feast and at the same time get some good exercise as you "canter" through a park.

✳

Pentecostal Wind Day. Fifty days after the movable feast of Easter we celebrate Pentecost, the feast of the Holy Spirit's descent upon the apostolic community in flaming tongues and a great wind. *Spirit* in Hebrew is the same as the word for wind. While invisible, the effects of both can be seen — and their presence felt.

27

As you pray "Come, Holy Spirit," in these days of preparation for the celebration of the feast of God's Wind, consider what kind of holy wind you want to come to you according to Beaufort's scale. In 1806 Admiral Sir Francis Beaufort of the British Navy composed a scale of winds ranging from zero to twelve in intensity of strength. The following scale is the U.S. National Weather Service's adaptation of Beaufort's scale, with zero being calm or less than one mile of wind per hour. The following numbers are statute miles per hour:

Light Breeze	1-5	Fresh gale	39-46
Gentle Breeze	6-12	Strong gale	47-54
Moderate Breeze	13-18	Whole gale	55-63
Strong Breeze	19-24	Storm	64-72
Fresh Breeze	25-31	Hurricane	73 or more
Moderate gale	32-38	Spirit Wind	?

Come, Holy Light, Blessed Breeze, and do not disturb our quiet prayer and comfortable worship. Come, Godly Gentle Breeze, and rouse us, but do so gently with no sudden surprises and with no radical demands. Come, Mystical Moderate Breeze, and reaffirm for us that all things must be done in moderation, never with excessive zeal or damage to our existing positions. Come not, Fresh or Strong Godly Gales, lest our church be shaken to its foundations with God's urgent call to change. God protect us from Whole Gale, Storm and Holy Hurricane Winds, lest we be blown away by the Holy Spirit! Amen (and check your wind sock, lest God fail to answer your prayers).

---

28 **Handgun Memorial Day.** Here in the United States, almost twice as many Americans were killed by firearms as in Southeast Asia during the Vietnam War decade of 1963-1973. The 46,752 killed in that conflict have a beautiful war memorial in Washington, D.C, while the 84,633 killed on the home front lack even a plaque. The United States has the world's highest death rate from firearms per capita, with a new gun being sold in the last years of the Second Millennium at the rate of one every 13.5 seconds.

Memorial Day is celebrated on the last Monday in May and provides an opportunity to remember those who have lost their lives on the home front because of our American obsession with guns. May the new millennium help us to let go of our Old American Wild West myths about gun-carrying cowboys and about shoot-outs on main street. Jesus quoted a folk saying of his day that is just as valid today as it was two millenniums ago: "Those who live by the sword will die by the sword."

On this Handgun Memorial Day we can ask: Will the new millennium see the passage of laws in America like those in other civilized countries prohibiting the ownership of guns other than hunting firearms?

---

29 **Birthday of Patrick Henry, 1736.** Patrick Henry is a canonized American revolutionary saint, whom school children know for his famous cry, "Give me liberty or give me death." Yet, eight months after that stirring speech for liberty he ordered "diligent patrols" to keep Virginia slaves from accepting the British offer of freedom to any slave who would join their side.

Patrick Henry, who himself owned slaves, spoke with a forked tongue, as the Native Americans would say, when he proclaimed that slavery is "as repugnant to humanity as it is inconsistent with the Bible and destructive of liberty." He justified this repugnant evil of owning humans as slaves by offering the sad tale that, "(he)...had three children as well as a wife to support...(and) knew he had to make a living in some way."

<hr>

Use the birthday of this American patriot to examine your conscience about what you believe to be true but fail to enforce in your personal life. Do you believe that prejudices based on race, age, religion and gender are evil? If so, speak out against them. Even more, vote and labor to remove them from our country which proclaims liberty and justice for all.

The Healing Power of *Pentecostal Red* Day. The color for the feast of the Holy Spirit is fire-red. So if you are dealing with some affliction, dress in red today. In England, from the fifteenth to the seventeenth centuries, the color red was considered to have healing properties. Patients suffering from a fever were dressed in red nightgowns, and their rooms were filled with red-colored objects.

30

<hr>

Since clergy wear red vestments for the feast of Pentecost and churches are filled with red flowers and banners, is this a sign that the church is sick? Regardless of the age, the community that Jesus left to continue his work of proclaiming the Good News always seems to suffer from some sicknesses. Religious institutions suffer from motion sickness and resist forward movement and change, like paralyzed patients pleading with their physical therapist to stay just where they are. Churches of all faiths also suffer homesickness, the disease of nostalgia. The older the church, the more it seems to suffer longing for the good old days.

Your local church may suffer from these and other illnesses. Take a few moments for a medical examination of your church — and your spiritual life. Mindful that disease can be contagious, consider dressing all in red the next time you go to church.

---

31 **Feast of the Visitation of Mary to Elizabeth.** Today's festival celebrates the day when Mary of Nazareth hurried to visit her relative, the aged Elizabeth, whose wrinkled womb had been visited by God with a child. Her son John would become the famous John the Baptizer, who would prepare the way for Mary's son, Jesus.

When the Angel Gabriel responded to Mary's surprise that the Holy Spirit would fill her womb, she was told that aged Elizabeth was also pregnant by the Spirit and that, "with God, all things are possible." That angelic message is as joyously true today as when it was first spoken, and it should become part of our daily prayer. It could be added to the prayer of the Hail Mary and to the Lord's Prayer, perhaps just before the final Amen.

Repeated frequently, this six-word phrase gives us hope for this day and for each of our tomorrows. With God, all things are possible: the removal of war, exploitation, the sin of racial prejudice and all the present evils of the world.

Two millennium ago, as she greeted Elizabeth, Mary sang about the great revolution in which the poor and hungry would be raised and the rich and powerful cast down. She rejoiced that God's age of justice had come – or, rather, that it had begun, for it is still coming. Mary, the mother of Jesus, is the patroness of the patient, as today she still awaits the fulfillment of her song of prophecy about God's reign. We need her charism of patience: Perhaps the new millennium will see a new feast in her honor to inspire us: the Feast of the Most Patient Heart of Mary. While that sounds much like an existing feast in her honor, today a most patient heart is needed as much as a most pure heart.

Also on this day in 1900, at 3:52 A.M. the folk hero railroad engineer John Luther "Casey" Jones died at the throttle of the Cannonball Express on the way from Memphis to Canton, Mississippi. With his hand on the brake trying to slow down his train, he slammed into the rear of a stopped train. Casey Jones was speeding in an effort to make up for lost time, but his final act was an attempt to save the lives of his passengers.

Pray, today, for the gifts of this feast. Pray first to possess holy patience as we work zealously, itching with impatience, for full social justice and equality for all. At the same time, remembering the fate of Casey Jones and the Cannonball Express, if you find yourself speeding to make up for lost time, pray for the grace to slow down before it is too late.

✳

THE

MONTH

OF

JUNE

June may be named for *juniores*, the Latin word for "youngsters," who were honored during this month. Others believe the source of its name is Juno, the Roman queen of the goddesses. The Dutch name for the sixth month was *Zomermaand*, for "summer month" since that season begins on June 21. The Old Saxon name was *Lida aerra*, meaning "joy time" — appropriate for weddings and the end of school. June weddings are considered lucky since Juno was the patron of women from birth to death. Reflect on other reasons why this new month might be "joy time" for you.

Birthday of Brigham Young, 1801-1877. After the assassination of Joseph Smith, the original founder of the Church of Jesus Christ of Latter-day Saints, the Mormons, Brigham Young in 1844 became the chief leader of the church. To escape religious persecution, Young led the great Mormon migration west to found what is today Salt Lake City, Utah. Brigham Young was a stern moralist and a brilliant leader, and was a present-day saint for nineteenth century America.

Dayton Duncan says of the 1847 exodus of the Mormons led by their Moses, Brigham Young: "In the evenings there would be no card playing. No checkers or dominoes. No dancing or fiddling. A bugle at 8:30 P.M. signaled all to retire to their wagons to pray. Campfires were to be extinguished by 9 P.M. and the bugle sounded again at 5 A.M. It was the most disciplined westward migration in American history." This was indeed a pilgrimage and a holy migration; in fact, if St. Benedict (480-543) had written the Rule for migrating monks, these Mormons would have been living it out.

The title of "saint" in the first communities of the Risen

Jesus was another way of saying "Christian." The New Testament makes frequent references to the early followers as "the saints." Today, to be called a saint would likely produce beet-red blushing and confessions of unworthiness. Sadly, the title "saint" has been reserved for those who are celibate, unmarried and childless, whose life work is involved in church ministry or who have died meritoriously for their faith.

What the new century needs are not early-day or latter-day, but present-day saints, who by being called "saints" are reminded to live ordinary lives in an extraordinary way. The new century needs married saints with children, grandparent saints who are extraordinary in their continued care of their children and their children's children. The new century needs present-day saintly politicians, saintly movie stars, saintly accountants, saintly janitors, gay saints, single-parent saints and divorced saints. What would the world be like if every church were called the Church of Jesus Christ of Present-day Saints?

One last reflection on Brigham Young's exodus: Every ten miles on their westward migration the Mormons would leave messages for those who might follow them. These messages, left in boxes attached to twelve-foot poles, told where the nearest good water or best campsite could be found. It would be a holy practice for you, as a person on a spiritual pilgrimage, to in some way do the same.

---

2 **Armageddon AIDS Day.** The Lord Buddha, which means "the enlightened one," is the title given to Siddhartha Gautama (about 563-483 B.C.). This founder of Buddhism is today's feast's patron of good health. In chapter sixteen of the Dhammapada, Buddha writes: Let us live in joy, never hating those who hate us. Let us live in joy, never falling sick like those who are sick."

Those who suffer from the sickness of millenniumitis experience bouts of depression and gloom about the approaching disaster of Armageddon. They suffer from a breakdown of their spiritual immune system and so easily fall victim to prophecies of disaster. This affliction is not restricted to those who see the crossing of the millennium as the approaching End Days; it is often shared by others who view society and religion as being in a grave crisis. As a healer, Buddha prescribes a cure: "Live in joy, and you will not fall sick like those who are sick with gloom and doom."

⚜

As if it were your home address, "live in joy." Let health, holiness and hopefulness be your residence. The end of the Second Millennium marks two thousand years since the birth of Jesus of Nazareth. He proclaimed the joyful tidings of the Good News that the reign of God had arrived. Those who claim to believe in his message and to be his disciples cannot live in gloom and dark despair, but only in joy.

Even if large parts of society and the world, while professing to be Christian, remain unconverted by the message of compassion and love proclaimed by Jesus, that is no reason for you to live in gloomy despair. God's work of liberation, which in ancient speech was called "salvation," has already begun, and so we should dress in joy, as well as work, pray, worship and live in joy.

Today, ask yourself where you live.

✳

A Monkey's Wedding Day. The expression, "a June bride," reminds us that this month is the favorite for weddings. It is said that the sixth month was named for one of Rome's leading families, the Juliuses, and was initiated by the celebration of the festival of the Roman goddess Juno on the first of this month. She was the protector of women throughout their lifetime, and it was an old Roman belief that she brought good fortune to all marriages begun in her month.

June is indeed filled with beauty and blessings. But, like every marriage, it also has its share of pain and hardship. So, be aware that today, or any day, you might be an invited guest at a *monkey wedding* — an old South African expression for the simultaneous occurrence of rain and sunshine.

⚜

Today, if you are aware of something unpleasant happening simultaneously with something enjoyable, don't be resentful or angry at whatever is "raining on your parade." Instead, you can smile and say to yourself or others, "It's a monkey wedding day" and be grateful for the sunshine.

�֎

4 **Feast of the First Ford Automobile, 2 A.M., 1896.** Early on this day in 1896 in a brick work shed in Detroit, Michigan, Henry Ford and his associates began an American revolution. As they completed work on his first automobile, an age of making the automobile available to the common person began. The first road test of his car had to be delayed for an hour or so because the genius Ford had overlooked a minor detail: His car was wider than the door of the brick work shed! Some bricks had to be axed down by his workers to widen the opening.

꧁❀꧂

This June day would be ideal for enjoying a leisurely drive in your car — and an ideal day to be grateful for Henry Ford's invention that has given so much freedom and pleasure to so many. Also, it can be an occasion to feel better about yourself the next time you forget something or make a mistake. If a genius can overlook an important detail such as the size of the door through which he must drive his invention, you needn't get down on yourself when you miscalculate a project or forget to plan ahead — or even when you forget where you placed your car keys.

✖

5 **Feast of St. Boniface.** Today we celebrate the patron saint of Germany and also of beer brewers. Even though large numbers of German immigrants have settled in the United States, the celebration of their patron saint's feast, unlike the Irish celebration of St. Patrick's Day, has little if any celebration. Perhaps this is because of their practical, hard-working, serious

Germanic nature. Yet it is never too late to have a revival of a festival. So if you have German ancestors, hold a personal or family celebration on this feast of Boniface.

This saint, born in England, is often shown in art chopping down the pagan sacred oak tree of the god Odin. St. Boniface converted Germany to Christianity and personally crowned Pepin as the Christian Emperor of the Franks. On his way home to England, while passing through present-day Holland, Boniface was brutally martyred by "unconverted" Frisians.

◈

The warm days of late spring are a time when beer drinking has a saint's touch to it. Consider celebrating this Germanic holy day by raising a glass of beer with a toast to Boniface the Bold. Those who seek an excuse for another cool drink might consider resurrecting the old custom of St. Boniface's cup. According to tradition, which may have been conveniently invented by those thirsty for a "frosty one," it was said that Pope Boniface I, who took the name of the famous saint, granted an indulgence to anyone who might drink to his health. (An indulgence was a spiritual reward taken from the treasury of the Church won by Christ and the graces of the saints. It was applied to an individual to reduce his or her time in purgatory by a specified number of days or years. The widespread abuse of this practice of granting indulgences was a primary target of Martin Luther's reforms.)

If on a hot June day you are *indulging* in killing your thirst, consider using this toast when drinking with friends: Raise your beer, iced tea or lemonade and say, "Here's to the good health of Pope Boniface and the health of each of us. God willing, may none of us ever die of thirst here or in hell."

Being American means being culturally and spiritually rich. Since few Americans are pure-blooded and since we all are readily exposed to an assortment of ethnic traditions, we have at our disposal a variety of patronal saint's days to celebrate. So, rejoice today and honor St. Boniface with a brief prayer or a cool brew. As with the revival of Octoberfests in the U.S., this feast gives all of us — whether German, Irish, Italian, Vietnamese or mixed ethnic background — an opportunity to revive and celebrate our abundant cultural, spiritual heritage.

✡

---

6 Feast of X-Rated June, the Loss of Virginity Month.

While June is known as the wedding month, it is also the month when approximately forty-five percent of young Americans lose their virginity. According to a study of 4,306 young people by the psychologist Joseph Lee Rodgers, regardless of race or gender, hormones are more active when the days are warm and long. The entire summer, with its vacations and free time, provides opportunities for sexual encounters, but June ranks first for first-time sex.

∗※∗

June would be a good candidate to become Sex Awareness Month. Like other such commemorative occasions, perhaps it might have its parades, postage stamps and special programs. But beyond the hoopla, Sex Awareness Month could make parents, educators and churches aware of the need to speak about human sexuality as one of God's greatest gifts. It could be an opportunity to cultivate a spirituality of sexuality, an awareness that responsible sex can bring us closer to God. Just as the horrors of hell are given more attention than the delights of heaven (When was the last time you heard a sermon about the delights awaiting you in paradise?), so the dangers and evils of sexuality predominate. On the other hand, television and Hollywood sell sex glamorized, artificially attired and separated from a living commitment of love and sacrifice.

Conspicuously absent from the canon of officially named saints in the Catholic Church are those who have lived and died in the joys of married sexuality. The refusal to allow priests to marry or married men to become priests speaks loudly of the Church's view on sexuality.

Married or not, take pride today in your sexuality and in all your body which is made in the divine image.

✡

Do Something X-Rated Day. Have you done anything X-rated recently? If not, consider today as an opportunity to do so. The rating "X" is given to films and other art forms that have excessive sexual content. However, the third to the last letter of the alphabet should not be limited to that meaning alone. An "X" is also the sign of the cross of St. Andrew, whom tradition says was crucified on a cross in that shape with his arms and legs spread wide. As we saw in the April 23 entry, the cross of St. Andrew is used as the background for the British flag over which the cross of St. George has been added.

7

Today, if you are called upon to be stretched beyond your limits by an act of service or kindness, as was St. Andrew, embrace with love this invitation, and do something X-rated in the pattern of Andrew's cross. In fact, a good examination of conscience at the end of each day would be to ask: Have I done anything X-rated today? While we usually believe we are already stretched to our limits, there is always a bit more time, money, energy, dedication or love that can be called forth. What practice or inner attitude can you cultivate in order to be ready to do something X-rated when your life requires it? What can you do to make sure that you have the inner spaciousness to respond, just in case you are blessed with such an Andrewian opportunity today.

✸

Georges Buffon's Evolutionary Theory Day, 1757. The French naturalist Georges de Buffon is credited with one of the early theories of evolution, a unique one at that. Buffon's eighteenth century theory suggested a reverse evolution, holding that an ape had evolved backwards from a man, a donkey from a horse.

8

As time bridges the Second and Third Millenniums, the seemingly humorous reverse evolution of Georges Buffon should be given a more serious consideration. The normal paradigm of personal and cultural evolution is promotion, the continual growth in status over one's lifetime, requiring us to be always ascending. Those judged successful are measured by how high they climb on the ladder of life. Promotional evolution, however, is a cause of excessive stress, and the inability to perpetually climb upward leads to low self-esteem and attacks of failuritis.

In all walks of life, instead of always going uphill, consider adapting Buffon's theory and begin going downhill. As a follower of Buffon, you could move upward until midlife and then begin to descend. The company president, for example, would begin to descend during middle age, first to vice-president, then office manager, continuing in reverse evolution until at the time of retirement the work of a janitor would be taken on. In religious institutions, the bishop would descend to priest, then to lay person in the pew. University professors would end their teaching careers as freshmen. Those who live in affluence would take on simpler and simpler lifestyles. And the religiously wise would become spiritually humble and poor.

As you struggle with the hectic pace of life today, consider your own experiments in Buffon's reverse evolution and see if you are not happier, healthier and holier going downhill.

�֎

---

9 **Birthday of Cole Porter, 1892.** Today honors a man who gave the world some beautiful love songs with witty and sophisticated lyrics. Among Porter's best-known songs are: "Night and Day," "Begin the Beguine" and "Let's Do It." SSt. Cole Porter is one of the leading secular patron saints of this month of love, marriage and romance. Love possesses the magic to set feet dancing and to cause songs to spring to our lips.

Cole Porter also wrote several musicals, including "Kiss Me, Kate" and "Can-Can." A high art form, musicals are plays where the actors sing instead of reciting their lines. Today, many consider them artificial since in ordinary life people do not suddenly begin singing. This position is only half correct, however. It is true that singing no longer is part of daily life. Yet that's a sad commentary, for music is the language of love. Yes, musicals, whether describing the ecstasy of falling in love or the agony of falling out of love, are museums of what once was normal in everyday life — singing. But to this extent churches are also museums, since in worship song and music are not luxuries but are essential to the message.

✦

God created crows and canaries; while they have different-sounding songs, both are music to the divine ears. Regardless of your voice, use Cole Porter's birthday as a special invitation to sing even a few lines of a favorite song. Be brave and sing to your spouse, friend or lover even a few lines of a love song. Liberate your singing from the solitude of your shower, and sing on the way to work and even at work.

If at age 16, 61 or 86 you feel "in love," by all means sing out. You might even consider becoming a born-again child, making up your own music and lyrics as you once did many years ago.
✦

Founding Day of Alcoholics Anonymous, 1935. 10

Alcoholics Anonymous has been instrumental in liberating millions from the slavery of alcohol. Its success is founded in good part on a deep spiritual belief in God — by whatever name you wish to give this Reality beyond yourself. It is also based on companionship with others who are in the process of, or are seeking to begin, becoming free, and on a confession of faults. Those who have been thus freed, along with their friends and family, should acknowledge the inspired creation of this group called AA.

✦

This remembrance day is the beginning of the celebration of freedom and liberty that comes to a climax on July 4th. AA teaches us that liberation is never an accomplished reality but is rather an ongoing one. Aware that addiction comes in many more forms than drugs and alcohol, begin this preface to Independence Day by continuing your personal liberation.
✦

11 **Speed Records Day.** While October 14, 1947, is the date of the first supersonic aircraft flight, today we celebrate a prehistoric ancestor to that anniversary. In 1947, Captain Chuck Yeager, piloting the Bell X-1 research plane, flew faster than the speed of sound. Today, in the midst of bug season, we honor all of nature's fliers. Second prize among the fastest of these fliers goes to the dragonfly, which reaches speeds of over sixty miles an hour. And the gold medal goes to the male horsefly, which reaches speeds of over ninety miles an hour — only, however, when in hot pursuit of a mate!

⁂

The speed with which we attend to matters is affected by a multitude of factors. We can achieve the speed of a horny horsefly when we are deeply interested in the project at hand. When we are not, we usually fail to come close to a dragonfly's speed. Instead of putting off a task you find unpleasant, consider making it your first project today. If you stay with it and break through the "dread barrier," you may find a release of energy that allows you to do all your work at record-breaking speed.

✶

12 **Patron Saint of Nudists, St. Onuphrius.** For sixty years, says the saint's legend, Onuphrius wore no clothing, and his nakedness was covered only by his very long beard and hair. Fortunately for his vocational call, Onuphrius was not a Siberian saint but an Egyptian hermit of the fifth century. He was chosen, perhaps with tongue in cheek, by the cloth-making guilds of the Middle Ages as their patron saint.

In India, even to this day, there are holy ones who go about totally naked as a sign of complete poverty. Among those Hindu saints is Mahadeviyakka, a twelfth century woman ascetic, who also went about naked, covered only with her long hair. Her prayers are flaming furnaces of devotion for her Lord and Lover. One of her prayer-poems goes like this:

> People, male and female,
> blush when a cloth covering their shame

comes loose.
When all the world is the eye of the Lord,
onlooking everywhere, what can you
cover or conceal?

Perhaps the seeming madness of naked St. Onuphrius is only holy sanctity, for indeed nothing is concealed from the eye of God who made all things good.

❧❀❧

The urge to return to the unclothed freedom of Eden is a primal secret longing. In the last centuries of the Second Millennium it was resymbolized in novels, art and movies by the longing for exotic island paradises of the South Pacific. This does not seem to be a longing of the native peoples of Alaska or northern Canada, but for us who live in moderate climates it does express itself in various ways during these warm summerlike days.

If you feel yourself thus tempted to abandon as many clothes as possible, do not feel guilty. Rather, call upon St. Onuphrius, the patron of the nude. And you may want to be grateful today that God has not called you, like St. Mahadeviyakka and St. Onuphrius, to the vocation of witnessing to the naked beauty of being made in the image of God.

✴

White Trash, Nigger and Other Garbage Words Day. 13

Years ago during the days of racial segregation, white children sometimes teased black children with chants like,

Nigger, nigger, never die,
Black face and shiney eye.

A standard reply by a black child to this taunt would be,

I don't eat cabbage,
and I don't eat hash.
I'd rather be a nigger
than poor white trash.

"White trash" appeared in print in 1833 as a form of the highest contempt among black slaves for white servants as the lowest of the low. "Nigger" stems from the Latin word for black, *niger*, and first appeared in print in 1786 in a poem by Robert Burns. Through the early years of the last century of the Second Millennium, the term "nigger" was often used without contempt. However the Tulsa, Oklahoma, *Tribune* helped cement it as a term of derision when in the June 1, 1921, edition it blamed an uprising in the city's ghetto on "the bad niggers...the lowest thing that walks on two feet." Governor Eugene Talmadge of Georgia took the term to a new low when in February of 1942 he was quoted in an article in the *American Mercury* as having said, "No niggah's as good as a white man because the niggah's only a few shawt year-ahs from cannibalism."

⚜

Children's rhymes like "Eeny, meeny, miny, mo, catch a nigger by the toe," make us aware of how deeply ingrained is the tendency to discriminate. And the taunt of "white trash" shows the equal tendency for those on the lowest rungs of a social ladder to try to find someone they can place even lower.

The horrible sin of racial and religious hated has a long history and won't easily be overcome in one or two generations. Such discrimination is not likely to disappear unless all garbage words, all negative and even jokingly prejudiced remarks are removed from our speech.

Use this day to examine what words you use when referring to those who differ from you with regard to their race, religion, sex or sexual orientation. If you find you are still using discriminating terms or engaging in off-color humor about such persons, then "wash your mouth out with soap" as a prayerful purification.

✴

---

14 Flag Day and President Harding's Radio Address, 1922.

While today is famous for celebrating the Stars and Stripes, our national flag, on this day in 1922 a president was first heard over the new invention called the radio. As President Warren Harding spoke at the dedication of the Francis Scott Key Memorial in Baltimore, the nation marveled that they could actually hear his voice by means of the new wireless invention.

⁂

Less than eighty years later, it is becoming increasingly difficult to be marveled or to engage in the act of marveling. Originally the word meant "wonderful things," from the Latin *mirabilia*. While the word wonderful is still in daily use, few of us are ever wonder-full. We who no longer can be astonished are impoverished by this loss of a sense of profound wonder, so profound as to fill us to the full.

What may be required in the new century is a new kind of martyr, one who embraces the martyrdom of marveling. A martyr is one who chooses to suffer death rather than renounce religious principles, one who is willing to sacrifice what is precious for a religious reason. In an age of lost innocence, only children can gape in open-mouthed wonder at some magician's trick, only the childlike remnant can marvel at a spring flower or "Ahhh" at a word of truth. Sophistication requires us to suppress whatever wonder might be left, so as to not appear delightfully surprised by anything.

God works a million marvels a minute, for those with eyes to bulge and mouths to gape open in wonder. By being astonished at a sunrise, an infant's smile or being loved by someone, you "witness" to a world filled with God's wonders. Blessed are those who sacrifice their sophistication and allow themselves to be marveled.

✯

UNIVAC Day – First Commercial Computer, 1951. **15**

Today in Philadelphia in 1951, the first electronic digital computer built for commercial purposes was dedicated. It was designed by Dr. John Mauchly and J. Presper Eckert, Jr., who had designed ENIAC, the world's first electronic digital computer in 1949. They attempted to develop a computer business but experienced financial problems, and Remington Rand took over their business.

⁂

The ENIAC computer of 1949 was so large that it occupied

an entire city block. At the end of the twentieth century, a chip of silicon only a quarter-inch square has the same capacity as the original ENIAC computer! Take time today to be filled with wonder at advances of technology like UNIVAC or like Kurzweil's Reading Machine and prepare yourself to be even more amazed by what will appear in the next few years.

Yes, how wonder-full is Kurzweil's Reading Machine, which can read printed English books aloud to the sight-impaired. It presently reads at speeds half again as fast as normal speech. This machine uses an electronic camera which can scan practically any typeface. It feeds images into a minicomputer which produces synthetic speech.

Whether or not they are aware of it, those who experience being full of awe in the presence of something wonderful are also full of prayer. A profound prayer begins the very moment we are awakened by that which awes, that makes us speechless or causes us to proclaim, "Wow!" Whether it's something spectacular in nature, the birth of a child or a marvelous new human invention, all that produces wonder opens us to communion with the Divine Mystery. God is the Ultimate Wonder, the Eternal Awe-full One, who brings angels and humans to their knees in adoration. If today you are awakened by something wonderful, rejoice and bow your head in adoration of the hidden Divine Mystery.

✳

---

16 **National "Ain't Today's Youth Bad?" Day.** This is a good day to lament the sad state to which our modern youth have fallen. Reflect on whether you agree with this quotation as a summary of today's youth: "Our youth love luxury. They have bad manners, contempt for authority; they show disrespect for their elders, and love to chatter in place of exercise. Children are now tyrants, not servants of their households. They no longer rise when their elders enter the room. They contradict their parents, gobble up their food, and tyrannize their teachers." If you agree, brace yourself, for these words were written by Socrates, the Greek philosopher, in 400 B.C.

❧❀☙

Socrates' comments make us who are adults hearken back to what they said about us when we were teenagers. Today is a good day to rejoice in the goodness and promise of our young people, and to abstain from criticism and negative comments about their behavior and attitudes.

✳

Celebrate Hero Day as You Water Your Lawn. 17

Summertime brings out the garden hose and sprinkler and provides an occasion for today's festival, which honors the inventor of the rotating sprinkler. About the time of the birth of Jesus Christ, a Greek engineer invented a device that was a kind of primitive steam engine. His name was Hero, and his device is used today in your rotating lawn sprinkler.

It is estimated that ninety percent of all scientists who have ever lived on earth are alive now! Since 1950 more scientific papers have been published than in all the millenniums before that date.

Scientists and inventors are creating new devices which may not find their way into common use until the year 4000 A.D. When their ideas finally find a practical use, the names of the inventors and scientists may no longer be known. Today can encourage us to become anonymous heroes and heroines by refraining from having our names plastered on all our good works and ideas.

✳

Arkansas Law Ruled Unconstitutional Day, 1959. 18

In the early years of his administration, Governor Orval Faubus closed schools in Little Rock and continued to maintain de facto segregation. On this day in 1959 his practice was judged by a three-judge federal court to be unconstitutional. This was another historical day in the long struggle of African-Americans to remove the barriers of segregation.

The sin of segregation has been the diabolic breeding ground for more social evils, injustices and inequalities than can be counted. Beginning in the days of slavery and then made into law after the Civil War, segregation based on the color of a person's skin has directly contributed to many of the other social evils that have grown up in the second half of the twentieth century.

Segregation was not limited to public transportation, schools and drinking fountains; it was also strictly practiced by almost every Christian church in America. Perhaps some day in the new millennium we will see all churches hold a national day of repentance for segregation. On that day, let all church bells toll. Led by their bishops or presiding officers, let all church members beg forgiveness from their African-American brothers and sisters for their sins of segregation. It shall be a day of fasting and penance not only for the failure to condemn slavery and segregation as morally evil from the very beginning but also for the fact that "white churches" practiced this sinful separation within their own walls.

Why wait for that day? Today can be a day of private repentance for your past — and even present — sins of segregation and discrimination.

�҂

---

19 **God in Our Dreams and Decisions Day.** The prudent take ample time to make important decisions in life. They invest much thought in the process of making a decision as they weigh and balance all the factors involved. Much more important, however, is how we live out our decisions. Today or the next time you must make a decision, remember that God is in the decision but the devil is in the details of how we live out life's decisions.

⚜

God dwells in our hopes, dreams and aspirations, calling us always to greatness in little and hidden ways. Yet it is wise to be cautious of how we handle the details, which often make us lose sight of the dream. So the next time you find you have forgotten your dream because you are being tormented by details, pray this short prayer: "Be gone, Satan!"

�֎

Prejudice Promotion Day. Being guilty of prejudice can be virtuous, so today begin to practice being prejudiced. This behavior is usually defined as "an adverse judgment or opinion which is formed without knowledge, or a proper examination of the facts." In this sense of the word, prejudice is a mother sin that has produced great litters of evil and hatred based on others' race, religion, gender, ethnic background or sexual orientation.

However, it's not that kind of prejudice that this day celebrates — but, rather, reverse or positive prejudice. Positive prejudice sees others to be as good and intelligent as I am without prior evidence to support that judgment. Then it treats them on that equal or even superior basis. It prejudges all to be teachers possessing some important knowledge, skill or ability which can be learned.

Approach everyone you encounter today as a person who wants to work hard at his or her task in a way that promotes dignity and the ability to live a decent life. See in everyone a being eternally chosen by God to reflect to the world a unique facet of God. Thus, treat everyone with dignity, as a walking sacrament of the Divine Mystery.

✦

Practice positive prejudice today with the innocence of a dove but also the wisdom of a serpent. The latter is a healthy judgment based on the awareness that everyone has faults. As a rule of thumb, be more like a dove than a serpent, but realize from self-knowledge the human tendency to fall short of Godly behavior. Yet, if more and more people began to practice this kind of positive prejudgment of others, it would take only a short time for the world to become the kingdom of God.

✖

21 **Summer Solstice Festival.** This day marks the year's longest day of sunlight. When humans lived more of their time out-of-doors, this long day was the occasion for all kinds of feasting, bonfires, dancing and celebration. Since December 21 the setting sun has been moving constantly north along the horizon; today it pauses briefly before again beginning its journey southward.

The human body is prehistorically programed to react to the extended hours of sunlight by being active for longer periods. Yet, regardless of how long or short the day, Thomas Edison has had a great effect on that inner programming. Indoor lighting has reset the body's biological clock, especially in those who live in industrialized countries. If you live in the United States, electric lights have shifted your body clock by four to five hours, so that it seems you are living part of your day on Hawaii time.

According to Dr. Charles Czeisler of Boston, each night when you switch on an electric light you are unknowingly taking a drug that effects how you will sleep.

Without using electric lights, let your body dance tonight to the ancient prehistoric delight of staying up late as the sun lingers in the western sky. Turn out the lights earlier and enjoy an old-fashioned sleep. A recent University of Florida study has shown that Americans at the end of the twentieth century were sleeping one and one-half hours less each day than in the 1930s. The report revealed that most adults sleep seven and one-half hours a day and that more and more they are sleeping less and less.

Use this pre-Christian holy day of the sun to respect the natural rhythms of your body. Use it as an occasion to examine the degree to which you live in harmony with creation's clock set by the seasons, the sun, the moon and the stars.

✬

22 **Pay Your Electric Bill Day.** Lights and air-conditioning can make June's electric bill look like those of mid-winter. As you pay your bill, consider this Pedestrian Prediction in 1955 by John von Neumann of the Atomic Energy Commission: "There is little doubt that the most significant event affecting energy is the advent of nuclear power....A few decades hence, energy may be free — just like the unmetered air."

⚜

More than four decades after that prediction by a nuclear scientist, energy in any form is far from free as air. Wise are those who know that nothing in life is as free as unmetered air. While the twenty-first century may provide solar and other forms of inexpensive energy, will any of them really be without its own particular cost?

Free is a trap-word. Whenever you see it printed on junk mail or in a store window, proceed with great caution — or turn and run the other way. This four-letter word works magic on even seasoned shoppers since it seduces by playing upon sloth and greed. *Free* promises no labor, no sweat or effort, yet what can be achieved without labor? *Free* promises no money spent and thereby none lost. Yes, who can resist the thought of getting something for nothing?

So beware of predictions and promises for free energy. Even if there is no surprise cost to your pocketbook, there may be an even more expensive hidden cost. Slavery, for example, provided "free" energy in the form of slave labor. Yet it has exacted an enormous moral cost on the human spirit. And besides the surprise financial costs of nuclear energy, is there not also a greater potential cost to the health of humans and the environment?

✷

The Birthday of the Rearview Mirror, 1906. In her 1906 book, *The Woman and the Car*, Dorothy Levitt, a pioneer woman motorist, provided the inspiration for the modern rearview mirror. She advised women to carry a hand mirror in the car's tool chest located under the driver's seat. Levitt suggested that the lady's mirror could be used not only to restore her makeup after a windy drive but could also be held aloft

23

frequently to check on the traffic behind her.

❦

Today, as you glance in your rearview mirror, say a small prayer of gratitude for Dorothy Levitt's idea about being a good driver by watching the traffic behind you. Prayer is also a rearview mirror in which we can glance at the end of the day to see where we've been and what we've done or failed to do. Looking backwards is essential for those on life's highway, for knowingly or unintentionally we can be responsible for many accidents along the way.

In interpersonal collisions at home or at work, it is easy to be a hit-and-run driver and leave the scene of the accident without acknowledging responsibility. In a hurry to accomplish your goals in conversations, you can "hog the road" and cause others to seek the safety of the shoulder. At the end of the day, by taking a brief time to look in the rearview mirror of prayerful reflection, you can see more clearly the patterns of your "driving" behavior.

Blessed are those who before going to sleep look into their rearview mirrors. By this simple prayerful practice they can adjust their course to be kinder, more considerate and more loving as they travel the high road of life.

✴

---

24 Midsummer's Eve, the Birthday of John the Baptist.

This feast was strategically placed on this day to be six months from the birth of Jesus. Speaking of Jesus, John said, "I must decrease and he must increase." From now on the hours of sunlight begin to decrease until the winter solstice, which has the fewest hours of daylight. Because of calendar changes, these feasts are not precisely on the dates of the solstices, but they do capture the spirit of the seasons. Tradition and customs have fittingly held this as Summer Christmas, as an occasion for celebrations, feasting, dancing, bonfires and the giving of gifts.

❦

Why give gifts to those you love only on Christmas, birthdays or anniversaries? Today can be a surprise gift-giving day, the resurrection of the ancient Summer Christmas and an occasion to celebrate. In the modern world of work-work-work, such surprise celebrations of gifting and feasting can help insure that we will not become clones of the machines that fill our lives. Machines *never* have holidays.

Machines also work without taking a break to relax, visit or rest. Nor do machines have fiestas or ancient celebrations like the feast of St. John the Baptist. Although efficient and dependable, machines do not pray or play. While these mechanical servants, who serve even the poorest persons, are hardworking and faithful to their daily tasks, they should not be imitated. Even a casual glance at the behavior of contemporary people in industrial countries shows an ever increasing similarity to the patterns of machines. Leisure time is shrinking for humans, it seems, in proportion to the advances in technology and the number of machines taking over human functions!

The old Sabbath Law required that beasts of burden and slaves be given a day of rest along with God's people. Would giving machines rest by unplugging them on Sundays and holy days be one way to remind us humans not to let machines be a model for our behavior?

25

Feast of St. Molaug. Known also as Molloch and Lugaid, this Irish monk is the patron invoked to heal headaches and insanity. He is renowned for being the first Christian missionary to the Highlands of Scotland.

On this feast make yourself a holy cord of Molaug as a cure for headaches. Simply take a piece of string or cord and tie seven knots about an inch apart. Then ask St. Molaug's blessing on it. When you next have a headache, tie the Molaug cord around your head about midway down your forehead. Even if you're not cured of your headache, it will be a sign to those with whom you work and live that your head is causing you pain, thus making patience difficult.

Recalling that this holy Irishman is also the patron against insanity, you can also wear the holy cord of Molaug if someone or something is "driving you out of your mind." Or you can carry it in your pocket, using the knots in the cord as prayer beads. Prayerfully fingering the cord of Molaug will help you keep your wits about you in the midst of being driven crazy.

⚜

Also this day in 1951 marked the first commercial color broadcast of television by CBS, which had spent eleven years and $5,000,000 to develop this new technology. At this time, however, no color TV sets were owned by the public, and it would be months before they'd become available. Yet, colorized or not, if TV gives you a headache, consider wearing a St. Molaug holy cord.

✯

---

26 **Long Living Day, 1920.** On this day in 1920 the United States Bureau of Public Health proudly announced that since 1901 the average life expectancy had increased from 49.24 years to 54.09 years.

Ancient Egyptians lived an average of only 33 years and so saw the completion of only one or two pyramids a lifetime, since each of those massive monuments took over twenty years to build. At the time of the building of the cathedral of Notre Dame, which took 137 years to complete, the average Frenchman lived only 45 years.

By contrast, the U.S. space program was able to place humans on the moon, a work that required only one-sixth the span of an average adult life at the time.

⚜

As you enjoy living longer today than your ancestors in the Roaring Twenties, reflect on what you are doing with your life. Consider the story of the three men who were building the great cathedral of Notre Dame. A visitor stopped and asked, "What are you doing?" The first stonemason replied, "I'm just making a living." The second replied, "I'm taking care of my family, feeding my wife and children." The third stonecarver said with great pride, "I'm building a great cathedral!"

✴

Feast of the Sauk Indians' Trail of Tears, 1831. On this day one of the many Trail of Tears was begun. Black Hawk, the leader of the Sauk Indians and General Edmund Gaines of the U.S. troops reached an agreement for the Native Americans to leave their homes in Illinois. They were moved across the Mississippi River into Iowa. In the spring of 1832, nearly starving to death from lack of food, they returned to their old corn fields in Illinois.

27

Seven years later, in midst of the wintry December of 1838, the Cherokee Native Americans from Georgia and southeastern Tennessee, numbering over 14,000, were removed by force from their homeland. They were force-marched by 7,000 U.S. soldiers into Oklahoma so that 7,000,000 acres of Cherokee land could be seized by white settlers. It was truly a "Trail of Tears," the term originally referring to the death of 4,000 Cherokees in 1835 during the enforcement of the fraudulent treaty of New Echota.

Between 1825 and 1860 approximately fifty plays were written and performed in America, portraying stereotyped and romantic images of Indians. At the same time, entire Indian tribal nations were being forced off their lands, abused and killed to make room for greedy settlers. In the twentieth century motion pictures continued to create the myth of the American Indian and to glorify the wholesale stealing of their lands.

≈⊙⊛⊙≈

The Jewish Holocaust Memorial Day remembers those killed as part of Hitler's "final solution to the Jewish question." Perhaps a new American Memorial Day is needed to remind us of our country's "final solution to the Indian question."

Such a memorial would provide an opportunity to look at the land upon which you live and know that it is stolen property. Sin is both personal and social, present and past. Individuals, nations and even churches can and do sin. When it comes to the need for repentance and pardon, there is no shortage of reasons to ask forgiveness of God and others.

�֎

---

28 **"What Would You Do In a Disaster?" Day.** The latter part of the twentieth century witnessed a revival of interest in the 1912 sinking of the ocean liner, the Titanic, with its loss of 1,513 lives, 80% of whom were men. Most people view the Titanic as the worst sea disaster in history. Yet far more disastrous was the 1945 sinking of the German vessel *Wilhelm Gustloff.* A Russian submarine torpedoed it in the Baltic Sea, causing the loss of close to 8,000 lives, most of whom were women and children.

A recent survey in the *Pittsburgh Post-Gazette* revealed that over ninety years after the Titanic only 35% of men would give up their seats in a lifeboat to children or women who were not in their immediate family. The survey also revealed that only 54% of men would give up their place in a lifeboat for their mothers, and only 67% would do so for their wives!

❧✦❧

The gallantry of gentlemen in the first decade of the twentieth century failed to survive until the twenty-first. This survey seems to say that the heroic love of which Jesus spoke, "There is no greater love than to give up one's life for one's friends" (Jn. 15: 13), is becoming an endangered species.

For whom would you give up your life? For whom would you sacrifice your life jacket or your seat in the last boat to safety? For whom would you become an exchange hostage? Would you do it for a family member, for a friend, for a stranger? The questions on this "What Would You Do in a Disaster?" Day might provide interesting conversation in a gathering of friends or around the family supper table.

�֎

---

29 **Feast of Saints Peter and Paul.** Today's twin feast first commemorates Simon, the apostle who was renamed by Jesus as Peter. He was chosen to be the servant of the servants of the servants of God, the leader of Jesus' small community after his death. This is also a festival commemoration of Saul, who became Paul. He was a latter-day apostle whose writings and journeys in Greece and Rome spread the new religion of Christianity. As legend holds that the twin brothers Romulus and Remus were the founders of the city of Rome, so Peter and Paul were viewed as the founders of the first Christian community of Rome. They were both martyred in Rome for their religious beliefs. Paul, being a Roman citizen, was beheaded, while Peter was crucified on a cross.

⚜

St. Peter is the patron, naturally, of fishermen and net makers. He can also be the patron of all who deny Jesus out of fear of the consequences. Simon Peter three times denied that he was one of the Galilean prophet's followers, or that he even knew Jesus. Pray a prayer to Peter, the holy coward, on your way home after a gathering where you denied being a follower of Jesus' way. If you remained silent, or joined in the laughter in order to avoid being criticized, as others told demeaning jokes about African-Americans, Jews, Asians, gays, women or any group that is discriminated against, then Simon Peter can identity with your pains of guilt.

Embrace your silent denial of your religious beliefs with sorrow. Then, do as Simon Peter did; turn your cowardly behavior inside out and become a martyr for your beliefs. At his own request Peter was crucified in a silly way, upside down. Your personal martyrdom may be to look silly in front of others by refusing to laugh or engage in the violence of prejudicial speech and humor. The new century needs more such martyrs who die yet live.

Paul might be called a latter-day apostle because he did not personally know Jesus of Nazareth. Yet this cofounder of the Church was as zealous as any apostle who had firsthand knowledge of Christ. Paul can thus be a patron saint for all of us who are called to be latter-day apostles and to proclaim the Good News. We know from his letters that St. Paul struggled to bring peace and unity to those in the early church who were at odds over various issues. Disagreement over rituals, requirements and the nature of the church is nothing new, and St. Paul can help pass on much grace to those who desire healing and reconciliation in the midst of bitterness and conflict. A further reflection of St. Paul can be found in the January 15 entry in this Almanac.

✳

---

30 The End of the Month — a Take-It-Leisurely Day.

As we have seen, there are many who believe the end of a century, an age or a millennium to be wrought with danger and impending doom. But how is the end of a millennium any different than the end of June, or of any month? Yet, as the future races forward and becomes the present, the potential for dangerous changes hangs heavy in the air. In response to such impending change, many people *create* emergencies. If you find this to be the pattern in your business, your religion or your personal life situation, strive to practice this response from ancient Chinese wisdom: A Chinese proverb to live by states, "Always take an emergency leisurely."

✵

The wise prepare for the future by living today and each day with thoughtfulness and reflection. By definition, an emergency is just an emerging situation which appears suddenly and demands immediate action. Yet contemporary life seems to have transformed the living room into an emergency room; moreover, the future will flood upon you with ever greater speed. While life's various emergencies require that we act quickly, we also need to take them leisurely.

We need to create a space of prayer in the midst of an emergency, a prayer that can slow down the flood of events and invite our timeless God into the situation. Consider having a mini emergency drill today by taking some minor emergency and treating it in a leisurely and prayerful manner. Make it a slow-motion picture and incorporate enough quiet and calm prayer into the situation as to also make it seem like a silent motion picture.

If you daily live out the profound belief of *Immanuel,* that "God is with us," when the unexpected suddenly emerges and demands immediate attention, you can respond with grace, peace and even leisure.

THE

MONTH

OF

JULY

The famous Mark Anthony named this month in honor of the legendary statesman and general, Julius Caesar. This seventh month had previously been called *Quintilis* because it was the fifth (*Quinque* is Latin for five) month in the old Roman calendar. Its Saxon name was *Maedd-monath* since at this time of year the cattle were turned into the meadows to feed. If a new calendar were created, this month's name might be changed to "Liberty" to honor both great revolutions, the American and French, which are celebrated in this month. July is also the high season for vacations, a word that comes from the Latin *vacatio*, which means freedom.

Creation Out of Nothing — Nanotechnology Day, 2031. This date marks one of the great breakthroughs of the twenty-first century, bringing humans a giant step closer to creating out of nothing, to being co-creators with God. "In the beginning..." the Bible teaches, there was nothing, and out of the absence of matter, God created the world. By the end of the twentieth century, scientists were developing major discoveries in creation. For millenniums, humans had been able to create things only by working with existing matter: chairs out of wood, buildings out of stone or swords out of metal. The term for this new field of science, *nano*, from nanometers, billionths of a meter, was coined by K. Eric Drexler in 1981.

With this technology of manipulating atoms and molecules, any material, food or substance can be created more efficiently and abundantly than even nature can. Molecules floating in an unceasing stream can be put together like Legos. No longer science fiction, this is the fulfillment of the vision of Richard Feynman, who in 1959 began the work of atom-by-atom manipulation that is in the process of revolutionizing material science.

One application of nanotechnology is making materials out of diamond, which has more than fifty times the strength-to-weight ratio of steel. Construction of spacecraft out of pure diamond could reduce their weight by a factor of fifty. Furthermore, fantastic uses of this technology make possible the creation of entirely new foods and materials for construction and even the repair and reconstruction of body tissue and bone. Holy and awesome is such a vocation of being a co-creator with God.

❧❦❧

Eye has not seen, nor ear heard, what awaits us in the new century and millennium. Cloning and other scientific experiments cause some religious leaders to cry, "Frankenstein! Contrary to God's law!" The prejudice of religion that science is dangerous or even diabolic has a long history. May the new century begin a new era of collaboration between religion and science and a new appreciation of the rapid and radical advances in our world.

What are your feelings — positive or negative — about such amazing new advances such as nanotechnology?

✯

---

2 Feast of the Early-Fulfilled Mini Computer Prophecy.

An issue of *Popular Mechanics* magazine in 1949 made this startling prediction for the future regarding the shrinking size of computers: "Computers in the future may weigh no more than one and a half tons." Laughing, and pointing to the ENIAC computer just put into use that same year — it occupied an entire city block — many readers said, "That future is a long, long way off!"

The wristwatch you are wearing contains more computing power than existed in the entire world before 1961! The cost of the science of computing is 8,000 times less than it was in the 1970s. Today is a feast set aside for awe-full prayer.

❧❦❧

Beholding a rainbow or the ocean or standing on the rim of the Grand Canyon can fill us with a sense of awe. We can be likewise struck with wonder when looking up in the center aisle of a great medieval cathedral.

Let the watch on your wrist call you to awe-full prayer as you reflect not only on its marvelous and lightweight technology but on how inexpensive it is. The shrinking cost of computer technology makes the marvel of telling time on your wrist the equivalent of getting a Boeing 747 for the price of a pizza.

O my God, Awe, Ah, Wow!

✳

Carroll Day, a Feast to Work for Freedom. Preparing for our national celebration of the adoption of the Declaration of Independence, today we commemorate Charles Carroll, who was one of its signers. He was a devoted patriot, public servant and the only Roman Catholic to sign the Declaration. As he affirmed that document of freedom, Charles Carroll was aware that it did not fully apply to him. As a Catholic, he was prohibited from holding public office in his home commonwealth of Maryland. There, as in the other colonies, Catholics could not be lawyers and could not even teach the young.

Fully aware that his signature on the Declaration was an act of treason against England, Carroll was the only signer who also appended his address, adding, "of Carrollton," Maryland. It seems he wanted to be sure the British would know where to find him when they came to hang him.

❦

The independence and freedom of all is a work that remains unfinished. You along with all the other citizens of our country have the honor and duty to work to bring full freedom and equality to all. While defending your own liberty and independence can spur you to take risks, are you willing to labor for equality among peoples even when it does not directly involve you?

If you are a man, are you willing to labor and take risks to insure the rights and equality of women? If you are white, are you truly zealous in promoting the rights of those of color? If you are heterosexual, are you willing to stand up and seek the full rights and equality of gays and lesbians?

The Fourth of July is more than a time for picnics, ball games and fireworks. Let it be a Festival of Freedom Fighters in the pattern of Charles Carroll.

☙❧

Also, today is the **Feast of St. Thomas the Apostle**, the patron saint of doubters. Being a saint of balanced passions, he was as fiery in his defense of his beliefs as he was in questioning them.

4 **Independence Day, 1776.** King George III wrote in his diary for this day, "Nothing of importance happened today."

The king of England closed the cover of his diary and perhaps yawned, not knowing what had occurred that day in faraway Philadelphia, Pennsylvania.

While we celebrate the *courage* of those who signed the Declaration of Independence, it seems they themselves were quite cautious. It was not until January 19, 1777, that the Continental Congress made public the names of those who had signed the Declaration. Historians suggest that Congress may have feared that if the revolution were to fail the signers would die as traitors.

☙❧

While the Fourth of July celebrates courage, we can also use today to celebrate prudence in moderation, as did the original signers of the Declaration of Independence. Jesus admonished his disciples to avoid martyrdom, if possible. "When they persecute you in one town, escape to another" (Mt. 10: 23). The key is *moderation,* for excessive prudence cloaks cowards in pious respectability. Jesus practiced what he preached, and on numerous occasions escaped from those who sought to kill him for his bold proclamations. However, when he was faced with the ultimate threat in Jerusalem, he embraced his martyrdom as the will of God.

Mindful of Jesus' words, and the delay of the original signers of the Declaration in releasing their names, practice the paradox of courage and prudence.

�֎

The Day After Any Revolution Festival. History has shown repeatedly that the day after a revolution, many revolutionaries becomes conservatives. Political revolutions, religious reformations and social revisions have all had "time limits." As a result, reforms must be subject to frequent reincarnations, rebirths of their revolutionary dreams.

5

❧❦❧

Every reformation or revolution is a special kind of story, not a history story, but a to-be-continued story. By contrast, every institution does all within its power to insure that revolutions are not like ongoing cliff-hanger adventure series. Rather, institutions embalm revolutions by making them historical occasions to-be-remembered.

While the Jewish and Christian religions keep ritual remembrances of the Exodus, do they really want one today? While the United States, with the ritual of flags, parades and fireworks, keeps the memory of the American Revolution of liberty and freedom for *all*, is it really eager for such a revolution to continue today?

�֎

The Festival of Wasted Days. Recalling the diary entry of King George III on July 4th of 1776 that nothing important happened, consider if today may be the same for you. James Boswell, the noted eighteenth century Scottish writer, frequently told his friends about the most wonderful day in his life. The unforgettable event of that day — one which had made a lifelong impression upon him — was his father taking him fishing. He relished telling of their hours together alone. One of Boswell's friends found the story fascinating, so he obtained the diary of Boswell's father and turned to the treasured date. There he saw

6

a brief entry, "Went fishing today with my son; a day wasted."

❧⚬❀⚬☙

By the last couple of years of the twentieth century, time had grown so scarce that a poll revealed 85% of Americans reporting that they had no spare time. Leisure is required not only to take a child fishing but to create lifelong memories with those you love. Time misers hate to "waste" one solitary moment, time being as precious as money. Blessed are the generous who throw away hours and days in reckless, loving waste, refusing to measure the value of time spent by the amount of money earned or work accomplished.

✴

---

7   **Dying to Look Good Day.** Looking like you're dying or frying is surprisingly still considered a sign of beauty and health! Fashion promotes the tanned look, which could more correctly be called the *singed* look. While an obvious overdose is called a sunburn, a good tan is actually a singe, a "superficial burning of the edges (of the skin's surface)...." It's been clearly shown that this singeing leads to skin cancer, which kills more people in America than any other kind of cancer. Someone dies every hour from melanoma!

In the fourteenth century, like today, people wanted beautiful, brilliantly white teeth. This was sometimes achieved by a process which, next to extraction, became the major dental operation. The dentist of the day, a barber-surgeon, would first file the patient's teeth using a coarse mental file. Then he would daub the teeth with *aquafortis*, a solution of highly corrosive nitric acid. The patient would go home with beautiful, shiny white teeth, but not for long. The process caused destruction of the teeth's enamel, which would lead to massive dental decay a few years later. Yet, even when these grim consequences were acknowledged, as with tanning, vanity won out and the process of acid cleaning of teeth continued in Europe until the eighteenth century!

❧⚬❀⚬☙

Having a great tan, looking cool smoking and other pursuits of vanity come at a high price. Few if any of us are free of vanity, and so today is "Mirror, mirror on the wall, am I not the fairest — and sickest — of them all?" day. What high price do you pay today to look good? Since aging is the enemy of vanity, what price are you paying to look other than your real age?

Love of oneself is essential, for it is the beginning of love of neighbor. Love yourself today by first embracing the reality of who you are and loving that reality. Proper grooming and style of dress can highlight who you are, but not by trying to disguise who you are. Such vanity can cause you to lose rather than enhance your identity.

✷

Making Yesterdays Full of Memories Day. Professor Harold Hill is the dynamic, flamboyant salesman in Meredith Wilson's musical *The Music Man*. Professor Hill attempts to get Marian the Librarian to go on a date with him. With all his charm, he asks her to meet him by the footbridge of a stream in the city park. Marian wants to go but is fearful, so she refuses, saying, "Please, some other time. Maybe tomorrow." Hill, the ever-persistent salesman, continues to try to tempt her to meet him at the bridge, but she continues to find excuses to postpone the date. At last, in exasperation, he says those marvelous words worth remembering, "Pile up enough tomorrows and you'll find you have collected nothing but a lot of empty yesterdays."

8

Remember that each entry in your Almanac has a ✷ Star-Date with an empty space for you to record your personal historical events. Using it may help you find your life full of full yesterdays. Recording significant events will remind you to do other, new significant events and not to put them off. Adventures and new experiences await us each day, but we postpone and delay them until a better day, which is always some tomorrow day. "Some other time, later, next year..." are ways we usually greet invitations which are uncomfortable because they are new and involve risks.

At the same time, we need to open all our plans and activities to God's hand. The Prophet Mohammed said in the Koran, "Do not say, regarding anything, 'I am going to do that tomorrow,' but only, 'if God wills.'" The Arabic word for this is *Inshallah*; it is a beautiful prayer word when some new adventure is proposed: We shall accomplish this by the end of the day — *Inshallah!*

Today, when a new adventure rings your doorbell, or some new experience knocks at your back door, pause and remember Marian the Librarian's polite protest, "Please, some other time, maybe tomorrow you can come back." Pray for courage and for a long life full of memories of marvelously rich yesterdays and say, "Welcome, come in, you couldn't have chosen a better day to visit. I'm ready to have a new adventure — *Inshallah.*"

✳

9

Feast of Saint Ephraem the Sourpuss. In 363 the Iranians, called Perisans in those days, invaded Iraq, called Mesopotamia at the time. In the wake of this war, Ephraem, a Christian deacon, fled to live the rest of his life in a cave. He was given the title "Harp of the Holy Spirit" because he composed numerous hymns. Yet Ephraem, the ancient scrolls state, never laughed or smiled. Our Father, who are in heaven, deliver us from temptation and from saints who never smile or laugh — even as they compose music! This feast of Serious Ephraem is a good day to petition Rome to canonize funny saints, those holy women and men who by their good humor make us, and God, smile.

❧⚓☙

Studies show the muscles in the face are capable of over 250,000 different combinations of expressions! We also know that it takes many more facial muscles to frown than to smile. Today, give your facial muscles a rest and smile more. Each day we have a basic choice: to be a sourpuss or a sweet-and-smiling-puss (puss is American slang for mouth or face, from the Irish *pus* for mouth or lip).

Ralph Waldo Emerson said that our face reveals what the spirit is doing. It does not lie but makes a faithful confession. Poor Ephraem, while a holy man, must have had a sour soul.

It's strange that religion seems to require a sober if not sour appearance lest the world think we are having too good a time enjoying life here on earth. Laughter is rare in holy places, and often among so-called holy people.

Religion is not the only one guilty of causing a sour face. In daily life, where hardships seem to abound, wearing a smile and being happy is usually considered a sign that you don't comprehend the problems facing the world and, therefore, must be simpleminded. If you monitor gatherings of friends and family, notice how often conversations center on the negative subjects: how bad is life, young people, the world, their work, their..., the litany of woes goes on and on. Beware if you lack any problems that make you grim faced, for others will start giving you some of theirs to carry. The issue isn't problems – everyone has problems. Rather, it is how you respond to them. For the soul, problems are the stuff of holiness, the raw material for working with God to transform our various situations into opportunities for greatness.

As you go about your activities today, remember that your face is the window of your soul. Don't pull down a window shade, wearing a half-face to cover what's in your soul. Rather, by spiritual exercise make your soul full of God – and so, your face full of joy.

10

Women and Wyoming Day, 1890. This day in 1890 marks the entrance of Wyoming into the Union as the 44th state. In 1869, while Wyoming was still a territory, it gave women the right to vote. In 1890, it was the first state to do the same, granting women their equal rights in electing public officials. Wyoming was prophetic, which means "speaking for" (usually the ending "...God" is implied), for prophets live ahead of their time. The Women's Right to Vote was not passed in the two houses of Congress until 1919. After being ratified by the necessary thirty-six states, it did not became law as the nineteenth Amendment to the Constitution until 1920.

July is Freedom Month, and today's remembrance should remind us that the work of liberation, as we see with recovering alcoholics, is never completed. Women continue to lack full equality with men in professions and business — either in equal wages for equal jobs or in equal opportunities for advancement — and also in some male-dominated religions. Live ahead of your time and proclaim in whatever way you can the full and equal rights of women, and all who are subject to discrimination because of ignorance or fear.

---

11 The Feast of Non-Pilgrims.

The Feast of Non-Pilgrims. This is a good day to stay home instead of going on a pilgrimage to some holy shrine. As you sit at home today, ponder these words of the fourteenth century Kashmiri poet, Lal Ded:

> I was passionate,
> filled with longing,
> I searched
> far and wide.

> But the day
> that the Truthful One
> found me,
> I was at home.

The Catholic Church proclaimed the year 2000 to be a Jubilee Year. All Jubilee Years have historically been occasions of pilgrimages to holy shrines, as special opportunities to deepen one's faith by a more direct contact with the holy. Religious shrines are places made holy by a variety of reasons, such as divine and saintly visitations, miracles or a long history of holy use.

Yet the practice of Christians making pilgrimages, especially to the Holy City of Jerusalem and the various sites of the life and death of Jesus, did not begin until the fervor of the faith had cooled. Aflame in the first centuries of the early church was the belief that the Risen Jesus could be experienced even in a brief pilgrimage to a neighbor. There was no need for places of sacred space, for churches or shrines. Rather, the faithful ones' homes were holy because they were the places of worship and celebrating the Lord's Supper.

To see the Risen Jesus today, make a pilgrimage to your neighbor's house or visit with a family member. Or pray where the Truthful One can find you — stay home!

✴

Feast of Non-Pygmy Vision. In 1943 Thomas Watson, chairman of IBM, said, "I think there is a world market for maybe five computers." Pygmies see as well as others, but being very short, their field of vision is limited in perspective. Jesus frequently went to pray in the mountains. There, symbolically, his vision was broader; he could see prophetically over the horizon and into the future. Those today who limit the power of faith, prayer and hidden acts of kindness view reality with pygmy vision and dwarf imagination. Doomed to shortsightedness are those who can only imagine what can be seen by looking at the present and, therefore, must live out pedestrian prophecies. Jesus could and did imagine a promised land, God's domain, which he called the kingdom of God.

12

※⚜️※

If you wish to visit the Promised Land, broaden your vision to see it in your home, office or workplace. Dwell in the same reality in which Jesus lived: an age of justice and equality for all, where the poor and weak are treated with respect and outcasts are welcomed. The failure of the reign of God to come in full vision is a failure not of prayer but of imagination. Blessed are those who can live in the greatest nation on earth, Imagi-Nation.

✴

Seeing the Beautiful Everywhere Day. A tenet of Zen masters is worth reflection today: "Everything exists according to its own nature. Our ideas about what is beautiful, valuable

13

and correct exist inside our heads, not outside them." To take the step to empty your mind of preformed ideas based on various principles about what is beautiful or valuable can allow you to step into paradise. Everything created by God is crafted according to its nature and purpose. God the Divine Artist does not create anything ugly, anything that isn't precious. Yet, with our minds we often deface Eden's artworks, making treasures into trash.

⚜

Today is a Feast of New Eyes. Practice looking at your daily world with God's eyes and so see everything and everyone as of supreme value and of breathtaking beauty. A billion times a day, God smiles upon all of creation and says, "You, you, you, and you — and all of you are beloved and upon you my favor rests."

Jesus healed the blind, not only those who physically lacked vision but those who lacked God's way of seeing the poor, sinners, outcasts and those forced to the margin of his society. Allow the Risen Jesus to heal your eyes today as you see with eyes cleansed of prejudiced thoughts about what is, and what is not, beautiful.

✻

---

14 **Bastille Day — French Independence Day.** Following the example of the American Revolution, the French people revolted against their king. The French Revolution of 1789 began as mobs stormed the royal prison called the Bastille. Today marks that event and is the national holiday of independence in France.

After their revolution of 1776, many Americans rightfully expected it would inspire other oppressed peoples to seek their independence and so were enthusiastic in support of the French people. Then, in the 1790s, shortly after the French Revolution, Americans had an opportunity to support a revolution for liberty and freedom much closer to home when the island of Haiti revolted against France and sought its independence. However, in 1803, the slave-holding president, Thomas Jefferson, preferring a Napoleonic colony to a free black republic in the Caribbean, secretly gave France the go-ahead to invade and crush the young independent black republic. This action was supported by slave-holding planters in America, who feared that a revolution by blacks in Haiti would inspire slave revolts in America — which it did. When Haiti won out in its struggle, despite America's siding with Napoleon's French Empire, the United States did not extend diplomatic recognition to Haiti!

Recall the Almanac entry for July 5 and how "the day after the revolution, its revolutionaries become conservatives." Bastille day is an excellent opportunity to test your desire for all peoples to be free and independent. The Jubilee Year of 2000 marks a starting point to celebrate those revolutionary words of Jesus in his hometown synagogue, "I have come to proclaim liberty to captives, and...to let the oppressed go free..." (Lk. 4: 18). Consider celebrating each year as a Jubilee Year, and each day as a Jubilee Day, by doing all in your power to set the prisoners free!

Feast of Saint Swithin. The English saint, Swithin, died in 861. His most celebrated miracle revolved around his desire to be buried not inside a church (as was then a custom) but outside in the graveyard next to the church so rain could fall on his grave. When his remains were dug up to be enshrined inside a cathedral in 971, it rained for almost forty days! So arose the British belief that if it rains on July 15, St. Swithin's Day, it will rain for forty days.

15

Today is the feast of a saint who is a double patron: for and against rain. This day is an occasion to enjoy a good July rain shower and to marvel in what is usually taken for granted — falling rain. Three and one-half millenniums ago, in 1525 B.C., the Egyptian troops of Thutmose I invaded Syria and were dumbfounded by what they reported as "the Nile falling from the sky!" Thutmose's soldiers, having come from the cloudless land of the Nile, were fascinated when they first encountered rain, which they thought must be falling from some great river in the sky.

If rain should fall on this feast of the patron saint of rain, use it as another occasion for wonder-full prayer, the cousin of the prayer of adoration. To adore is to "pray before," *ad-ora*, and to pray before falling rain should not be restricted to farmers after a long drought. Gene Kelly's musical movie *Singing in the Rain* is not only a classic of modern dance but of childlike delight in playing-dancing-singing in the rain. Few of us are inclined to such "madness" for fear of catching cold, ruining a hairdo or simply getting wet. Yet today, or on any day blessed with a summer shower, if you are so inclined to experience one of the holy wonders of creation, despite the shock of family and friends, by all means, go Swithin Singing in the rain.

✷

---

16 **WD-40 Day.** This wondrous if not magical spray was invented by Norman Larsen in 1953 to keep moisture off Atlas Missile nose cones. Larsen was successful after his 40th try at developing a water displacement formula and so named the formula for the event WD-40.

Keep a can around the house or office, and whenever you're trying to get something to work, let the label remind you not to give up your efforts after twenty or even thirty-nine times. Interestingly, when he circled the world in 1964, John Glenn was covered with WD-40 from head to foot!

Besides keeping moisture off missiles, airplanes, electrical circuits and preventing corrosion, it's good for countless other uses, such as taking the squeak out of new shoes, removing sap from garden tools, cleaning clogged spray-paint nozzles, removing price labels off glass and plastic products or removing chewing gum, tar and crayon from most surfaces. It makes easier the removal of dead insects from the hood of your car, and many claim that if you spray it on fishing bait it will hide the smell of human hands and thus be a better lure.

❧❦❧

Once again, the practical life and the spiritual life should not be separated. Consider having a can of WD-40 in your home prayer shrine to remind you to be persistent in your prayers and to pray for every request at least 40 times. Also, if you have hostile feelings toward someone, write the person's offense in crayon on a drinking glass and place it before you when you pray for the person. At the end of the prayer, take your WD-40 and spray the drinking glass. As the offense is removed, let it be wiped away from your heart as well.

�

Feast of the Flight of Wrong-Way Corrigan, 1938. 17

On this day, Douglas G. Corrigan, alias "Wrong-Way," took off from New York for California, only to land in Dublin, Ireland. He had requested, but failed to receive, a flight exit permit to fly to Europe and claimed that he had lost his way. Despite his illegal action, Corrigan became a national celebrity by his clever mistake.

❧

Those who wait for permission to do daring things will sit on the runway of life for a long time, if not forever. Today celebrates the SSt. (secular saint) Wrong-Way Corrigan, who is the patron of those who find creative ways to do what is forbidden by regulations and laws. SSt. Corrigan is also the patron saint of those who are willing to take risks in life.

In 1971 Pope Paul VI spoke to all Christians, not simply Catholics, when he said, "It belongs to the laity *and clergy* (author's addition) without waiting for orders and directives, to take the initiative freely and to infuse a Christian spirit into the mentality, customs, laws and structures of the community in which they live." Surely, Paul VI understood community to be an inclusive word referring to both the secular and spiritual, so use the Pauline Privilege for taking initiative in the spirit of Wrong-Way Corrigan.

�

National Garage, or Rummage, Sale Day. 18

July is a popular month for holding that great American suburban flea market called a *garage sale*, in which your unwanted goods are offered for sale at a low price. In former times it would have been called a rummage sale, more correctly, *arrumage*, meaning "to load a cargo ship." Goods were often damaged in loading and unloading, and sales of these damaged objects were called arrumage sales. With time, unsold rummage became old; along with out-of-style and used clothing it was usually "unloaded" to a charitable organization.

Reflect when you are inspired to give clothing and other objects to the poor if you are "unloading" your arrumage goods. They are "damaged" because they're no longer in style or almost worn out. If you are so inspired, reflect on this story of a missionary priest from a foreign land who spoke before a pious woman's parish society. At the end of his talk he asked, "Ladies, do you have any old vestments, altar cloths and so forth?" The women responded eagerly, "Why yes, Father." The missionary replied, "Then burn them!"

Moral: Don't just assume your discards are of value.

19 **Richard Blechynden Day.** At the St. Louis World's Fair in 1904 an Englishman named Richard Blechynden had the fair's tea concession. On one hot day his hot tea had few if any buyers. To compensate for his loss of business, he did something unthinkable for an Englishman; he served his tea in glasses with ice.

In some parts of Colonial America, even hot tea was a novelty. When tea first came to the American Colonies, some women served the tea leaves with sugar or syrup and threw away the hot water in which the leaves had been prepared.

Celebrate Richard Blechynden Day as you savor that popular summertime drink, ice tea, with a toast to the clever Brit. Also, if you have a conversation with friends on this July day, consider some unthinkable solution to a problem you may presently have.

As the tea was thrown away in the early days of the American Colonies and the tea leaves served, are you throwing away something today that may in the next century become a practical necessity as well as a delight? Ask yourself too if you only complain about a present sad situation — like having no market for hot tea on a hot summer day — or do you creatively adapt to the situation with radical innovations?

✳

Feast of St. Margaret, Patroness of Women's Liberation. 20

A saint of the early church, Margaret of Antioch became one of the great models in the Middle Ages. Hers was one of the voices Joan of Arc heard in prayer, and she fearlessly took on the duties of what only men had previously done. Margaret's voice is one that many women today could pray to hear in their prayers.

The story of Margaret is legendary. Because she was holy, the devil was drawn to Margaret; he came once as a great dragon and swallowed her alive, like Jonah. In the belly of the dragon Margaret held tightly to her cross, which grew so large it split the dragon wide open, enabling her to emerge unharmed. Because of this she is the patroness of childbirth. She is also the perfect patroness of Women's Liberation: In another diabolic attack, Margaret knocked the devil down and stood on his neck, saying, "Lie still, you fiend, under the foot of a woman."

❧⚘☙

July is Independence and Liberation Month, celebrating a freedom story that is ever to-be-continued. Today, we can pray this prayer:

> Holy Margaret, come and aid the birthing of women
> in all cultures, institutions and religions of our world
> as full equals with men in all things,
> in all places, and at all times.

✳

The Great Garage Laboratory Day. *Garage* is a 21

borrowed British word referring to a room on the wing of a house or a separate building near a house in which a car or cars are parked. Popular at the end of the twentieth century as a place for sales of unwanted belongings, as the July 18 Almanac entry celebrated, it is also useful as a laboratory for new inventions.

In 1896 Henry Ford began experimenting with his gasoline engine in his kitchen. Needing more room, he soon moved to a garage shed in Detroit. Similarly, Walt Disney moved to Hollywood in 1923 to live with his uncle. He began his first cartoon film work in his uncle's garage in Los Angeles. Likewise, C.E. Woolman began his aerial crop-dusting business in a former gas station garage in 1920. From cotton field dusting he moved on to carrying mail and passengers. He named his new company Delta Air Service and later redecorated the garage as a lounge for his passengers.

Silicon Valley began in a garage rented in 1938 by William Hewlett and David Packard. Their experiments with an audio oscillator moved on to computers. In 1940, Ruth and Eliotte Handler rented a garage to make giftware with Lucite, the new plastic innovation. In that garage in 1958, Ruth dreamed up the Barbie doll, and the Mattel Toy Company was born. In 1975, Stephen Wozinak moved into Steve Job's garage to produce their personal computer; it became the first headquarters of Apple Computer. Buddy Holly and the Crickets created rock and roll in a garage in Lubbock, Texas. In Pleasantville, New York, DeWitt and Lila Wallace rented a garage-apartment and began writing and editing *Reader's Digest*.

<hr/>

The next time you go into your garage, pause a moment and look at it with new eyes. Perhaps the spirit of some new invention, toy or household product, music or movie, magazine or new company is just waiting to be created.

This National Celebrate Your Garage Day provides an opportunity to reflect on using that space for more than parking your car and storing your equipment — consider making it sacred space. A stable, the ancient, great-grandmother shed of today's garage, was also the birthplace of God's new creation, Jesus Christ, the birthplace of a new covenant. If you need a place to reinvent your prayer life or to visit with God about new ideas for how to reinvent your life, consider spending some quality time in your garage.

✴

Feast of St. Mary Magdalene, Patron Saint of Sinners. 22

Biblical scholars tell us that Mary of Magdala is confused with the unnamed sinful woman who anointed the feet of Jesus. It was reported that Jesus drove seven demons out of Mary of Magdala, and so she had her fill of evil spirits. This may mean that she was suffering from a severe illness or literally that she was beset by a terrible case of possession. Yet despite the suggestion of recent scholarship, Magdala Mary remains, by legend and tradition, a woman who knew the sins of the flesh.

Mary is also one of the Gospel's most honored women, privileged to be the first apostle sent by the Risen Jesus to bear the "good news" of his resurrection to his men disciples. She is also Mary the Brave, who dared to stand near Jesus' cross as he was crucified.

❧❀❧

While most professions have their patron saints, and all kinds of sicknesses and afflictions have theirs, St. Mary Magdalene can be the patron of all us sinners. If seven evil spirits had taken up residence in her heart, then she knows the strong tidal pull of evil. While tradition has made her the patroness of "fallen women," we all fall weekly or even daily in our attempts to walk in the footprints of Jesus. Paradoxically, she is also a patroness of contemplatives, which can be attributed to the legend that in her later life she retired to a cave in the wilderness. Contemplatives are those who seek to live in the perpetual presence of God in the midst of daily life, and so Mary of Magdala is the perfect saint to point the way. For if you are fully aware of how much God has forgiven you, you cannot help but be absorbed in deep love of the Divine Pardoner. Every lover knows the power of that release. A life of sin, even when one seems to be possessed by evil, can thus be the doorway to becoming a contemplative saint.

St. Mary Magdalene, protect us from the pious affliction
   of seeing ourselves as "honorary" sinners.
By honestly confessing our faults,
   help us to become so drunk on divine forgiveness
   as to love God and one another with great passion.
Show us how the best apostles of the Good News
   are former major league sinners.

⭐

23 End of the World by Poison Gas, 1800 Million B.C.

Another July revolution is commemorated today as we remember
when a major part of life on Earth died in the great Oxygen
Revolution. Primitive life on planet Earth began absolutely free
of oxygen, which is needed for plants and animals to live. As
oxygen began to be formed from seawater, it was a deadly
poisonous gas for organisms unequipped to deal with it! For
almost half the history of Earth, formation of sulfates and rich
iron ores eliminated the oxygen produced by the growth of
plants. This natural geochemical process was finally exhausted,
and a gigantic global change occurred, for all intents and purposes
bringing about the death and end of a world.

The author and philosopher, Alfred North Whitehead, said,
"It is the business of the future to be dangerous....The major
advances in civilization are processes that all but wreck the
societies in which they occur." Such was the arrival of oxygen
which is so essential for life on this earth; it destroyed an existing
primitive life culture as it gave birth to a new one.

⁂

The twenty-first century as a force of the future was in a
hurry and crossed over the line of the millennium before the
year 2000. Also in a hurry were the social, religious and global
changes it carries with it. Radical changes in society that once
took centuries, now seemingly take only seconds. The dangerous
future will be a healthy home only to those who can adapt to
the radical changes that will come with it. Blessed are the
adaptable, for to them the future will not be destructive.

Adaptation is the art of being flexible and able to let go of what once was comfortable and well known. It requires the grace of being as new as each new situation and of being able to reinvent yourself not simply to fit in but to prosper in the new.

The changes of the future can seem like a poisonous gas to the lungs of the soul. Yet we are all blessed with a marvelous capacity for adaptation, the ability to grow and flourish in new life conditions. Practice today for the future (which could be as close as next week) by experimenting with newness and change in your life.

✳

Learn to See Day. The Native American elders teach the necessity of looking at the world twice if you truly want to see what's there. Reeducate your eyes today to look carefully at things as common as an ant or the way sunlight falls on a leaf. Then look again as you focus your eyes on the edge of what is visible. Seeing what is "on the edge," the Native Americans believe, allows you to see visions, the unspeakable, the holy ones who are invisible, and the other side of the natural. They teach that those who only see what is before them are blind.

24

⚜

Jesus said, "Let those with eyes *see*." Practice today looking twice at as many things as possible and you will be blessed, for blessed are the eyes that see. The great seventeenth century poet, William Blake, once observed, "If the doors of perception were cleansed, one would see everything as it is, infinite."

What is needed for such seeing is not new glasses, but a vision cleansed of habit and routine, of what is limited only to the surface of things. Today could be a day to wash out your eyes by closing them and letting the healing powers of holy darkness wash over them. Pray the prayer of the blind, "Lord, that I might see," and then open your eyes to the infinite.

✳

25 Pedestrian Prophecy and Aquarium Day.

"Television won't be able to hold onto a market it captures after the first six months. People will soon get tired of staring at a plywood box every night." The 1946 prophecy of Darryl F. Zanuck, head of Twentieth Century Fox Studios.

⚜

Summertime, and the fish are jumping — rather, swimming for hours on television as people stare at their small plywood box. Several summers ago, the cable television company that serves Columbia, South Carolina, directed a camera full-time at an aquarium in order to occupy a vacant channel. The cable company was waiting until September to start up their science fiction channel. When the new channel replaced the swimming fish, the company was swamped by complaints for the aquarium show. They wisely found another channel which now runs the fish program continuously for fourteen hours a day.

Fish are natural gurus for those who would like to meditate. Watching fish swimming can be soothing, relaxing and even fascinating. Next to a home-chapel or a prayer corner, an aquarium may be the surest way to find solitude and a meditative soul. It's also an excellent place to sit in front of, in silence, when you and someone else in your house have had an argument or when you're stressful or overdrawn. You can simply sit quietly as these underwater magicians, with a swish of their tails, remove your stress.

Consider, today, how a glass aquarium is almost identical in appearance to a TV set, but the contents are often far superior. If you own a TV set, perhaps you should also have an aquarium.

✺

26 Feast of Sts. Joachim and Ann, Patrons of Grandparents.

The names of the parents of Mary of Nazareth appear in a first-century source of Christian faith. They are the most renowned grandparents in history, their grandson being Jesus of Nazareth. Today honors all grandparents who are indeed grand and wonderful second parents; their genetic gifts are part of our

DNA inheritance. Grandparents usually do not have to discipline their grandchildren and do not live with them, and so they are freer to give parental love in that unique way that is sometimes called "spoiling."

⚜

Today is also the birthday in 1875 of the famous Swiss psychiatrist, Carl Jung. He met and began working with Sigmund Freud in 1907, but by 1912 they had professional disagreements and parted. Grandparents can encourage and support grandchildren when parents fail. One wonders on this feast of the patronal saints of grandparents, if the great Sigmund Freud was blessed with loving, with "grand," grandparents. In 1864 Jakob Freud said of his son Sigmund, "The boy will come of nothing!"

⚜

Grandparents are accused of spoiling their grandchildren. Yet, can any child or adult be spoiled by too much love? Ask yourself: What really spoils a child and creates a rotten adult?

Today is a perfect occasion to remember your grandparents by a telephone call, a visit or by prayer. If you are a parent, help your children to learn about their grandparents by telling them stories about their grandmas and grandpas so they will be able to understand themselves better. Also, spend some time today, perhaps on the way to work, remembering your grandparents. As you do, see if you can identify their DNA, as well as their spiritual gifts, in you.

✳

Feast of a Cure for Millennium Motion Sickness. 27

July is the peak of the vacation season as people take to roads, skies and oceans on their annual absence-from-work time. Many travelers suffer from motion sickness, which can turn a holiday into the horrible. Some of those so afflicted use Dramamine, while those who travel by car often simply choose to be the driver, since this seems to reduce the dizziness. Moreover, a scientific study from Britain states that ginger is more effective than Dramamine in stopping motion sickness. Asian food markets sell candied ginger, which can be chewed while traveling. You can also take two 500-milligram capsules of ginger an hour before you leave on your trip and one or two more capsules every four hours while traveling.

While ginger may remove a highway traveler's dizziness, is there some herb to relieve millennium motion sickness? While moving forward into the future is said to challenge us with change, Tom Peters of the Tom Peters Seminars says, "Forget change. The word is feeble. Keep saying 'revolution.'" While revolutions usually brew for years, when they come, they do not amble along. For those unprepared, they come with the speed of lightning. To help us with the rapid motion of revolution, some herb or drug stronger than ginger and Dramamine put together is needed.

⚜

Ginger is a plant of tropical Asia whose root stock is used as a sweet favoring. It is used to make ginger ale, ginger beer and gingerbread. As we have seen, it also reduces the ill effects of motion sickness. However, it has yet to be proven as an effective herbal medicine for rapid forward movement — as in revolutions and the variety of approaching eras and ages.

Yet, being "gingerly," being cautious and careful, in how you approach rapid change may be a potent medication. To gingerly greet the new century means rejoicing in the new while testing its value to enhance rather than threaten life. While one meaning of gingerly is "to treat daintily," it is hardly possible to be dainty with a revolution! A more accurate strand of the DNA code of the word gingerly is from the old French word meaning "of noble birth."

To approach whatever changes the new century will hold, and we can be sure there will be many, we need a good measure of nobility, of dignity, confidence and kindness. This is poetically conveyed in the expression *noblesse oblige*, which means to be benevolent, kind and honorable to others in keeping with the responsibility of persons of high birth and rank.

Christian Baptism includes an anointing with the same chrism oil once used for anointing kings and queens. Christians, by their spiritual birthright, belong to a royal priestly family through their incorporation into Christ. If anyone, then, can embrace gingerly and without anxiety the dizziness of the rapidly moving new era, surely it would be a disciple-believer in the Risen Jesus.

✺

Birthday of Beatrix Potter, 1866. This English author and illustrator gave us the classic *The Tales of Peter Rabbit* and other wonderful fantasy stories. To balance the diet of daily grim news, try a little fantasy reading today. Why should fantasy be restricted only to childhood?

For many at the end of century twenty, more than half of their need for fantasy was met by the daily news! In 1997 a survey showed that 64% of Americans obtained their news from television, 27% from newspapers, 5% from radio and only 1% from magazines. When those who watched television news were asked if they believed the news they received to be true, only 34% of Easterners said they did, and only 54% of Southerners. If less than half of the population doesn't believe news reports, is it because the news is incorrectly reported or simply that it's perceived as a form of fantasy?

❧✥❧

Beatrix Potter's story of Peter Rabbit is not credible as fact, and is readily understood to be a fantasy. Reflect on what the percentages might be if a survey were taken on how many people believe in the credibility of the Good News, the Gospel of Jesus Christ? Hearing or reading the Good News is one thing, believing that it is a credible way to live in the contemporary world is another. Believing in Jesus as the son of God is one thing, but it is quite another to take seriously his words about never returning injury for injury, loving your enemies, living without anxiety for tomorrow like the birds of the air, forgiving each other without limit, caring for and becoming like the poor and other radical examples of the Good News. Ask yourself if you believe what you hear on the evening television news is true; then ask yourself if you truly believe what Jesus taught is how God wants — and expects — you to live.

✵

---

29 Feasts of Sts. Martha and Mary and SSt. Earl Tupper.

The two sisters who frequently entertained Jesus of Galilee and his band of disciples are known for being patronesses of opposite virtues. Mary is the patroness of contemplatives who sit and ponder the mysteries of God's Word, while Martha is the patroness of hospitality, household chores and kitchens. The home of a person with a wholesome, balanced spirituality would have a shrine to both of them. A rocking chair with a stand for a cup of coffee or tea would be a fitting shrine of St. Mary the contemplative, while a welcome mat, a broom closet, the laundry machine or the kitchen stove could be shrines of St. Martha. Both sets of shrines can be holy places, and both need to be visited daily with prayerfulness and an awareness of their unity in helping us become holy.

⁂

Today also honors a secular saint who is the perfect companion for the saint of the kitchen, Martha. Earl Tupper was a Du Pont chemist who in 1945 produced his first polyethylene bathroom water tumbler. Plastic kitchen bowls had all been rigid until Tupper introduced indestructible, low-cost, flexible plastic containers of seamless beauty in various pastel shades. Earl Tupper is a patron for all who wish to respond to the approaching changes of a new century with creativity and imagination.

He was inspired to offer his new Tupperware to the public through in-home Tupperware sales parties. By 1951 his infant company had become a multimillion-dollar business. So successful were his in-home promotion sales that he discontinued selling his product in stores. By 1954 Tupperware sales had topped $25 million. Earl Tupper's next move can also be an inspiration for us today and in the tomorrows of the future: In 1958 he sold his business for an estimated $9 million and disappeared! Eventually he became a citizen of Costa Rica and died there in 1983.

⁂

Martha, Mary and Earl Tupper are a transmillennium trio who can inspire us to three needed virtues. Mary calls us to be contemplatives and to take time to reflect on the rich treasures of God's Word so as to be wealthy in the age of God. Martha invites us to enflesh God's Word by daily housework and hospitality, which finds both the chalice and cooking pot to be holy. Earl, our secular saint, can inspire us to be inventive, to try new ways to reach others with whatever is our "product."

Saints Mary, Martha and Earl together might inspire us to close all churches for one year. Instead of going to church for worship, people would have in-home Tupperware-style prayer and Eucharist parties. Earl found that he could sell more at home than in stores; who knows what religion might discover by copying this creative idea.

�֎

Festival of the First Color Motion Pictures, 1928. 30

A new kind of color called Technicolor arrived and the world ended — the world of black-and-white motion pictures. George Eastman exhibited this new creation on this day in 1928 in Rochester, New York. The first showing featured colorful goldfish, peacocks, butterflies, flowers and pretty girls in brightly colorful dresses. Upon seeing this new wonder, the president of RCA predicted that someday television would be in full color.

Eleven years later in 1939, MGM used both color and black filming to create the motion picture *The Wizard of Oz*. While it was intended to be a prestige motion picture, it was a box office failure and a money loser. The critic for the *New Yorker*, Russell Maloney, wrote in his review, "I sat cringing before MGM's Technicolor production of *The Wizard of Oz*, which displays no trace of imagination, good taste or ingenuity." After eighteen years of being entombed, this flop reappeared in 1956 on television. It went on to become a classic annual production, with millions and millions of fans. Some maintain that it looks better on the small screen of your television set than on the theater big screen; others say that it was just ahead of its time.

Some works of art take time to be appreciated, and some things need a new generation to appreciate them. Herman Melville's *Moby Dick*, the classic story of the great white whale and the struggle between good and evil, is almost universally considered to be one of the greatest novels ever written. Yet when it appeared in 1851, it was misunderstood and ignored. It and Melville's other books had to wait for over seventy years before they even began to be acknowledged for their creative genius.

If today you find a flop on your hands, remember the *Wizard of Oz* and *Moby Dick* and smile; perhaps your creation arrived before the world was ready to appreciate it. Also, if a work you are asked to judge appears to be lacking "in good taste or ingenuity," with no trace of imagination, pause before pronouncing judgment and again remember *The Wizard of Oz*. And when you strive to accomplish a breakthrough in the struggle between good and evil or justice and injustice, remember Herman Melville, who in 1891 died in poverty and obscurity thinking his writing and life had been a failure.

✳

---

31 Anniversary of the First U.S. Patent, 1790.

Two hundred plus years after the issuing of the first U.S. patent, perhaps someone will secure a patent for a Portable Rapid-Adaptor Pacer. Like the heart pacer, the PRAP will allow its wearer to quickly adjust to the need to abandon the old and slip into the new. Peter Drucker wrote in the *Harvard Business Review*, "Every organization has to prepare for the abandonment of everything it does." Drucker doesn't say that companies should prepare to change but to *abandon* what they are presently doing.

His advice burns like a fuse on a time bomb for those who realize that tomorrow will not be just a new copy of today! *Prepare* is a key word in his challenging statement. Prepared, you can meet the challenge of the future, even if you are not wearing a PRAP. Unprepared, you will not so much be a spectator as a participant in a disaster. We can look to 1939 for a striking example of a pedestrian prophecy of the unprepared. Writing in *The American Mercury*, George Fielding Eliot said, "A Japanese attack on Pearl Harbor is a strategic impossibility."

※※◎※※

Whatever you consider impossible today, whether a potential disaster or a great blessing, may come across the horizon in only a few years, or even tomorrow. The angel Gabriel, who announced to Mary of Nazareth her critically important role in God's Dream for the re-creation of a new world, told her, "...with God all things are possible."

Holding that angelic message next to your heart as your Portable Rapid-Adaptor Pacer will prevent heart attacks from surprise, fear or shock when the impossible suddenly becomes a reality. The next time you are tempted to say, "Impossible!" think again. You may say instead, "Not impossible — perhaps even very likely." Today is a feast day for examining the impossible in your life and work, and being open to how the impossible might become a reality.

✴

THE
MONTH
OF
AUGUST

M·D·XX·

This eighth month, once named *Sextilis* (it was then the
sixth month), received its present name in 8 B.C.
from the Roman Emperor Augustus Caesar. *Augustus* is
a title meaning "venerable" given to the Roman Emperor
and then passed on to his successors. Looking at your yard,
you may wish to return to the Old Saxon name for this month,
Weod-monath, "weed month." (Originally the Saxon for
weed did not mean an alien plant but vegetation in general.)
Or you may desire to return to its name in the French
Republican calendar, *Thermidor*, "the hot month."

Don't Wait for Orders Day, or the 240-Z Festival.

1

The easiest way not to be called on the carpet by the boss and
charged with making a mistake is to only do what you are
ordered to do. So, today, celebrate taking the initiative: Don't
call and ask what to do — just do it.

In the later part of the twentieth century when Nissan was
attempting to penetrate the U.S. sports car market, they sent
Yutaka Katayama to explore American interests and needs. He
suggested to Nissan headquarters in Japan that they use a
powerful name for the car they intended to import into the U.S.
He proposed names like *Lion* or *Tiger*, but headquarters remained
firm in their belief that Americans wanted an English image to
their sports cars. When the first cars rolled off the ship onto
American soil, Katayama was horrified to see their nameplates
read *My Fair Lady*. It seems that one of the top executives of
Nissan was fond of the musical *My Fair Lady* and had used his
authority to name the new car.

Katayama did not call the home office in Japan with his
problem; he simply pried off the nameplate and replaced it with
240-Z, which was Nissan's internal design number for that model.
The car became a legendary success and began the trend of

giving sport cars numbers instead of names.

⚜

Those "in the field" or on the front lines have a closer and better view of the situation than those at the top. It's surprising for one at the very top, Pope Paul VI, to propose others taking initiative. As we saw on July 17, he said in 1971 that "It belongs to the laity, without waiting for orders and directives, to take the initiative freely and to infuse a Christian spirit into the mentality, customs, laws and structures of the community in which they live."

Even if you are not a Roman Catholic, these historic words should inspire you to act in the secular and religious community in which you live. Laity and clergy as well should respond as Katayama did and act when the occasion demands it.

To act on your own initiative for the good of the company, the church or society can make you a martyr. If the cause is good, then the cost is worth the risk.

✺

---

2 Secret Composer of "Old Folks at Home" Day, 1851.

Stephen Foster wrote the classic song, "Old Folks at Home," commonly known as "Swanee River." However, fearful of the prejudice of "Ethiopian songs," and wishing his name to be associated only with more genteel compositions, he sold the performance rights to Edwin P. Christy. Christy was a famous minstrel, and it was his name that first appeared as the composer on the music.

⚜

Stephen Foster's fear that his reputation would be tarnished by prejudice, slander or innuendo is a fear known to each of us. Our reputation — how we are known by the public, the general estimation of our character as good or bad — is a deeply rooted and strongly motivating concern. Each age and culture has its own scale for judging a reputation based on external evidence. Yet Jesus harshly condemned those who were eager for a good reputation, who wore a mask like the Greek actors, or hypocrites.

He condemned those who prayed in a way to impress others and not out of love for God. Jesus never seemed to worry about his reputation and so provided a clear example for his followers. On the contrary, by associating with outcasts, those forced to the margins of his society, he earned a rather negative reputation — and so gave a bad reputation a good name.

Consider following Jesus today and being known for your bad reputation. Use an old rule of thumb to determine the degree of your humility. How much do you fear your reputation would be destroyed — and how ashamed would you be — if some hidden truth about you were made public? It's not that your deep, dark secrets need to be made known, but if what is hidden ever does become known, embrace it not as a disaster but as the royal road to true humility and holiness.

✳

The World's Most Famous Port Day. On this day in 1492 Christopher Columbus departed from the port of Palos in Spain on his journey of discovery to the New World of the Americas. However, it's not the Port of Palos but the Port of Doubt from which the truly adventuresome explorers have departed on voyages of great discovery. Port Doubt has been, and still is, condemned as diabolic and heretical and so has been feared by many as the gateway to hell and destruction. Yet without passing through the fertile departure point of Port Doubt, history's most fascinating discoveries of enlightenment would never have been made.

3

꧁◐꧂

Today, check your log and find the last time you pulled up anchor in Port Doubt and sailed off into the blinding fog of questions marks. Reverence your doubts about your faith, for being rock-sure isn't what Jesus said would save you or move mountains. The Aramaic word he spoke that is translated as *faith* is better rendered as *loyalty*. The difference between being loyal to Jesus and to his vision and believing in dogmas and creeds is as great as the distance from the Indies to Spain. Creeds give prayer patterns to basic beliefs, a much needed religious identity and an essential religious foundation. Yet Jesus was not distressed by human doubts; it was the failure to be loyal to him and his mission that saddened him the most.

※⚘※

This day in 1960 marked the first phone conversation in which voices were bounced off the moon, a great accomplishment for U.S. scientists. Many in various parts of the world doubted that this was possible, as many also doubted the feasibility of the moon landing. However, coyotes, wolves and dogs have been bouncing howls off the moon for millenniums.

✦

---

4 *Peine Forte et Dure* **Day, England, 1350.** "Pain, hard and long" was the term describing the capital punishment of "pressing" that was practiced in the Middle Ages. Torture was commonplace as the preface to execution. Every local castle had a stretching rack, a drowning pit and a device for pressing, along with a gallows. Heretics and witches were pressed to confess their guilt, as were Jews, Christians accused of "living with a Jewess," those who spoke out against the king or the Church, as well as those suspected of various crimes such as robbery. If the accused pleaded their innocence, or remained silent as did Jesus before his judges, they were pressed until they confessed or died in the process of coming to the truth.

An accused person would be forced to strip and lie on the floor with arms and legs spread-eagle and tied to stakes. The torturer would apply weights to the chest one at time, making breathing labored, but careful not to kill the accused too soon. Kept alive for days, the accused's weights would gradually be increased. Large stones were used until King Henry IV improved the ancient art by specially constructing iron weights similar to today's body building devices. This practice only ended in England in 1741, twenty-some years before the American Colonies rebelled against the Crown.

※⚘※

Peine Forte et Dure is more common today than in the Middle

Ages! It's not criminals, real or falsely accused, but ordinary people who now are being "pressed" by the iron weights of added commitments, more work, the ever-ticking clock, family, social and church obligations and deadlines. In Medieval times only adults were tortured. Today, even children are squeezed by parental pressures to achieve and to meet many commitments once only placed on adults. Little League, extra-school activities, church classes and a long list of kiddy *Peine Forte et Dure* are laid upon them, so that like adults they have little free time.

Are you being so tortured? Unlike the olden days, however, it's not done by some masked fiend. You yourself are the torturer who daily adds more and more weights, squeezing you to near death. Is it possible that such a high percentage of Americans vote in favor of capital punishment because they themselves are daily experiencing an ancient form of it?

5

The Feast of the Impossible. Lord Kevin, who was president of England's Royal Society in 1895, said, "Heavier-than-air flying machines are impossible." Lord Kevin's pedestrian prophecy should be a reminder never to use that uncreative and limiting word *impossible.*

One example of the impossible is using the Bible to escape from prison, yet it was done – literally. In Dorchester County, Maryland, two inmates escaped from jail with the help of the stiff cover from the Bible in their cell. With patience they used it as a pry tool to open a defective lock on the jail door that led to a fire escape – and to freedom.

The next time an airplane flies overhead, take a few minutes to pause and ponder the future. Say aloud to yourself this prayer of hope: "Just as heavier-than-air flying machines are possible, so is ________________." *(Fill in the blank with your favorite dream for tomorrow.)*

Also, today, use your Bible to escape. Opening the Word of God and reading it in faith may give you some ideas of possible ways to escape from an impossible situation in which you presently find yourself imprisoned.

✵

---

6 **Hiroshima Memorial and Electric Chair Day.** Today remembers the 130,000 who died in the atomic bomb explosion which leveled 90% of the city of Hiroshima on this day in 1945. Without warning, the lives of hundreds of thousands, if not the whole world, were radically changed on this day.

Admiral William Leahy of the U.S. Navy, speaking to President Truman earlier in 1945 about the millions of dollars spent on research for the atomic bomb, said, "That is the biggest fool thing we have ever done.... The (atomic) bomb will never go off, and I speak as an expert in explosives."

❧❦❧

Also today in 1890, Harold Brown invented the first electric chair. Five brief years after New York City customers began to use the new invention of the electric light bulb, New York State set up a commission to explore electrical alternatives to hanging. Brown and a fellow inventor experimented on fifty cats and dogs rounded up at night (they were alleged not to be pets but strays). First a cow and then a horse were killed by electrical current (crowds of thousands later attended Brown's electrocutions for entertainment), and by June 4, 1888, the governor signed a bill making electrocution the legal capital punishment of the state.

The first electric chair execution, of William Kemmler on August 8, 1890, was so botched that several witnesses fainted; others were nauseated and fled the room. *The Buffalo Express* predicted, "Kemmler will be the last man executed in such a manner."

❧❦❧

On this day of death and destruction, pray that capital punishment will be put to death. The end of the twentieth century found the majority of Americans in favor of this futile and inhumane form of dealing with crime. In 1890, thousands were not shocked, but actually flocked to attend Brown's electrocution of animals! What kind of men and women would find such a sight entertaining or fascinating? In the year 2090, will people react with the same shock when told of how the citizens of our time saw nothing morally wrong in taking human lives by electrocution, gas chambers and lethal injection?

Capital punishment — the taking of the *head*, from *caput*, by various methods employed in Christian countries, such as stoning, hanging, beheading or being drawn and quartered — was once the occasion of massive festival gatherings. Such executions did not deter crime; in fact, the crowds of the curious actually were used by pickpockets to great advantage.

America prides itself on being a Christian nation. So perhaps the best way to end the immorality of capital punishment would be to restore crucifixion as the only legal means of capital punishment. The executions could take place on a wooden cross, using nails, and could be performed in the middle of the city square. All would be invited, free of charge, to witness and enjoy the execution of justice.

✮

Ice Gratitude Day. In the midst of the heat of summer we in the modern world take ice for granted. Yet not long ago ice was a luxury and a means of support. In the 1800s ice harvesting was a thriving business in New England. Ice from frozen lakes and rivers was cut into blocks by ice harvesters and shipped around the world. One of the largest shipments, carrying over 200 tons of ice stored in sawdust, was sent to India. Considering the distance, it is amazing that half the shipment arrived.

This harvesting of natural ice in the winter continued until the invention of machines that made ice. What is surprising is that no ice harvesting company invented either ice-making machines or refrigerators. It seems they were "frozen" in their perception of the scope of their business and were unable to creatively envision making ice other than the natural way. Massachusetts' inventor, Jacob Perkins, developed the first refrigeration compression machine in 1834. This was refined with the use of ammonia by Carl von Linde between 1873 and 1875.

On what for many of us will be a hot August day, if you decide to enjoy an iced drink, use it to toast Jake Perkins. Also ponder if, like the ice harvesting companies, you are frozen in your thinking when considering the possibilities for change in your life, marriage or business. Defrost hard-held beliefs about tomorrow, and make them as flexible as flowing water.

✳

8 Day to Remember the 1925 KKK March on Washington.

On this day of infamy, some 40,000 white-robed Klansmen and Klanswomen marched proudly down Pennsylvania Avenue. This massive demonstration was to show the public the Klan's strength during its resurgence in the early 1920s. A city ordinance prohibited the wearing of masks, so the Klan marched in bold pride without hoods.

As their strength grew daily, so did the fear of blacks, Jews and Catholics, who were the targets of Klan hate and violence. This secret militia operated without fear of the police or local law enforcement officials. The Klan was judge, jury and executioner of African-Americans being held for questioning or even suspected of a crime. As these horrible racial murders took place, uniformed and elected law enforcement officers looked the other way — or were even involved as members of the Klan.

The Klan was organized in 1866 by ex-Confederates and used whippings and lynchings to terrorize ex-slaves and their white supporters. It was officially disbanded in 1869, but its members continued to prevent blacks from voting. The Klan was resurrected in 1915 and became anti-Semitic and anti-Catholic as well as anti-black. By the mid-1920s it had a membership of between four and five million. It strongly contributed to the defeat of Alfred E. Smith in his 1928 bid to be president because he was Roman Catholic and so was considered unsuited for the office. It visibly resurfaced again in the 1960s in response to federal civil rights laws and instigated racial confrontations. Near the end of the century the spirit of the Klan reappeared in various hate groups that claimed to be above the law.

⚜

Ancient is the hated of others because of differences in race, nationality, religion or sexual orientation. While today laws and law enforcement agencies may try to protect citizens from physical acts of hate, no laws can control minds and hearts. The removal of hate comes only with love. "For hatred can never be removed by hate; only by love. This is the ancient and unalterable law," said the Buddha. Jesus spoke that same law, saying that there is only one law: to love God and to love your neighbor as you love yourself. Buddha said that the hatred of discrimination is removed when we wisely discriminate, that is, when we refuse to allow our minds to harbor thoughts of hate and revenge. In the Buddha's words, "'He was angry with me, he attacked me... did me wrong, robbed me' — those who dwell on such thoughts will never be free of hatred."

✻

Sins of Obedience Memorial Day. On this day in 1945 the crew of an American plane dropped the second atomic bomb, devastating more than a third of the Japanese city of Nagasaki, killing or severely wounding 75,000 people. If the Allies had lost the Second World War and the crew of the plane that dropped that atomic bomb had been tried as war criminals, their defense would have been, "We were only following orders." C.P. Snow wrote, "When you think of the long and gloomy history of man, you will find more hideous crimes have been committed in the name of obedience than have ever been committed in the name of rebellion."

Individual Klansmen who tortured and hung blacks might say, "We were only following the orders of the Grand Dragon of the Klan." The firing squad at an execution or prison officers who activate an electric chair are not guilty of murder but only of obedience. Ever since Adam and Eve, disobedience has been viewed as sinful, yet, as C.P. Snow observed, obedience has been the source of history's most hideous crimes. There is a long litany of "sins of obedience": the torture and killing of mentally deranged people considered witches by the Catholic Church's Inquisition, the forced baptism of Medieval Jews, the slaughter of innocent noncombatants in countless wars, the

Nazi Holocaust, the Vietnam My Lai Massacre and centuries of crimes of genocide. Those responsible have kept guilt at arm's length by asserting that they were only being obedient and following orders.

In the government, the military or the business world, following orders is not only a virtue but essential for promotion. In religious orders and communities of men and women it has been raised beyond a virtue to a vow – the vow of obedience being equal to the spiritual states of chastity and poverty.

This August Memorial Day is an opportunity to examine your virtue or holy vow, your admiration or blind acceptance of the value of obedience. To assist in this reflection ask yourself a few questions: Does a temptation to disobey a "negative" instruction or law – one that seems to hinder the good of another human being – bring back memories of being punished as a child for being disobedient? Can you recall a time when being rebellious was encouraged – or can you personally ever recall being praised by someone in authority for being disobedient? Does the present ritual of adult baptism need to be amended so that along with a promise to deny Satan and evil, there would be a solemn promise to be disobedient to all laws and requirements that limit love, compassion, freedom of conscience, and the good of others and oneself?

Regardless of whether such a vow of disobedience is ever publicly made in the ritual of baptism, it *is* implied if you are baptized into Jesus Christ and not simply into an institutional church. For when you were baptized into Christ, you were made one with Jesus, the divine disobeyer of Galilee, the rebellious Immanuel who freely and boldly disobeyed all laws that limited the scope of God's love and freedom to heal. On the personal seal of Thomas Jefferson it was written, "Rebellion to tyrants is obedience to God." Jesus was and is the model of obedience, but his obedience was to God, not toeing the line to antiquated laws, narrow village customs or oppressive civil and even religious codes and laws.

Civil War Events Become Good Theater Day, 1861. 10 Less than a month after the battle of Bull Run, Charles Gayler's *Bull Run* was a smash hit in New York City. Between that date and 1862 over five Civil War plays were theatrical successes in New York. Among them was one that would have played well a hundred years later, *How to Avoid Drafting* by Henry Seymour.

The television movie of the Jonestown Kool-Aid slaughter in 1978 appeared 513 days after the disaster. The TV movie of the Waco, Texas, Branch Davidian fiery disaster appeared only 34 days after the event, a fifteenfold contraction of time. Yet this was four days longer than it took for Charles Gayer's *Bull Run* to appear in 1861. Media exploitation of disasters is not a recent vice.

❦

Also, today, take heed when taking advice from others and be your own judge. When Louis B. Mayer was considering buying the motion picture rights to the book *Gone with the Wind*, he was given some "sound" theatrical advice. Irving Thalberg, the MGM producer, advised his boss, "Fact is, Louis, Civil War pictures have never made a dime."

If war makes good theater both on stage and in motion pictures, why doesn't peace? If lives of gangsters and violent action-heroes make good theater and great profits, why don't lives of holy people? If cults who embrace mass suicide make good theater, why don't communities who embrace the poor and promote good in the world? The answer to such questions is also the answer to the absence of prophets and holy heroes and heroines in our contemporary society.

If you find yourself being tempted by God to become a prophet or a holy person, remember the advice given to Louis Mayer and don't ask your friends what they think of the idea.
✯

Feast of St. Clare of Assisi. Companion in poverty and 11 dear friend of Francis, Clare renounced her future as the daughter of a rich merchant and in 1212 joined Francis in his spiritual revolution. She founded a community of women committed to poverty and service; they wore no shoes, ate no meat and slept on the ground, owning nothing.

She and Francis were powerful prophets, not by speaking out against the excessive wealth of the church but by scandalizing the church through their radical living of the Gospel. Francis and Clare lived the life that Jesus wanted for his followers: they embraced a holy life of daily communion with God, a simple life lived without anxiety over material possessions, a life of nonviolence and harmony with all creation. They embraced the poor and rejected, social lepers and outcasts, and found joy in such a radical life.

In 1958 St. Clare became the patroness of television, which needs more than one patron saint. Clare was chosen because of the time in 1253 when she was aged and sick, unable to leave her cell, and thus unable to attend Christmas midnight Mass. When she heard the nuns singing, she prayed, and on the wall before her she saw clearly the manager in Bethlehem!

⁂

May St. Clare help each of us when we watch the evening news to truly see the hungry, poor and suffering in our slums and in the world. May she heal us of dull-vision, that unique blindness created by television that afflicts us when we see poverty and suffering on TV and daily, making us grow less compassionate. Dull-vision makes us blind to suffering in our personal daily lives, on the street corner or in our local ghettos, toward the poor or people of color. May Clare of Assisi heal us of the dull-vision that blinds us when we enter a church and fail to see the lack of holy simplicity in our parish church appointments, music, prayer and ritual.

Pray, today, that God would grace the world and churches of the new century with holy people who are silent but scandalizing prophets. They will speak to us not in sermons, revivals, retreats or workshops, but by their lives and actions will shout that the life Jesus proposed *is* possible.

❋

Gold Discovered in the Klondike Day, 1896. Shout it from the rooftops: "Gold in the Yukon!" The discovery of gold three miles from Dawson in the Yukon Territory of northwest Canada was the second largest gold rush in North American history. Communication wasn't instant at the end of the nineteenth century, and it wasn't until June of 1897 that the news of the discovery reached the United States. Within a month, thousands were on their way to strike it rich, and by 1898 there were 25,000 people in the Klondike region.

12

※❦※

On this August day start your own gold rush by not rushing. The gold deposits that have been discovered had always been there — whether in the Klondike, Colorado or California — they had only been overlooked. As those fortune hunters a hundred years or more ago abandoned their daily work to go in search of gold, go on a search today without leaving your home or work. Stop rushing and look for the golden treasures hidden beneath the surface of your daily life, family, home or yard. Abandon as many deadlines as possible in order to be "rushless," and thus better able to search for the wealth hidden beneath the surface of your life.

Deadlines not only blind, they are deadly to prospectors of the real. A deadline is a final demarcation line beyond which one is not permitted to go. It began not as a corporate term but as prison talk. In the Civil War the original deadline was a line seventeen feet from the inner stockade in military prison camps. No prisoner could cross that line without being shot. While deadlines are not literally lethal today, they do assassinate the ability to find treasures in the ordinary. They poison pleasure in work and living, and in time they are hazardous to the health of body, soul and spirit.

✭

Pedestrian Prophecy Day, 1948. "Landing and moving around the moon offers so many serious problems for human beings that it may take science another 200 years to lick them"

13

꧁☙❦☙꧂

The future for some things comes with lead feet; for others it comes wearing wings. While inventions and discoveries fly — making sudden appearances, sometimes centuries ahead of schedule — religious and social reforms and the removal of social injustices usually walk with the feet of mountains. Religious and political leaders, when speaking of the new, customarily caution moderation and patience.

Curiously, NASA, medical research centers working on cures for cancer or other killer diseases and new weapon designers are never cautioned with moderation or encouraged to be patient. Yet impatience is a virtue when we seek solutions to injustice and inequality. Aware of the affluent level of life in first world nations like America, may the new century hold a radical reversal: May inventions wear lead shoes and moral reforms wear wings.

In your personal future, examine what your material and spiritual goals are wearing and consider reversing the traveling equipment in those two areas. A minute's meditation from the Jewish Talmud: "Condemn no man and consider nothing impossible, for there is no man who does not have a future. And there is nothing that does not have its hour."

✺

---

14 **Social Security Passage Day, 1935.** On this day in 1935 Congress passed the Social Security Act. While now high on the endangered species list, this magnificent law was an important step toward justice in our society through the sharing of wealth. Those with money at the time attacked this Act as being un-American, socialistic and the beginning of communism. Some even predicted that recipients would have their social security numbers tattooed on their arms! The poor of the 1930s, on the other hand, saw it as the lifting of a terrible burden, the fear of the future in their old age. Remember and pray today, and when the opportunity arises, vote. Pray for the awakening of a social conscience so that the near future will hold remembrance days like today. Pray that we don't have to wait till 2035 for a Social Health Care Act that gives to all citizens the right to proper medical care and a Social Home Act that gives to all citizens the right to proper shelter. Health care and shelter, like public education, are the shared responsibility of the citizens of a nation "under God."

⁂

Religion in America has been and continues to be lived out in a more robust way than it is in Europe. It has been noted that Americans are a hyperreligious people, but this vigor has been described as "a mile wide and an inch deep." Jesus reminds us that it is not those who cry out, "Lord, Lord, we love you," who will enter the reign of God, but those who do the will of God. The Bible makes it very clear that proper care for the oppressed, the alien, those who are hungry, sick and homeless is the will of God. If we are truly "one nation under God," then should not security, health, housing and equality for everyone in society be a foremost national priority?

This August day is a good day to go for a swim. Yet, rather than wading an inch deep in your religious beliefs, why not plunge deeply into the will of God?

✵

Feast of the Assumption of Mary, the Mother of God. 15

This August feast of the Blessed Mother Mary was once a great festival day of feasting and leisure — but no more! This day, like almost all 365, is now simply a workday. In the 1890s predictions were made that workers would have two-day weekends along with vacations of three to four weeks, but such leisure was half a century away for most. In Europe and America at the end of the nineteenth century, men, women and children worked twelve-hour days every day except Sunday. Holy days were oases, like random Sundays scattered throughout the year, in which Sunday's obligations of no work and time spent in leisure were to be observed.

The 1890s predicted a future of more leisure and even the civil right to sometimes do what you want instead of always having to be working. Yet the rise of industry had no room for even sporadic leisure days. The hardworking lower-class, dreaming of being middle-class, made idleness, the negative name for leisure, into a vice.

Yet, that hoped-for and predicted dream of a time of leisure persisted. As one example, a French physician of the day, Paul Lafargue, who was married to Karl Marx's daughter, wrote a pamphlet called *The Right to Be Lazy*. His work promoted a shorter work week, more leisure and better pay for workers.

The long-awaited future has arrived, yet few today experience the joy of being lazy or engaging in leisurely activities. Americans are working longer and more days than in the middle of the twentieth century and have less, if any, leisure time. It is paradoxical that homes for the aged who are physically unable to work are sometimes called "rest homes."

On this once-upon-a-time holy leisure day, spend some time thinking about how you can make your home into a rest home. Be like a prisoner making plans for how to escape from the prison workhouse of daily life, where the vast majority of your fellow and sister Americans are incarcerated.

Holy Mary, Mother of God,
    on this feast of your assumption into heaven,
    pray for us.
Inspire us to rest in peace and leisure today,
    so someday we can share eternal rest
    with you and your holy son.

✴

---

16 **Plain as the Nose on Your Face Day, 1782.** Today is the wedding anniversary of Wolfgang Amadeus Mozart. On this day in 1782 he married his bride, Constanze Weber. The marriage was the source of sour wine for his biographers, who embraced as dogma Mozart's creed, "Next after God, papa." Yet his marriage was an integral part of his creative life. The number of musical compositions of this genius has been recorded at

626, beginning with minuets written at the age of four and concluding with his famous *Requiem.*

Perhaps Mozart's most unusual composition was written for his mentor, Franz Joseph Haydn, who challenged his prized pupil to write a musical piece that the elder composer could not play at first sight. Within five minutes, Mozart dashed off what appeared to be a simple little piece. The mentor Haydn launched into it with great confidence. Halfway through the score, Haydn found that his left hand was at the bottom of the keyboard, while his right hand was way up at the top. To his amazement, the score required the performer to play a single solitary note right in the middle of the keyboard. Haydn stopped playing and said in disgust, "It is impossible for anyone to play this music!" Mozart then sat down at the piano, rapidly played the first part of the score and arrived at the critical section with his hands at opposite ends of the keyboard. At the precise moment required in the musical score, Mozart leaned over and struck the "unplayable" note with his unusually large nose!

Mozart's wedding anniversary is a good day to take a second look at some impossible problem in your life and realize that the solution may be as plain as the nose on your face! Why do we fail to see what is obvious? Some psychologists suggest that when faced with a problem that seems impossible to handle, a unique form of blindness develops. No problem is without a solution; the real problem is the willingness to see and acknowledge it.

End of the World Day — for Permians, 225 Million B.C. 17

Every thirty million years some massive catastrophe occurs in the earth's history that is for many the End. The evidence of one such disaster was found in fossils dug up near the Russian city of Perm, which gave its name to the age of amphibians brought to light by these fossils. Today's entry marks a true cataclysm, a sudden, violent calamity of disastrous proportions. It marks the earth's first truly devastating extinction, effectively ending the era of amphibians. Between 280 and 225 million years ago, seventy-five percent of all amphibian species and more than eighty percent of all reptilian families vanished!

The disaster was the result of great havoc in the oceans, where fifty percent of marine organisms vanished from the earth in a few million years (which are geological minutes). Prehistoric mountains, the grandparents of the Appalachians, Rockies and Alps suddenly shot out of the earth with violence. Perhaps a sudden violent sunspot or an explosion of a supernova caused the drastic geological and climatic changes. Yet as one earth ended, a new one appeared: the age of the reptiles.

Prehistoric history shows that in any cataclysm those who are hardy and resilient survive the disaster as well as the aftershocks of the calamity. Also, new species evolve out of the disaster, species who are able to adapt to the new era. The future will include the End of the World: the end of the present world of certain giant corporations, small businesses, institutions and even religions.

Examine yourself on this End of the World Day to see if you are extinction-proof. Take an adaptation examination: Do you function well when sudden changes are introduced into your life? Do you respond with denial and rejection when new ideas are proposed? Do you enjoy change?

Rather than "Remember Pearl Harbor!" a fitting slogan for these End Times would be "Remember the Permians!"

---

18 Day of the First Successful Brain Transplant, 2031.

Today the world learned of the first successful human brain transplant, which was performed in the Ukraine. In January of 1997 a leading U.S. neuroscientist, Dr. Robert J. White, stated that medicine was on the verge of being able to successfully transplant a human brain. Dr. White said that after considering the moral and ethical implications of the operation he thought such a procedure was not only acceptable but "a moral imperative" in certain cases. The operation, he said, would require a "head-trunk" transplant, the transferring of one person's head to the body trunk of another, because of the difficulties in removing the human brain from the cranium. Dr. White stated that the donor would be someone whose brain was fully functioning but who was dying from multi-organ failure. He predicted in 1997 that within fifty years or less research in the spinal cord would make this surgical process possible.

At the end of the twentieth century critics objected seriously, calling his proposed operation Frankensteinish, since the human brain is the container of human identity and memory. Dr. White was a devout Catholic who attended Mass daily, had ten children and was even a member of the Vatican's Pontifical Academy of Sciences. However, the Vatican charged that he had crossed the ethical line, calling unethical the transplants of brain and sexual organs, which "assure the personal and procreative identity of the person."

⚜

If your lunch break conversation is lifeless today, consider asking your coworkers their opinion on brain-head transplants. Before racing to declare such a transplant impossible and unethical, remember that all transplants of human organs were once declared immoral and unethical, as were many other commonplace medical procedures.

As you explore this question, keep in mind that the church and the great scholars in the Middle Ages believed, as did the Greek philosopher Aristotle (whose philosophy was the basis for Medieval theology), that the heart was the place of intelligence, not the brain. In fact, Egyptian priests embalmed every organ of their dead, except the brain, which they threw away as being of no value. And so, up to the Middle Ages, a heart transplant (if possible) would almost certainly have been considered a violation of the identity of the person. Moreover, at that time, even medical autopsies were forbidden as sinful.

Note: Thirty-four years ago, in 1997, Dr. White, who ten years previously had successfully transplanted the brain of one monkey into the body of another, spoke of his future. He said he was considering moving his brain transplant research to the Ukraine where his experiments might be carried out with "less of the reflection of heavy publicity."

---

19 **Human Slavery and Evolutionary Scriptures Day.** "A believing slave is better than an idolater, even though you might admire him," said the prophet Mohammed in the Koran. Moses, in the Jewish Scriptures, forbade the enslavement of Hebrews by Hebrews, but permitted making foreigners into slaves of the Hebrews. Jesus did not condemn slavery and shockingly called his disciples to be slaves, a term later softened to *servants*. St. Paul urged slaves to be obedient to their masters.

God spoke to Mohammed, dictating the divine message of the Koran. God also spoke through Moses, Jesus and St. Paul. God acts in the world as God finds it in each age and culture. God's Dream of the fullness of equality and justice for all, however, is ever evolutionary. While Jesus did not condemn the horrible status of making humans into beasts of burden for another's service, he did strike a mortal blow at the roots of slavery in his commandment to love one another.

God's revelation does not stop when the pen of any particular sacred writer is laid down, regardless of the age. The Prophet Mohammed said it so well, "If all the trees on the earth were pens, and God should change the oceans into seven seas of ink, the Words of God would still not be exhausted."

If today the Bible or the Koran is quoted to you condoning or approving some injustice, like Mohammed, you might respond, "God isn't finished speaking, the holy books to date have only begun to reveal the Word of God."

Speak more, All Holy One, in the new century.

---

20 **Pedestrian Prediction Day, 1926.** In 1926 Lee de Forest, the U.S. inventor called "the Father of Radio," made this prediction about the future: "While theoretically and technically television may be feasible, commercially and financially I consider it an impossibility, a development of which we need waste little time dreaming."

⚜

Today is Waste Time by Dreaming Day, not the kind of dreaming we do asleep in bed but our wakeful vision of what might be. What is frequently called God's *will* could also be called God's *dreaming*. God's vision for how creation and the world should be is a dream that has been shared with each of us. Prophets, visionaries and mystics have been gifted with pieces of God's dream, helping to flesh out important pieces of the living vision for all of us. When Jesus began his public ministry, he related Isaiah's vision of the reign of God, the age of God's justice and equality, to a "Jubilee Year," an extended time of great blessing which was beginning as he spoke. The Jubilee "Year" 2000, which extends well into the twenty-first century, is a time for paying special attention to God's dream.

God's dream is not alien to your deepest dream for yourself. God seeds the divine dream among our personal aspirations so that each of us has a share in helping the sacred vision become a reality. Today is a good day for beginning to see our time wasted dreaming about the *impossible* — which is another way of describing God's dream — not as wasted time but as prayer time.

✻

Believe in Yourself Day. In 1933 the famous and talented dancer, Fred Astaire, took a screen test for MGM studios. A memo was written about him by one of the directors of MGM which read, "Can't act. Slightly bald. Can dance a little." Fred Astaire had that memo framed and kept it over his fireplace in his Beverly Hills home.

21

The family of Louisa May Alcott, the author of *Little Women*, advised her that in light of her limited talents she should find work as a servant or seamstress.

Beethoven's teacher called him hopeless as a composer.

⚜

Determine, today, to pursue your gifts with a passion, regardless of how those gifts are viewed by others, especially by so-called experts in the field. Receive with a grain of salt the voices that criticize your dreams and aspirations. Deep within each of us are two self-critics whose voices we hear daily. The first criticizes our failures and mistakes; the other praises our talents and work. We need to listen to both voices to make progress in life, not letting the voice of one drown out the other. If one has to be louder, let it be the critic who praises rather than the one who condemns.

Perhaps we all need obstacles to sharpen the desire of our dreams, but don't let those obstacles destroy your dream. Believe in yourself and your God-given gifts today.

✳

---

22 National Bicycle and Liberation Pedaling Machine Day.

This August celebration honors the riding machine called the bicycle (*bi* meaning "two" and the Greek *kucklos* meaning "wheel"). It was invented in 1839 by a Scottish blacksmith named Kirkpatrick MacMillian. In the 1890s, the "safety" bicycle, which is similar to the model we know today, was a new national fascination. It was also considered a threat to society!

Unlike the previous models, which had small back wheels and a large front wheel with metal tires, this bicycle had wheels of equal size with a type of rubber tires, making it much more functional and useful. Yet *The Georgia Journal of Medicine and Surgery* said that this "pedaling machine" produced dangerous female disorders, especially at exhilarating speeds which threw the female body forward against the bicycle, arousing unnatural sexual feelings in the young maiden. Booksellers further complained in *Scientific American* that "people are rushing about on wheels, days, nights and Sundays, and no longer read anything." Naturally, as with any new invention, the clergy lambasted bicycling as utter idleness and so a vice, not to mention that it allowed young people to ride away from the very watchful eyes of their parents.

By 1895, over ten million bicycles were in use in America,

their success challenging even the horse and buggy — for bicycles did not need to be fed and sheltered. Also, for the average woman the bicycle was a liberation machine, allowing her to venture beyond the walled boundaries of the home and the restrictive neighborhood. This "evil" and liberating fact was not overlooked by husbands and clergy.

⚜

By 1910, however, the pedaling machine fad died out, and the bicycle became the vehicle of children. Yet perhaps bicycles are in the process of being a reinvented fad for twenty-first century America as a means of conservation of energy, anti-pollution, better health and good exercise. This might lead us to examine if there are any other activities once the domain only of children that might be reinvented for leisurely, practical or spiritual use by adults in the twenty-first century.

✳

Visit the Zoo and the Rise of Segregation Day, 1870. 23

Racism and hate of African-Americans is an age-old American sin. After the Civil War in 1864, a popular Northern song was the "New National Anthem," *Nigger Doodle Dandy,* which ridiculed former slaves. By the 1870s most white citizens of the North turned a blind eye to what was happening to black citizens in the South. Gradually the Southern states deprived black citizens of the right to vote by complicated restrictions; segregation laws forced them into the status of second-class citizens. Even the federal government failed them when in 1877 the United States failed to guarantee blacks' civil rights, and an 1896 decision of the Supreme Court (*Plessy* v. *Ferguson*) upheld segregation. The legal disfranchising of African-Americans continued into the early 1900s. During this period lynchings rose to an all-time high.

As in India, a strong caste system was established, extending over all the public facilities Black Americans used. Separate water fountains, toilets, waiting rooms, seating areas in restaurants and public transportation all carried an invisible sign that read "Unclean." Rather than simply making African-Americans second-class citizens, they were demeaned to subhuman status. This inhumane attitude reached its height when the New York City Bronx Zoo exhibited an African-American behind bars, like a gorilla!

Sadly the American solution of segregation spread from the United States to South Africa, Bermuda and even to enclaves in China where Europeans held control. The sin of injustice exhibited in segregation and discrimination is like a cancer and spreads like any deadly disease, making the entire body sick.

❦

The disaster of slums and inner city ghettos is the harvest of sin, the sin of segregation. Crime, drug use, the loss of entire generations of African-American youth to life-patterns of prison and death are the harvest of sin, the sin of segregation. Although sin always has a dimension of personal responsibility, it also has a very real social dimension. Today is a good day to pray that part of the Lord's Prayer, "forgive us our debts as we forgive those who...." The sin-debt White Americans need to have forgiven is that of the horrible sin of segregation, for it is a sin which has bred even uglier and more deadly sins. And as White Americans face with honesty the sins of their ancestors, they must also honestly look within themselves at the disfiguration of prejudice bred by segregation.

The Jubilee "Year" of 2000 (which, again, extends well into the twenty-first century) is a Christian celebration that echoes the ancient Jewish Jubilee in which all debts were to be forgiven. Make this an August Penance and Repentance Day, a true celebration of Jubilee time.

✠

---

24 Day to Remember the St. Bartholomew's Massacre and the Outbreak of the Great Plague, 1572.

Two thousand Huguenot Calvinists were slaughtered in Paris in 1572 on this day which was the eve of the feast of St. Bartholomew. The two thousand victims were attending the royal wedding of Henry of Navarre and the sister of Charles IX.

Wishing to maintain her power, the de facto ruler of France, the queen mother, Catherine de Medici, was behind the murders as she played off the Calvinists against the Catholics. While this is the political answer given for the massacre, perhaps the real de facto reason was the Plague.

It was not the bubonic plague but the Bible plague that was now the scourge of Europe. The Black Death had swept across Europe and parts of Asia in the fourteenth century, killing as much as three-fourths of the population in less than twenty years. The Bible plague, like the bubonic plague, spread quickly from country to country. The bubonic plaque resulted from a bacterium *Pasteurella pestis*, transmitted by fleas who infected rats, who in turn passed it to humans. The Bible plague was caused by the virus *Theologitis pestis*, or *Deus Vult*, "God wills it." In that virus, stealing, the destruction of property, torture, killing and war were all exempt from the Ten Commandments if they were done to people of another religion. War was baptized and renamed "Crusade." Hate was baptized and renamed "God Wills It." Victims of the disease were any infidels, particularly Muslims or Jews, those of other Christian denominations or anyone judged as a heretic.

This highly contagious virus is ancient in origin, being found very early in the Bible. In the book of Joshua, the Canaanites (who were of a different religion) were exterminated by the invading Israelites in what some scholars call the first recorded genocide in history. The book of Deuteronomy gives the rules for holy wars, presenting such genocides as a duty imposed by God. Those who destroyed cathedrals and religious masterpieces of art in the sixteenth century could quote the Bible to support their actions, "Drive out all those living in that land, destroy all their religious images, and demolish their worship places" (Nm. 33: 50-52).

The Black Bible Plague, which was pandemic in the sixteenth century, is unlike the bubonic plague which ended within a hundred years. For the Bible plague remained rampant for over five hundred years. It could also be called the Black Death because this highly infectious disease was spread by black-robed clergy on both sides and by royal rulers eager to use the disease for political purposes. It has killed unknown millions, destroying thousands of churches and priceless religious art treasures by acts of vandalism. As with the Bubonic Black Death, it also was carried on board ships, primarily to the American Colonies, where it gave rise to anti-Catholic laws and religious discrimination on the part of Protestants. In Catholic countries it likewise gave rise to anti-Protestant laws. This disease of religious discrimination and bigotry which claims that God blesses hate is not restricted to Judaism and Christianity but has a long history within Islam, Hinduism and most other religions.

⚜

This has been a long but necessary Almanac entry since epidemics and diseases are of such great concern today for public health. AIDS is but one example of a highly contagious and deadly disease that appeared in the end of the twentieth century. Millions of dollars have been spent on "safe sex" commercials, literature with anti-disease information and the testing of possible victims. Equally essential is the need for "safe religion" information and testing. Take time to examine yourself today to see if you are infected with the Bible plague. Before answering with a quick "no," be sure that you don't have even a mild case of the disease of religious discrimination.

While the bubonic plaque still threatens certain parts of the world, antibiotics have greatly reduced its spread and effect. What are the antibiotics to stop the spread of the Bible plague and its personal injurious effect upon you? Be careful of churches and prayer groups; even watching religion on TV can be dangerous to your health. And when you do expose yourself to these highly contagious environments, it is wise to inoculate yourself with a good dose of the Spirit of unity, peace, understanding and nondiscrimination.

✳

---

25 **The Great Waiting Room Day.** Recently 3000 Americans were polled and asked the question, "What are you living for?" Over ninety percent said they were waiting for something significant to happen, for some change in their lives or the lives of those closest to them. Those who were middle-aged reported waiting for elderly parents to die so they could move on to the next stage in their lives. Others were waiting for their children to grow and move out so they could go on with their lives. There were those waiting to finish school or waiting to be married or unmarried before they really stepped into life.

T.S. Eliot's play *The Elder Statesman* shares his insight about waiting: "If I had the energy to work myself to death, how gladly would I face death!...waiting, simply waiting with no desire to act, yet a loathing of inaction. It is like sitting in an empty waiting room in a railroad station on a branch line after the last train, after all the other passengers have left, and the booking office is closed and the porters gone." Since ninety percent of those surveyed stated that instead of living they were waiting, perhaps our country has become one large waiting room!

⚜

Waiting rooms in the offices of dentists, physicians and other professionals are much like Eliot's railroad station waiting room: Other than old magazines and perhaps a television set with nothing worth watching, the rooms are dead space, a waste of time. On this Great Waiting Room Day, ask yourself the question in that survey: "What are you living for?"

Living is much more than waiting for something to happen; it calls us to fully experience whatever is happening. While some future event or change may indeed have a profound effect on your life, do not delay living to the full until that awaited event arrives.

✺

Corn Oil Day, or Happy Hogless Lard Feast. In 1899, chemist Dr. David Wesson discovered the first edible vegetable oil. The oil Wesson produced was a hogless lard originally called Snowdrift. Besides its cooking benefits, Wesson's corn oil has many practical household uses: the removal of oil-based paints from skin — in place of turpentine — the removal of water marks on wood furniture, the removal of decals and price tags, the removal of a splinter (by soaking the wound in corn oil to soften the skin for a few minutes, the splinter comes out easily). In

26

winter, to keep car doors from freezing, rub the gaskets with Wesson's oil to seal out water without harming the gaskets. Before shoveling show, coat your shovel with corn oil to prevent snow from sticking to the shovel.

Yes, the practical life and the spiritual life are one; so when the splinter in your neighbor's eye is making you itch to remove it, consider this ritual. Aware, as Jesus said, that we should first remove the plank from our own eye before operating on our neighbor's splinter, pour a bit of corn oil on your hands and rub them together for five minutes. During this time reflect on the nature of the 2' x 4' problem you have to remove and pray for the grace to see it. Then wipe your hands with a paper towel and thoroughly wash them in soap and hot water. You will now be ready, with God's grace, to perform the delicate surgical operation of removing your plank.

---

27 **Take Off Your Shoes and Go Outside Day.** You might want to read again the reflection for the 22nd of this month: It asked what childhood activities adults might reinvent. Today's feast gives one answer: Go barefoot! Infants and small children enjoy walking without anything between their soles and the floor or ground. Children delight in the feeling of the skin of their feet coming into direct contact with the grass and the earth. Adults, if they go barefoot at all, usually only do so inside their homes or around a swimming pool.

Yet a special physical and spiritual enjoyment can be found in going "native," in liberating your feet from the prisons of shoes and socks, slippers or clogs. In *Call Me by True Names,* the Buddhist monk Thich Nhat Hanh gives us a prayer for the feet:

> Walk and touch peace every moment.
> Walk and touch happiness every moment.
> Each step brings a fresh breeze.
> Each step makes a flower bloom under our feet.

Kiss the Earth with your feet.
Print on Earth our love and happiness.

✦

Today also celebrates the **Birthday of Mother Teresa** in 1910. Upon going to India, she learned the Hindu custom of removing one's sandals before entering a chapel, shrine or place of prayer. This custom is also practiced by many Christians throughout the East, as well as by Muslims, since God had directed Moses to bare his feet to the holy ground at the burning bush. All earth is holy, and this August day provides us with an opportunity to kiss the earth with our feet. If the place where you live lacks a lawn, find a park or some grassy place where you can take off your shoes and "kiss" the earth. Walk on the land barefoot even if it feels tender to your soles — it will be an invigorating tonic for your soul.

✦

Cadbury Schwepps Purchases Canada Dry Day, 1986. 28

On this day in 1986, Schwepps, the world's first soft drink maker, bought the wondrous carbonated 1904 creation of Toronto pharmacist, J.J. McLaughlin. McLaughlin had started a small plant to produce soda water which drugstores would use as a mixer for fruit juices. Trying to improve on existing formulas, he developed a new "dry" (nonalcoholic) ginger ale. Being an entrepreneur, he expanded beyond drug store counters and began to pioneer mass bottling of his product for baseball games and public beaches. In 1930 Canada Dry introduced a club soda to the market.

Club soda has countless practical uses beyond being a soft drink: As the liquid ingredient, it can make fluffy pancakes and waffles; it cleans grease stains from knit clothing, removes wine and other spots from a carpet, food stains from clothing and grease from car windshields. Use it to clean chrome and stainless steel and porcelain fixtures, and you can mix it with fruit juices to create your own original and inexpensive soft drinks.

✦

Again, the spiritual life and the practical life are one, and wise are those who remove any barrier between them. Soda, a "soft" drink, takes away hard-to-remove stains, suggesting what may be a useful life principle. When you encounter a difficult problem or person, consider treating what is hard with softness. President Teddy Roosevelt was famous for speaking softly but carrying a big stick. The carbonated-soda Christian speaks softly and carries no stick, big or little.

Stains on clothing and carpet should be removed by a carbonated beverage as soon as possible. The same is true for disagreements and unfortunate spills in marriage and family life. As quickly as you can, use soft words of reconciliation (which come in various flavors) and lovingly daub the stained area of a relationship. Never use a harsh abrasive to remove a hard stain.

✯

---

29 Old, Almost Worn-Out Clothing Day.

A recent poll by Louis Harris and Associates revealed the surprising fact that 73% of Americans are willing to wear clothes until they wear out! While almost three-fourths of us are willing, how many actually wear clothing until it is worn out? And while we might wear favorite old clothing in the summertime as we work outside in the yard or garden, would you wear old clothing to work or to a party?

If the will of a majority of Americans is to become a reality, perhaps what is needed is for the president, movie stars and famous sports figures to wear out-of-style, worn-out clothes. If you are one of the 73% who are willing to wear your old, out-of-style clothing, then you need to feel free to do so. If at a party you feel uncomfortable dressed in still-wearable but no longer in-style attire, you could say to your friends, "I'm sure you're one of the 73% of Americans, the majority, who believe we should wear our clothes until they wear out."

❧❖❧

Poll-taking and national surveys are popular forms of gathering information — or misinformation. Politicians use them to test the winds before setting sail, business people use them to adjust their sails to their sales and to reshape their products. Churches usually object to polls as weather vanes, even if they are moved by the Holy Wind, declaring that the church will not be swayed by democratic popular opinion.

Poll-taking can also collect illogical information as we see in today's reflection on Americans' willingness to wear old, ragged and patched clothing. While the data could be evaluated as a sign of a renewal of holy poverty and simple living, the poll's figures may be as foggy as a recent survey by *U.S. News* on the existence of heaven. In a nationwide survey 67% of adults said they believed that there is a heaven, and 23% said that they hope there is one. Only 8% seriously doubted heaven's existence, and 2% were not sure. However, when this same poll asked the same people if they thought they were going to heaven, 88% said yes!

✶

Anti-Uniform Day. Pope Celestine I (422-432) was disturbed because his clergy began wearing "uniforms," taking on clerical dress, and reprimanded them, "We should be set apart from others not by our dress, but by our conversation and the style of our lives."

30

Until after the Civil War, railroad conductors and mailmen refused to wear uniforms. In 1844, the police in New York City staged a strike against the proposal that they wear identical blue uniforms. The reason for such strong opposition to uniforms is that they were viewed as symbols of servitude — only butlers and maids wore them in the old country. On the other hand, parents with children in schools where uniforms are worn know the value of a uniformed dress code, which prevents not only expensive fashion warfare but also discrimination among children.

❧

Today's question for pondering: Do you wear some kind of uniformed attire as a dress code, symbolizing servitude to an institution, company, church or the fashion of the day? While youth are notorious for being rebels, they often dress themselves in uniforms of rebellion which are signs not of freedom but of slavery. Regardless of your age or the requirements of your work, how enslaved are you to style, to the opinions of others — or to the desire to be special or set apart?

✴

---

31 **Feast of St. Raymond Nonnatus.** Today's saint is the patron of childbirth since he was delivered by surgeons after his mother had died in labor; in fact, his Latin name means "not born." Wishing to minister to the Christians captured by Muslims, he went to Algeria and gave himself as a ransom in exchange for the freedom of another. He was ordered again and again not to spread the Gospel to his fellow prisoners, but he continued to persist in preaching, even to some Muslims, whom he converted. Islamic law prescribed death for this crime, but Raymond was given a reduced sentence. His lips were pierced by a red-hot iron spike; then a padlock secured his lips shut. The key was in the keeping of his jailer, who unlocked his lips only at meal time.

While the piercing of ears, nose and lips is common in our culture, today's saint challenges us not so much with piercing as with the cost of proclaiming the Good News of Jesus. St. Raymond is the patron of those who are willing, regardless of the cost, to speak out boldly against racial, religious and sexual discrimination, against injustice and oppression of the poor and weak.

~~~~~

Are your lips padlocked shut in the face of injustice because you fear rejection, ridicule or being accused of not understanding all the issues involved? On the other hand, have you considered padlocking shut your lips when you are in the middle of the kind of discussion which history has shown leads to strong disagreement?

As a child, you may have practiced this old ritual for keeping a secret: closing your lips and locking them with an imaginary key. Perhaps that childhood ritual could be an adult prayer both for opening your lips to speak for justice and for closing them to promote peace and limit the spread of gossip. A good morning prayer would involve both the unlocking and locking of your lips with the Key of Love as you say this brief prayer:

Gracious God, unlock the gates of my mouth
as you opened the lips of your prophets to speak for you.
Gentle God, close and lock my lips
so they will not condemn others
or give lip service to the violence in the world.
May they speak only of your love.

THE

MONTH

OF

SEPTEMBER

Mit Röm: Key: May: Freyheit.

Since once this was the seventh month, it is named after the Latin word for the number seven, *septem.* The old Dutch name was *Herst-maand*, "autumn month," since on the twenty-first of this month the autumn season begins.

After Christianity had been introduced to them, the Saxons called this month *Halig-monath*, meaning "holy month." They did so because it is crowded with holy days, among them being the Nativity of the Virgin Mary on the 8th, the feast of the Holy Cross on the 14th and the feast of Saint Michael the Archangel on the 29th. May it be a holy month for you as the summer season dies one more time and gives way to golden autumn.

County, State and World's Fair Day, 1939. The end of August and the beginning of September are fair times, and today we remember some predictions made at the great New York World's Fair of 1939. The millions of visitors at that fair wore buttons that proclaimed, "I Have Seen the Future." Today is the future they thought they had seen, and so it is time to see how the actual future matches what they saw. The future sixty years before the end of the century was filled with air-conditioned homes; bright, clean cities free of slums; new cars "built like raindrops...(that) cost as low as $200, and are able to race across the country in less than 24 hours, (while) a solution has been found to solve traffic jams."

Those 1939 visionaries further predicted: "America in 1960 is full of tanned and vigorous people who in 20 years have learned how to have fun...these people do not care much for possessions." Highways would be "two-ways...consist of four 50-mph lanes on each of the other edges, two pairs of 75-mph lanes and in the center, two lanes for 100 mph express traffic." Regarding medicine: "Cures for cancer and infantile paralysis have extended man's life span."

Today's remembrance of the future predicted in 1939 is a good lesson to begin this month of returning to school. The lesson isn't intended to be a humorous commentary but, like all teachings, a source of knowledge and wisdom. The coming decade or two will be a rich time for predictions by scholars, scientists, crystal ball readers and astrologers. When you are inclined to believe them, proceed with caution.

Learn from history that what is predicted in the far-off future has the habit of arriving much earlier than expected – or not at all. The future tends to be more like a surprise party at which the unpredicted and unexpected arrive on their own timetable, to the surprise and sometimes the shock of all. The future which contains dreams of cities without slums, an environment safe for creation and humans and the end of killer diseases is a future which will come not by fate but because it has become the goal of a people willing to spend the money, time and resources to see it come to pass. On this first day of September, ask yourself what you are willing to spend – not just in money but in time, talent and energy – to create a better future.

2 **The Tabloid News – a Hard Pill to Swallow Day.** Tabloids love the future, along with sightings of Elvis Presley and UFOs. Today, we honor the Burroughs, Wellcome and Company, who in the nineteenth century gave us the tabloid – not the *newspaper* but the *pill.* Prior to this, medicinal pills in Britain were both large and bitter. But the inventive Burroughs, Wellcome and Company compressed the large standard tablet into a small "tabloid."

In 1902 the *Westminster Gazette* began a new approach to journalism "...to give in tabloid form all the news printed in other journals." The inventors of the new small pill took the issue to court, contending that "tabloid" could only be used for their compressed tablet of medicine. They lost. The new millennium will provide an endless source of news for tabloids, which are half-sized newspapers with stories of the secret lives of stars, of the weird and fantastic, and of impending disasters.

⁂

The popularity of tabloids and pulpits that predict disasters of the new millennium speaks to a powerful hunger. For what kind of news about tomorrow are you hungry and thirsty? Your attitude toward today will reveal the makeup of your hunger. If your daily life is dull, routine and without wonder, then you will likely devour tabloid stories of two-headed babies, the discovery of the long-lost ark of Noah or the great tidal wave predicted to destroy San Francisco in 2022.

The next time you pass a tabloid rack in the grocery store let it be a reminder to check the state of wonder and awe in your daily life. If you do find your life to be routine and wonderless, take a real tabloid, a small "pill of pausing," a silent moment to stand in awe and wonder at a tree, a singing bird or your infant's first attempts to walk. The average home is full of such tabloids to cure the wonderless.

✳

Feast of September, the Back-to-School Month. This is the traditional month for schools, from kindergarten to college, to begin a new term. While going back to school is considered an activity for the young, let this day be an occasion to call you to return to learning. Alvin Toffler, author of *Future Shock,* observed, "The illiterate of the future are not those who cannot read or write, but those who cannot learn, unlearn, and relearn." As small children prepare for the beginning of school, where they will learn the famous three Rs, those of us who want to be literate of the future need to know the three Ls, the ability to learn, unlearn and relearn.

⁂

Whether your age is seven or seventy-five, set aside time for learning today. First, ask yourself what you need to unlearn. Take your time about this, for it is only natural to consider all knowledge gained as valuable. Be patient and search carefully through your personal Library of Facts of Life, Assumptions and Gospel-Truth Beliefs to see what needs to be unlearned and discarded. Then examine what you have learned in one way to see if it should be relearned in a new way. Finally, what is essential for living in the future that you should begin learning today? Play with these questions during all your recess periods this day.

Jesus promised that his Spirit would teach his disciples what they would need to know after he was gone. The Spirit of God is also the Great Holy Spirit Eraser, who teaches what needs to be unlearned, as well as the Spirit of the New, who is a coach for relearning what we thought we knew.

Come, Holy Spirit,
    and make my heart that of an eager child
    who is entering school for the first time.
Come, Holy Spirit,
    and help me unlearn what I learned as a child
    about God and my church and how the world should be.
Teach me how to respond to the sudden advances
    of science, technology and business on a global scale.
Come, Spirit of Creation,
    and help me relearn, in this new and complex world
    that places great stress on family and personal relationships,
    how to love beyond the circle of those who love me.
Help me relearn, Spirit of the New,
    so that harmony and peace might abound,
    the identity of those to whom God has been revealed —
    all peoples of all religions.
Come, Holy Spirit,
    and help me learn my three Ls.

✷

---

4 **Day of the End of the Postcard's World, 1888.** On this day in 1888 George Eastman patented his Kodak camera. "You press the button and we do the rest" was Kodak's slogan for the first folk camera, called the Brownie. What once had been only the domain of the professional photographer was now

possible for anyone. Kodak's camera was the first to use roll film instead of photographic plates and came factory-loaded with a hundred-exposure film pack. In 1900 the camera was made of hard cardboard reinforced with wood, and sold for one dollar. Americans in 1900 marveled at the new, almost magical world of instant photographs.

Eastman's name for the camera was chosen in honor of his manufacturing collaborator Frank Brownell and a reflection on popular cartoon characters of the day, elflike brownies. The early 1900s rage of the Brownie camera, however, was the End of the World for the professional photograph postcards, which had been such an enormous success just prior to 1890. The October 3 entry in this Almanac will further treat the rise and fall of the postcard.

⁂

Worlds do end, even if slowly, as new worlds arise daily with the coming of inventions and new advances. Prophets of doom who predict the End of the World from pulpits or religious tabloids are correct. The question is: *Which worlds* will end in the coming years and decades? Do you have personal or financial investments in a doomed world or institution? Does your world — or business — have a limited life expectancy? If your answer is no, look again carefully at your world. Spend some time today exploring how to prepare wisely for the parts of your world that may be becoming extinct.

✴

The Birthday of Jesse James, 1847. Jesse Woodson James was a bank and train robber in Missouri and nearby states during the Wild West era. He is credited with responsibility for the first train robbery in history in 1873. The hefty reward of $5,000 he and his brother Frank warranted reflects the folk-hero notoriety they gained by robbing trains. While they were compared to Robin Hood, no record shows they ever shared the wealth they gained from banks and rich train-travelers with the poor. In 1881 Jesse, using the name Tom Howard, moved to St. Joseph, Missouri, where he was shot five months later by Robert

Ford. Jesse James' dramatic death increased his fame, and he became a legendary folk hero of penny pamphlets.

Robbery, killing and violence should not be glorified, cried clergy, educators and parents in the late nineteenth century, and again, and again. In the 1930s a concerned parent wrote, "Our six-year-old has become gangster-minded this past year since he has been allowed to run the radio at his will." Radio networks stated that they were "only giving the public what they want," but social concern over violence on the radio mounted. "A law should be passed," claimed those who were disturbed by such shockingly violent programs as *The Green Hornet* and *Gangbusters*, which children could hear when they were allowed "to run the radio at will." The result was a new code announced by NBC and CBS: "All stories must reflect respect for adult authority, good morals and clean living.... Disrespect for parental authority must not be glorified or encouraged." Censored along with the radio, black-and-white motion pictures featuring machine-gunning gangsters, outlaw cowboys and bank robbers captured the imagination of the youth of that day.

⚜

Today, as in the 1930s, there is great anxiety about the effect of the media on the moral fiber of our children. Perhaps parents, educators and clergy were correct in being alarmed by the radio programs and motion pictures of the 1930s. It would explain why the vast majority of today's senior citizens turned into gangsters. The large number of violent criminals among our senior citizens, along with the high incidence among them of unclean living and bad morals must surely be the harvest of the media pollution of their youth. Today, society must pay the price for the 1930s when six-year-olds were allowed to listen to violent programs by running the radio at their will.

A historical parable to ponder.

✳

6 **The Birthday of the Book, 2800 B.C.** "School days, school days, good old-fashioned school days," even as recently as 1980, would not have been possible without books from which students could study. So often taken for granted, the wondrous invention of the book needs to be honored on this day. The convenient and portable book began more as a package of pages — or in the case of Assyria four thousand years ago as a collection of clay tablets. When the Egyptians, almost 5,000 years ago, invented papyrus, a form of paper made from plants now almost extinct, it allowed their "books" to be rolled up in scrolls and kept in a jar. The Greeks improved on this Nile roll-book by putting together a collection of smaller-sized pages which could be bound together by cords into a packet of pages. This was the closest ancient relative to the book you are reading at this moment. The Greeks named their more-portable improvement after the city which provided the paper of that day, Byblos. This, of course, is the source of our word Bible, which is more a library of books than a single volume.

Those in the Middle East used animal skins, usually of calves or lambs, and parchment or vellum was first employed around 165 B.C. In the second century after Jesus, the Romans made books by binding vellum pages together with a cord between thin wooden waxed boards, often made from beechwood. The wooden covers of these books may be the source of our word for "book," as the German *boc* means beech.

Surprisingly, since Johann Gutenberg's invention of the movable type printing press in 1436, basically no improvements were made on the design of that second century book. While pages made from paper instead of vellum were introduced, the shape and format of books has remained relatively unchanged through the end of the twentieth century. Yet as the plant that provides papyrus is now all but extinct, perhaps books soon will be too. Electronic books — computers — may signal the end of the world for the old basic book. To read more on the demise of the book, follow the circle of time around and examine the ending of the December 19 entry.

⚜

Columbus carried a book with him on his first voyage to the New World. It was Marco Polo's account of his thirteenth century twenty-two year expeditional odyssey to China and back. May the book you are presently holding inspire you on your life's expedition just as Marco Polo's book inspired Columbus. May this Almanac encourage you not to hug the shores with fear, but to sail forth on a voyage of learning about new worlds. May it be an odyssey of new ideas from books, from every person you meet and from the great book of creation.

Yet again, the spiritual life and the practical life are one, and that is especially true in the world of books. To give someone you love a good book is a rare and useful gift. A good book can create a Marco Polo adventure for those who are homebound by responsibilities. A good book is not only a handy handheld mentor and guide, it is also a holy tabernacle allowing the spirit of the gift-giver to reside in the home of a friend. The person who receives a gift book inscribed with a handwritten note can lightly finger the inscription with the same sense of the "holy" as Egyptian priests handled their hieroglyphics, their "holy signs," 5,000 years ago. Your signed book will likewise be a divine gift for your friend or loved one.

---

7 **Just Say "No" Day.** September ushers in not only school days but also the beginning of various programs, boards, committees and projects. September is the prime season for many organizations – from parent-school associations to parish committees – to enlist volunteers. The free gift of your time as a volunteer is a necessity in the contemporary world where so many needs must be met with ever shrinking funds. Volunteering has been shown not only to expand one's horizons, but to be a source of personal wellness and good health. Certainly, it is most beneficial for your soul to give of yourself, your time and talents.

If everyone volunteered a reasonable amount of time and energy, all the needs would easily be met. However, the number of those who actually serve is never enough to meet the demand. The result is inevitably that a few suffer from overextension. Stress flows directly from overcommitment – saying *yes* when you really want to say *no*. The *yes* response to being asked to do something is frequently a fire escape, a short-term way of avoiding confrontation or feeling embarrassed on the spot. But too many *yeses* create pain in the future and stress in the soul.

The clock is not large enough to provide hours adequate to do everything you might want to do, so it is important in this month of learning to learn how to say *no*. Knowing how to make distinctions, knowing the limits of your strength, time and responsibilities, will provide the ability for determining when you can say *yes* and when you should say *no*.

≈✹✹✹≈

No is only a tiny two-letter word, but it weighs a ton when you have to say it to your boss, pastor, spouse or children. *No* is also an important command word you need to say to yourself so as to have time for reading, prayer and leisure. Learning how to gracefully say *no* gives you control over your life and prevents you from becoming a victim of your own choices.

No can be a holy word; speak it like a prayer.

✴

Feast of the Nativity of Mary, Mother of God. Today is the birthday of the Blessed Virgin Mary, whom the archangel Gabriel announced would be the mother of our savior, Jesus Christ.

Along with New Age interest in various alternate religious expressions, the decades just before the end of the twentieth century witnessed a renewal of interest in angels. I once received an "exclusive" mail subscription offer to a new publication. Printed on the envelope were statements of what this new magazine would offer: *Discover alternative paths to good health. Unlock the healing powers of food. Encounter the world's wisdom. Hear angelic voices.* The dual implication was that by reading this magazine one could learn to hear angelic voices — and also that many people desired to do this.

If you are interested in hearing angelic voices, pause and consider the possible consequences: For Mary it meant the end of her quiet village world to become not only the mother of the Good News but also the suffering, sorrowful Mother of a holy crucified criminal. Remember also the price that Saint Joan of Arc paid for hearing angelic voices in her garden. For claiming to have heard such voices, and for following what they told her, dressing as a man and leading the French army to victory, she paid a high price. On May 30, 1431, Joan of Arc was burned at the stake as a witch and excommunicated as a heretic. While in 1920 she was officially raised to the rank of a saint by a church that claimed a clerical error, her world ended on May 30, 1431, because she was open to hearing angelic voices.

Holy Mary,
  Mother of God and Queen of Angels,
    intercede for me with God on this your birthday.
Grant me the grace to be spared from hearing angelic voices
    so that my present quiet and comfortable world
    may not end.

9 **The Feast Day of the Angel Israfel.** In 1831 Edgar Allen Poe wrote a poem he called "Israfel." It contains these verses:

If I could dwell
Where Israfel
Hath dwelt, and he where I,
He might not sing so wildly well
A mortal melody,
While a bolder note than this might swell
From my lyre within the sky.

In his Koran, the prophet Mohammed wrote of this angel, "...and the angel Israfel, whose heartstrings are a lute, and who has the sweetest voice of all God's creatures...." Yet Poe proposes that if he and Israfel were to change places, Edgar's songs would be bolder and wilder than the angel who had the sweetest voice.

As we celebrate on this feast of the Islamic angel, Israfel, whose heartstrings are a harp, examine today the instrument of your heart. Do your heartstrings during prayer play loudly and wildly a song of great sweetness, or do they sound a dirge of sad lament? As the poet Poe says, Israfel sings so "wildly well" as he accompanies himself on his heart-harp. That description prompts the question: Are my prayers wildly sung or simply droned out in the dullness of dry duty?

The Prophet Mohammed also said in the Koran, "God changes not what is in a people, until they change what is in themselves." What, then, needs to change within to make your heartstrings zing with zestful, wild and bold praise of God?

✣

Iron Retirement Feast, or Liberation Day, 1954. **10**
Previous to this decade of the 1950s it was necessary to spend up to twenty hours a week ironing shirts, skirts, tablecloths, bed linens and other things made from natural fibers. A new age arrived with the appearance of synthetic fabrics made from cellulose, acetate, nylon, acrylic and polyester that gave postwar clothing the name "wash and wear." The laundry-room drudgery of having to iron was greatly reduced, if not eliminated. Although thirty to forty years after synthetic cloth began to be used for clothing, there was a rebirth of cotton and other fibers, even these natural fibers were intended not to be ironed. Thus, those responsible for ironing were given twenty free hours a week in which to enjoy leisure and other activities.

❦

By the end of the century a gang of thieves had stolen all those twenty free hours, and one of the culture's greatest complaints was a lack of leisure time. What are the names of the robbers who have stolen your free time? Despite such ever-helpful household servants as fast-food, wash-and-wear, instant coffee and a host of others, you need to be ever watchful of your precious time, even if you can't identify your time thieves. If these years around the turn of the century are devoid of free time for the average person, what will it be like in the 2020s and beyond?

Be your own private detective and search your home for evidence of break-ins. If you find no such signs, consider whether your robberies might be inside jobs. Perhaps you should look for the fingerprints of your timesaving devices, your business and household mechanical and electronic servants, to see if they are stealing time from you when you're not looking. Today's question to chew on in your free time is: How are these "time-saving" thieves stealing time from me?

✹

11   **The Necessary Education of Feedback Festival.** This is a national day to honor the ancient source of knowledge recently renamed as feedback. The dictionary defines this process as the return of a portion of the output of a system or process. Feedback is any information about the results of the process itself. As information, feedback is essential for those seeking excellence.

Humans have a built-in need for feedback, or at least for partial feedback, the kind that is positive and praising. So great is this need that ingenious manipulations are employed to receive such good information. On the other hand, few, it seems, want to know the whole range of informational truth and nothing but the truth. Most of us become upset when negative feedback is given and reject any information critical of our work. Among those who want only half of the information, the positive feedback, are dictators, oppressive governments, churches, corporate leaders, bosses and also millions upon millions of ordinary people. Yet unless individuals or organizations, parents or popes are open to honest feedback, how can they achieve true excellence in the work they are striving to produce?

❧

Today's festival asks: Do you see criticism as purely *negative* feedback? When was the last time you asked someone to give you honest feedback, especially criticism of your work? Do you treat praise and criticism as having the same value? Do you treat it simply as information necessary for excellence and improvement? If it is just information, should one make you feel good and the other bad? Should one make you proud and the other cause shame? The learning rule of thumb is that one usually learns more from one's mistakes than from one's successes. The rule of the index finger is that one is usually blinded to one's shortcomings and mistakes.

The famous MGM movie producer Samuel Goldwyn spoke for popes, politicians and movie producers when he said to his junior executives, "I want you to tell me the truth, even if it costs you your jobs."

Try this prayer today:

Lord, that I might see,
   give me those who love me enough to tell me the truth,
   especially to criticize me with the same love
   with which they congratulate and praise me.

✵

The Feast of Silent Heroes and Heroines. In 1927 Harry M. Warner of Warner Brothers Studios said of talking motion pictures, "Who the hell wants to hear actors talk?" History showed Harry Warner that almost everyone did! The arrival of talking pictures, as with the Cretaceous extinction some sixty-five million years ago, meant the End of the World. Those who were victims sixty-five million years ago were dinosaurs, particularly the three-horned triceratops, a massive four-legged, plant-eating browser with a long horn over each eye and a short horn on its nose. In Hollywood those stars who spoke as if through a squeaky horn lost their jobs, their silent world ending in the disaster of sound.

12

⚜

Statues and sacred images are like silent movie stars, except they are stone still as well as silent. Use today's pedestrian prophecy as a springboard to jump into a pool of questions. Would you want to hear voices from holy pictures and statues of saints? Imagine the impact if instead of being like silent movie stars who appeared on the silver screen, the images of saints would speak...shout...cry out to all who came into church. What might your favorite saint or the Mother of God or Jesus on the cross say or shout to you if given the power to speak instead of simply looking at you with pious faces?

�֎

---

13 The Birthday of the Picture Window, Around 1955.

Though the precise date is not possible to determine, sometime in the mid 1950s the new one-level American ranch-style home appeared. This home, departing from the typical two-story house, was based on earlier designs by the celebrated architect, Frank Lloyd Wright. His principle was that structures should harmonize with their environments and blend with nature. The new mid-century home had its own driveway and connecting garage, a backyard cement patio and a large, sunny picture window. Wright designed this large window for the purpose of framing nature. It was not intended to face a street filled with other homes with their own large picture windows looking directly back.

☙❦❧

The moral of the day is: If you are buying or building a new home, "never buy a view you don't own." While the picture window failed to frame nature and usually required drawn curtains to protect the privacy of the inhabitants, a new picture window soon arrived. Television, with its little, to-grow-larger picture window would be what families sat in front of, not the one that faced outdoors. Unlike the picture windows of the ranch-style middle-class home, this new picture window would in a couple of decades be part of every home.

If the view out your window looks onto nature, do you use it, or do you limit yourself to looking into the moving picture window of your TV set?

✖

---

14 Feast of St. Notburga, Patroness of All Lowly Servants, of Fast-Food Workers, Dishwashers, Busboys and Behind-the-Scenes Drudgery Workers.

Saint Notburga was a peasant woman with one eye who was a

lowly servant in the great castle of the Count and Countess of Rottenburg. Mocked by the ever-demanding countess because of her one eye, Notburga was given the lowest of duties. Discovered by the countess giving food to the poor instead of to the pigs, she was fired and thrown out of work – it seems the Countess of Rottenburg had an appropriate name. After the cruel countess died, she was said to be relegated to haunting the castle pigpens due to her refusal to give food to the poor, and an exorcist had to be called in to banish her ghost. Notburga now returned and was raised to the rank of castle housekeeper until she died around 1313. Besides being a model for all "drudgery" workers, she is also entitled to be the patron saint of priest housekeepers.

May you be inspired on this feast of Notburga to treat all those "not-beings" you encounter with great reverence. "Not-beings" comprise the army of lowly who both visibly and invisibly wait on you in the great castle of contemporary life. May St. Notburga inspire you to treat with respect those who fry and serve your burgers, gas station attendants, checkout clerks or those who clean up and work in the kitchen for minimal wages and usually no benefits. The commercial world is crowded with the lowly peasants of this age who are usually treated as non-beings and all but invisible. Each age, so it seems, has its peasant class to perform the drudgery deeds of daily life. Peasants tip their caps to the gentry, step out of the way and do not speak unless spoken to. St. Notburga, help me to not see myself as gentry but to be like the gentle Galilean peasant who treated the poor and outcasts not simply as gentry but as royalty, and who calls me to do the same.

An old Irish story captures this point. An Irishman was laboring away by the side of the road when a member of the English gentry came riding by and asked, "My good man, have you seen any gentry recently pass this way?" The poor tenant farmer tipped his hat and replied, "Not in the past two hundred years, my Lord."

15

Feast of the First Millennium, 1000 A.D. A celebration of ten centuries is today's feast. The last time a millennium was celebrated it was done so with the greatest of fear, as countless people believed it would be the End of the World. Since it was believed this would usher in the Last Judgment, religious fervor was at a high pitch. There were long lines of people anxious to confess their sins, as well as frequent religious processions and vigils at shrines of the saints. Those living in sin tried to live outside of it — at least during the passage of that infamous millennial crossing, and a few years on the other side for good measure.

While many thought of the millennium as the End, for others it was only the beginning. The explorer Leif Ericson, son of Eric the Red, is reported to have discovered the New World, having set foot on present-day Nova Scotia. While many miscalculating believers were looking to the sky for the arrival of Christ as King and Judge, others were looking up for other reasons: Documents mention several abortive human attempts to fly or to float in the air. Christian missionaries reached and converted Iceland and Greenland on this 1,000th anniversary of the birth of Jesus Christ. For the peoples of Greenland and Iceland it was not the End, but a new beginning. The end of the first thousand years and the beginning of the next thousand, then, was a mixture of millennium madness and exciting new beginnings. This Feast of Remembrance of the First Millennium is of such importance as to have several days of commemoration in this Almanac. The Ten Centennial Millennium — to be continued.

❦

Historians record the great events of the world — usually only those that favor their racial and political preferences. Yet countless unrecorded but significant personal dramas were occurring at the First Millennium Crossing. The Holy Crossing would be a good name for today's festival, in honor of the feast of the *Holy Cross*, which celebrates the cross on which Jesus was crucified. The Holy Crossing could add to that veneration of the cross of Christ a celebration of how unknown but heroic people deal with the mixture of private disasters and personal new beginnings that are commonplace in the decades before and after a Millennium Crossing.

�҂

Day To Mark the Extinction of the Automobile, 1943. 16

Not only would it be the End of the World for cars, but school
buses also would be doomed to the fate of the horse and buggy
— this was the prediction for the second half of the twentieth
century. In 1943 Harry Bruno, an aviational publicist, wrote,
"Automobiles will start to decline as soon as the last shot is
fired in World War II." Bruno proposed that the name of Igor
Sikorsky would replace that of Henry Ford, for his invention,
the helicopter, would be the new form of transportation. Bruno
added, "...instead of a car in every garage, there will be a
helicopter.... These 'copters will be so safe and will cost so little
that small models will be made for teenage youngsters. These
tiny 'copters when school lets out, will fill the sky as the bicycles
of our youth filled the prewar roads."

❧

Bruno's last image of the skies filled with flying teenagers
is a veritable prediction of environmental disaster. Pause today
to give thanks that Bruno's mini-copter future did not become a
reality, at least not in your lifetime. You can usually feel safe in
your own home from injury at the hands of the most accident-
prone group, teenagers. But what if you had to worry about
them falling from the skies and crashing into your roof? So if
on your way to work today you are forced to reduce your speed
to creeping in a rush-hour traffic jam, don't be stressed. Smile
and remember Bruno's prophecy of a carless society.

✚

Words Avoidance Day. 17

For better interpersonal relation-
ships, avoid using two words in particular: *should* and *must*. Those
who learn to remove these offenders from their speech and
replace them with other options will likely find their lives with
others greatly improved.

If you wish to make someone feel guilty or inferior, try saying, "You should..." — for it implies the other person should have either thought of or already done what you had in mind. Also lethal are "You must..." or "You need to..." or "You have no other choice but..." because these statements have such parental and dictatorial tones. Being a student is a lifelong occupation. After learning how to speak, a good student relearns what words should not be spoken.

※◯◆◯※

It's not "Read my lips," as President George Bush was fond of saying, but "Watch my lips" that's our motto for the day. Watch your lips as carefully as you watch your rearview mirror when preparing to change lanes to pass a car. If you recognize that a *should* or *must* is about to enter the conversation, replace it at once with, "One possibility is..." or "You could consider doing..." or "If you get the chance, you might want to experiment with...." Today is also ideal for remembering the old adage, "Those who offer advice when advice is not requested, need advice."

✻

---

18 **Mind-Thought Viruses Day.** The British evolutionist Richard Dawkins in the late 1970s proposed the concept of *memes*, or mind viruses. It was a seed idea that became a plant through the work of Aaron Lynch, a physicist who wrote the book *Thought Contagion*. While most people are cautious, if not anxious, about germs and the spread of viruses, they unwittingly overlook the deadly effect of thoughts. As with diseases, Lynch proposed that the spread of memes, thought viruses, depends upon how much fervor they inspire, how long each host carrier stays infected and how much resistance the virus encounters in the general population.

Memes germs do not have to be true or need to be able to be justified by rational thought; they survive and spread, like other germs, simply because they are good at surviving. Consider the thought viruses of racial or religious prejudice: While lacking in truth, they infect millions, each of whom in turn infects the people around them.

The world's great religions possess powerful memes; while they began as small and insignificant viruses, they spread worldwide. Other memes, like the radical ideas of the 1960s social revolution, became epidemic among certain sections of the population. Mainstream ideas usually meet little resistance while unorthodox beliefs are treated like the Black Plague. Ideas of the End of the World — like being struck by some great comet, some gigantic geological disaster or an invasion by aliens from outer space — are among the floating millennium-memes. These kinds of thought viruses spread quickly because the sense of urgency at the end of an era gives them greater power.

❧❦❧

The Buddha was more than two millenniums ahead of recent studies on the infectious nature of thoughts. He said, "With your thoughts you make your world. Think evil and as surely as the cart follows the ox, evil will pursue you." Buddha could have said, "With your thoughts you infect yourself and others. Think good thoughts and the contagion of compassion will fill your body and spread out to the world around you." Jesus of Nazareth, whose birth is the counting point for the millennium, likewise acknowledged the powerful influence of thoughts. He said that not only were the deeds of killing or adultery evil, so were the memes of such actions.

Some two thousand years ago, Buddha and Jesus signaled a radical shift in morality: Not only was committing an evil act forbidden, the very thought of it was equal to the act. Both saw that the world would not be changed by laws; it would only be transformed by the infectious thoughts of love and compassion.

The most powerful evangelization is to spread the good virus of virtue by first being infected yourself, then by coming into intimate contact with as many people as possible.

✴

Star Trek Anniversary — First NBC-TV Voyage, 1966. The premier of this program in September of 1966 provided no hint that this series and its characters would have a cult following that would extend well into the next millennium. *Star Trek*

19

portrayed a future in space where evil and good continued their ancient struggle begun on earth.

⚜

Whatever the new century holds, it will not be life without evil, greed and exploitation. The tomorrow imaged in *Star Trek* raises war to a cosmic level, dashing wishful thinking that space might be free of war. The personal future for you, however, can be "warless" if you work to make today and tomorrow free of waging wars, even holy wars. A world without war comes with a large price tag, as does a life of personal peace. Peace is costly, nonviolence is costly — are you willing to pay the price?

✳

20 Be Your Own Explorer Day.

In September of 1522, the Spanish navigator Juan de Elcano returned triumphantly to Spain, completing the first circumnavigation of the globe. On this day he was the toast of great festivals in Spain honoring him and the dead hero who had begun the expedition, Ferdinand Magellan, who had been killed by natives in the Pacific. Today, in honor of Elcano and Magellan, launch out on your own expedition to explore parts of yourself. You don't need a sailing ship or airplane, but perhaps a piece of paper and a pen would help.

Prepare for the expedition by writing five or ten incomplete sentences. Then sail forth like a bold explorer, without stopping to think, and fill in the blanks. Some sample incomplete sentences:

If I place others' thoughts above my own, _____.
If I am more self-assertive today, _____.
If I take responsibility for fulfilling my own needs, _____.
If I thought before I spoke, _____.
If I censored by own negative thoughts, _____.
If I took more time for leisure, _____.
If I....

This fill-in-the-blank exercise is suggested by Dr. Nathaniel Branden, a psychologist who encourages developing self-respect by determining your own goals in life and standing up for them.

⚜

You may not be inclined to leave the beaten path of your routine for such a written expedition. Think again. For to write down feelings, dreams and goals is to think them twice and to think them through. If you lack the time for this exercise, consider playing the game of the Three Coulds with yourself when you need to make a decision today. Before coming to some conclusion, playfully say to yourself, "I could _____, or I could _____, or I could even do_____." If this game becomes addictive, you will find that every decision has many possibilities, even when you feel you have no choices.

Today is also the **Feast of St. Eustace**, who was highly honored in the Middle Ages. The Spanish city of Madrid is dedicated to him, and the faithful throughout Europe considered him one of the Fourteen Holy Helpers, along with St. Christopher, St. Nicholas, St. Margaret and St. Barbara. This devotion reached cult status during the Black Plague. When faced today by a plague of choices, may St. Eustace help you fill in the blanks.

Birth of the Ballpark Figure, 1890. When you ask for an estimate or bid, you are often given a "ballpark figure." World Series fever is in the air during these days of late summer and early autumn. At this time of year in the 1890s, ballparks hosted not only baseball but also political rallies. Admission to these gatherings, unlike ball games, was free, and so attendance could not be determined by ticket stubs but had to be estimated.

Just as history is written by the winners, so in those days newspapers favoring a particular candidate for office would inflate the attendance figure at a rally. Likewise, a rival newspaper which supported the other candidate would produce a lower estimated crowd (a pattern still practiced today when it comes to various political marches and other demonstrations). This estimating of crowds a hundred years ago has given us the expression *a ballpark figure*, meaning a rough guesstimate.

This is also the **Feast of St. Matthew**, patron saint of the IRS and tax collectors. In his day, taxes demanded at the tollgate were much like *ballpark figures*, since the tax collector paid a general fee to the Roman government for the right to collect tolls and could then determine the amount of a tax. Tax collecting was a business — even if the collectors were hated and despised by the oppressed people — a business in which a profit was made by setting an estimated tax high enough to insure a good living.

Moral: Obtain all bids and estimates in writing, aware that an estimated bill may only awaken the itch of the ancient Roman tax collector in the person providing the service.

✳

---

22 Autumn Equinox — Invention of the Clock, 3500 B.C.

Today tells time by the most ancient method, by the sun's position on the horizon. September 21 and 22 mark the point at which the setting or rising sun is precisely halfway on its journey between its northernmost and southernmost points, making this the first full day of the autumn equinox. Our prehistoric parents found awe and wonderment in this day of equal light and darkness. What would your life be like if you only kept time by the changing of the seasons?

What would life be like today without clocks? Do not be ashamed if you would enjoy experimenting with living 5,000 years ago when the only clock was the sun by day and stars by night. Some Egyptian genius stuck a stick in the ground and watched how its shadow moved as the sun progressed across the sky. Then perhaps the unknown inventor placed pebbles or little sticks along the shadow's path to mark different settings around that first sundial.

Time marches on, and in the eighth century B.C. a precision timepiece was in use. It had a straight base and inscribed numbers rather than pebbles in its six time divisions. Five centuries later in 300 B.C., a Babylonian priest and astronomer named Berosus divided the sundial into twelve equal intervals or hours and the modern face of the clock appeared.

Water clocks, which kept time by the fall or flow of a quantity of water, were followed by clocks dripping sand through a vessel, leading to the invention of the hourglass in Europe in the first century A.D. This sand clock had to be turned over every hour to keep accurate time. When sermons preached by zealous Renaissance clerics in love with their own voices grew to be two hours long, technicians were asked to design a new clock. This "hourglass" clock measured time in more bearable divisions of fifteen to thirty minutes to assist the long-suffering faithful.

꧁ꕥ꧂

For an inexpensive, if not absolutely free, vacation, select some non-work day and hide all your clocks. Put away your wristwatch, place all your household digitals in drawers, and then escape to a day of measuring time only by your body-clock and the sun. Among other things, a Jubilee Year is intended to be a time for setting prisoners free. Celebrate a Jubilee Day today, and frequently, by being liberated from the slavery of the clock.

✵

Incognita Festival Day, 1806 and 6939. On this day in 1806, Lewis and Clark returned from their transcontinental expedition to the Pacific, which had begun in 1803 with the intention of exploring the newly acquired Louisiana Purchase, the unknown lands west of the Mississippi River. President Thomas Jefferson, who had conceived and commissioned the expedition, was one of the most brilliant men of his time. Yet in his extensive library of books on geography and natural history, this vast expanse of land was named *terra incognita*, the unknown land. At that time the Blue Ridge Mountains were thought to be the highest range on the American continent. It was believed that prehistoric creatures would be found in its upper reaches, that there existed somewhere on the great plains a mile-high mountain of pure salt and that volcanoes might still be erupting beyond the plains in what today is called the Badlands of the Dakotas. It was also held that there might be a waterway leading to the Pacific Ocean, and this belief was one of the major reasons for the expedition.

23

꧁ꕥ꧂

Also on this day in 1939 a six-ton monument containing a time-capsule from the New York World's Fair of 1939-1940 was unveiled in Flushing Meadows, New York, the site of the fair. The capsule contained various artifacts and general information about twentieth century culture. The date for the opening of the time capsule was set for the year 6939.

⚜

The year 6939! To prepare something to be explored so far in the future is a bold statement of hope. Hurrah for those who originated the idea and had the courage to set the clock on the capsule for such an awesomely distant year. But it's not just the year 6939 or the year 4939 or even 2139 that is *terra incognita*! In 1900, at the dawn of electric lights, telephones, automobiles and airplanes, who could have imagined the lay of the land in a mere fifty years! At the dawn of the twentieth century, few people possessed any of these inventions. Yet the pace of life even in the middle of the century was so much slower than the supersonic speed of how new inventions and discoveries have multiplied since then. Now *terra incognita* is not fifty years away but only a handful! Prepare for your arrival in the new and wondrous land by outfitting yourself today with not only a shockproof watch but a shockproof heart and mind — and especially a shockproof soul.

✳

---

24 Good Old Days Festival.

Yesterdays are looked upon with fondness for many reasons, being referred to not only as *old*, but as *good*. The passage of years possesses the enchanting power to erase the hardships and illuminate the happier times. Homes and restaurants are often decorated with antiques from Yesterday because they evoke so many warm and good memories. While the pre-wash-and-wear days of the early 1950s are among the Good Old Days, few of us would want to return again to spending an average of twenty hours a week ironing (see the September 10 entry).

Yet what are good yesterdays for some are the Bad Old Days for others. For most African-Americans any days prior to the 1960s and Civil Rights were the Bad Old Days. For the Chinese and other Asians, the Gay Nineties of the nineteenth century were the Sad Nineties, the Bad Old Days of the Yellow Peril fears. Like blacks, the Chinese imported into our country to work on the railroads were made into targets of hate, prejudice and violence. The immoral Yellow Peril prejudice continued to crawl like a poison viper from decade to decade through most of the twentieth century.

⚜

Today is the time to make the Good Old Days. And the best way to create good yesterdays is to lisp when you pronounce the word, saying "yes-to-today." When you say a bold, loving *yes* to all that each day brings, you affirm it as good. Saying *yes* to difficult problems that challenge you, to sickness that awakens you from sleepwalking through good health, and even to having too much to do, you can make today a yesterday to remember when you are in some nursing home with nothing to do. Practice making good yesterdays now by saying "yes-to-today" in as many situations as possible.

❉

It's Safe to Wear a Wristwatch Day. Peter Henlein of Nurnberg, Germany, who lived in the middle of the second millennium, around 1500, may be unknown to you, but today is a good day to applaud Peter and also Vernon Castle. Henlein's invention of the mainspring, a flat coiled steel band, is an essential element in one of our most useful instruments — the watch. Its name has religious significance; it springs from the Old English *waecce*, "to keep vigil," the duty not only of night watchmen but also of those who pray in the middle of the night.

25

Henlein's invention made it possible to carry a time-measuring device in days when clocks were large and bulky. The first watches themselves weren't small, being four to five inches in diameter and three inches thick. They were clunky enough that some nobility designated a servant to carry the device, to "watch" the time and announce it when asked.

As M & Ms were created so that World War II troops could

carry chocolates that wouldn't melt in their hands, so wristwatches were small pocket watches with straps that could be worn on the wrist by World War I pilots. As we saw on May 13, pocket watches were too difficult to remove while flying those early airplanes. After the war, the wristwatch lost its macho airman's image and even acquired an effeminate image, being called a "bracelet" watch. "Real" men now only carried respectable pocket watches. Enter Vernon Castle. He and his wife Irene were trendsetters from the postwar years into the 1920s. They were a famous Tango dancing team in both America and Europe, the Ginger Rogers and Fred Astaire of their day. When Vernon Castle began to wear a wristwatch, its image again changed and young men quickly began to imitate him.

⚜

Styles change, and sometimes rapidly. What once was male-only clothing has become fashionable for women. While women wear slacks, a prediction that twenty years from now men's fashions will feature skirts might well be laughed at. Yet, however strange a prediction for the future might sound, remember the women's bracelet watch and hold your laughter.

Moreover, remember that the spiritual life and the practical life are one, and wise and holy are those who never separate them. If you wear a wristwatch, it can be as religious an image as a cross or a medal worn around your neck, a pocket rosary or any portable religious reminder. To make your wristwatch religious, the next time you check your watch for the correct time, say softly to yourself these words of Jesus: "Be watchful, for you know not the hour or the day." Jesus encouraged his disciples not to let death sneak up and pickpocket them, but to always be vigilant. Seeing the time correctly is seeing that it is late, later than you think. It is time to soak up all the enjoyment of life that you can. Seeing the time correctly is seeing that it is time to be generous with your love and gifts. Seeing the time correctly is seeing that God's Time has arrived, that the reign of God is here, now, at this very moment. Knowing the correct and real time means living in that mystical time zone of Jubilee Time.

✵

Festival of September Song and Autumn Poetry. 26

Today marks the birthdays of George Gershwin in 1898 and T.S. Eliot in 1888. Gershwin's *Rhapsody in Blue* and *American in Paris* are artistic examples of his blending of folk and jazz elements to create a unique American music. Music, song and poetry truly feed the soul and are as essential to a full life as good, wholesome food. Unfortunately, they are usually seen as luxuries by hardworking, practical Americans. Many musicians and most poets struggle to be published and to make a living at their art.

Thomas Stearns Eliot sewed song and poetry together, as we see in his poem "The Game of Chess":

> O O O O that Shakespearian Rag —
> It's so elegant
> So intelligent.

Poets like Eliot have the ability to take snapshots of us at naked moments. In "The Hollow Men" he frames us in uncomfortable truth:

> We are the hollow men
> We are the Hollow men
> Leaning together
> Headpiece filled with straw. Alas!

Similarly, in "Cocktail Party," written in 1950, Eliot echoes poets and philosophers before him like Virgil, Milton and Sartre:

> What is Hell?
> Hell is oneself.
> Hell is alone,
> The other figures of it
> Merely projections.

❦

How much richer our lives would be if we'd daily add to our diets one poem to recite and one song to sing. Energy packed, full of divine vitamins for the soul are song and poetry. Increasing your daily intake would make your soul sing that great Gershwin hit, "I got rhythm...who could ask for anything more."

✹

27 **A Brand New America Day.** Thomas Jefferson once said, "We may consider each generation a distinct nation." The next time you pass a school bus you could say, "There goes a busload of immigrants on their way to a new nation." Look at your children or kids in a playground and say, "You will be citizens in a new nation unlike the one in which you are now living. Leave behind all the trash of this age. Discard any of your parents' old prejudices and structures of inequality."

Don't pack the immigrant bags of your children or other people's children with today's trash ideas of greed, values like "Get all you can and give as little as possible." Don't fill their pockets with stale chunks of cynicism. Don't clothe them in a wardrobe of examples of disrespect for those in authority, for the senior members of society or for the disabled. Don't give them eyeglasses focused only on Hollywood or sport stars as heroic models. Finally and most importantly, do not give them mirrors for modeling themselves that are really your unfilled desires and abandoned dreams. Let them be a new nation!

⚜

What wise Jefferson said about each generation being a new nation is equally true for religion! Each generation is a new church. Rejoice in that reality. Pray that the higher values your church couldn't bring itself to profess will be lived out in the next generation. No more beautiful, yet threatening, image exists for the new church, mosque or synagogue of the twenty-first century than children. Children, those who have not yet set their hearts and souls in stone, are the true Pilgrim People of God. Choose with great care what you pack in their exodus bags.

✶

28 **Feast of St. Wenceslaus, Patron of Czechoslovakia.** This saint, whose image appears on Czech coins as a symbol of the nation, was murdered by his brother Boleslaus. The Solemnity of his feast, according to the Old Hermit's Calendar, is celebrated on December 22 since he is the subject of a famous old carol. Wenceslaus was raised by his saintly grandmother as a good

Christian. Once he became king in 921, he was an aggressive Christian ruler. At royal banquets he would force all his guests, whether Christian or not, to recite the Lord's Prayer with him. Those who refused would be beaten without compassion. However, he was known for building churches, for his good deeds at night (see the December 22 entry) and for evangelizing his subjects.

This feast of an aggressive Christian evangelizer is a good opportunity to reflect on evangelization Zechariah style. That Jewish prophet told what happens when God takes full possession of a people. Of the "days to come," he wrote: "In those days, ten people from every nation on earth, of every language, shall take hold of every Jew, grasping his garment and saying, 'Let us go with you, for we have heard that God is with you'" (Zec. 8: 20-23).

To spread the Gospel is both easy and very hard. If you want to evangelize, first fill yourself to overflowing with the Gospel. Don't preach the Good News, *be* the Good News of justice, peace and equality for all. Don't grab other people by the lapels and try to sell them your faith. Rather fill yourself to the seams with God's love, and they will come and grab you by your lapels, saying, "I want to have what you have, since it is clear that God is with you."

"Those days to come" came two thousand years ago. Live today in prophetic time; the future full of God has arrived, you have only to live in that time.

Feast of Archangels Michael, Gabriel and Raphael. 29

St. Michael the Warrior Guardian of Heaven is to lead God's forces to victory in the final battle between good and evil. Devotion to him is the oldest among the three. St. Gabriel is the messenger of God known for his visit to a small village called Nazareth. There he gave Mary the invitation to become the mother of God's son. The angel Raphael's visits to earth are primarily recorded in Old Testament times, as this angel guided Tobiah on his quest for a bride and to find the means of healing his father Tobit and restoring the family fortune. In brief, Michael is the guardian, Gabriel the announcer and Raphael the guide.

❧❀☙

In the last years of the twentieth century angels began to be revived in art, television and motion pictures. This artistic Angelic Renaissance has rarely depicted awesome archangels but rather cute little cherubs with innocent smiling faces. The TV and movie variety have been adult humanlike angels of the helpful, guardian type. In either case, these "attractive" New Age angels have not appeared as fierce fighters of evil or bearing messages that would dynamically alter quiet lives.

Even church angels are usually refined, gentle, harp-playing kinds, whose hands are often folded in prayer. No wonder their devotion today is watered down. Perhaps the new century will see a real renaissance of angels in the style of today's festival of Saints Gabriel, Raphael and Michael.

Archangel Michael's prediction of evil's defeat in the final battle at the End of Time raises a good question. When Michael, God's commander-in-chief, has defeated evil, will the winner help the defeated enemy — as with Germany and Japan after World War II — back on its feet as a respectable member of a new society?

Note: On-line in 1997, the Vatican's new web site begun by Pope John Paul II, has three powerful computers running twenty-four hours a day and in six languages. These computers have been named Raphael, Michael and Gabriel.

✤

---

30 Good Health Day: Don't Rub Your Eye with Your Elbow.

First of all, the advice offered in the title of today's entry is impossible, so don't try it. This bit of folk wisdom is given to prevent the spread of disease, since the eyes, mouth and nose are portals for the entry of viruses into your body. The frequent washing of hands is recommended for good health but not because germs enter through the skin of your hands. Washing hands with soap removes germs which your hands might otherwise bring into contact with your eyes, mouth and nose. As Autumn, wearing a chilly wrap, comes to your door, so do fall colds.

Each age seems to give rise to a new disease or virus,

while ancient ones linger, such as *Yenta*, an especially contagious virus. *Yenta* is Yiddish for a gossipy woman who can't keep a secret and is endlessly talking. *Yentas*, however, come in both sexes. Yiddish scholars are not sure if *Yenta* was a proper name for a nonstop talker who loves to spread stories about others' problems and woes, or a version of the Italian *gentile*.

For good spiritual health, "Don't rub your eye or your *ear* with your elbow." The spread of gossip germs is highly contagious, and it's wise to take care about what enters your ear. The shortest distance between two points for a *Yenta* is from the ear to the mouth. The next time your ears are infected with the germs of gossip, wash your hands. Then take your ear finger (the little finger), and turn it twice in your right ear, repeating the action with your ring finger. As you do, pray, "Dirty gossip germs, climb aboard my fingertips, so you'll never ever be found crossing my lips." Then wash your fingertips and say, "O God, help me to never infect others with the dis-ease of gossip."

⚜

Today is also the **Feast of St. Jerome**, who performed for his fourth century world the gigantic solo feat of translating the Greek New Testament into the Latin edition called the Vulgate. He was known for a violent temper, extremely negative views on marriage and sex (having once proposed that a man who loved his wife too much was guilty of adultery) and his ascetical life as a desert hermit. Aware of his own sins, Jerome is often pictured striking his breast with a stone in an act of repentance.

⚜

Consider finding a stone that will fit full in the palm of your hand and calling it your St. Jerome, or Gerry, Stone. If during the day you forget to perform your anti-gossip ritual and you pass on one or more dark viruses, consider this night prayer: Prayerfully remember the person who was the subject of your gossip, then strike your breast three times with your Gerry Stone, begging God's pardon for the sin of gossiping.

✷

QVAESTIC·
NES

THE
MONTH
OF
OCTOBER

FAMA
IMMORTA

FRANCOFORTI AD
Mœnum.
M. D. LXXXI.

Octo is Latin for "eight," this once having been
the eighth month of the year in the Roman Calendar.
In the Gregorian Calendar, which we presently use, this is,
of course, the tenth month. Again, if we were to adopt a
new calendar for use in space, would it need to be inclusive
enough to reflect the unity and newness of those living
away from planet Earth? Would it incorporate
the Jewish Calendar, which dates from Creation
(fixed at 3761 B.C.E. [Before the Common Era]) and the
Mohammedan Calendar, used in Muslim countries (which
begins July 16, 622 C.E. [Common Era], the date of the
Hegira, the flight of the prophet Mohammed from Mecca)?
While in Old English this month was once called
Win-monath, meaning "wine month" or "vintage time,"
what might it be called in 2100 C.E.?

"It Will Never Get Off the Ground" Festival. The genius
and famous inventor, Thomas Edison, said of the airplane, "It is
apparent to me that the possibilities of the aeroplane...have
been exhausted, and that we must turn elsewhere." Even Wilbur
Wright told his brother in 1901, only two years before their famous
flight at Kitty Hawk, "Man will not be able to fly for 50 years."

1

This is the first day of a new month, a day to get projects
off and flying, bills paid and goals set. Today's pedestrian
predictions, along with similar predictions by other outstanding
inventors, should remind us to treat words like "impossible"
with great caution. Recall how we have seen that with God all
things are possible. In each of our lives are dreams and hopes
that have been filed away under "I" for *Impossible*.

As you begin October, take out that secret file and see what is in it. You will find dreams from your childhood and early youth that have yellowed with age. You may also find dream-plans marked "Impossible until I graduate or get a job" or "Impossible until after the children have grown and left home." You may also find new dream-blueprints titled, "Impossible now, but when I retire...." Postponing the impossible until the right time is akin to the old Chinese custom of binding the feet of girl infants so that when they reach adulthood they will have small feet. While culturally attractive, unfortunately it prevented most women from walking correctly.

Securing your dream-plans in your file marked "Impossible" or "Not for ten or thirty or fifty years..." prevents those realities from walking into your life today or in any tomorrow. While today's feast celebrates the dream of the airplane come true — and earlier than dreamed — it is also the Feast of Dead Dreams that were never even attempted. Pray today that the impossible realities which you dream about will lose the *im* and become *possible*.

✳

---

2 **Feast of the Guardian Angels.** Jesus spoke of God giving angels to watch over even the little ones. The religious culture of his day was crowded with spirits, angels and demons. It was believed that God gave to each blade of grass a guardian angel. People of the pre-industrial world, in all parts of the world and all cultures, firmly believed that spirits guard both persons and places. Out of that fertile spiritual imagination, we hold an image of angels given to individuals to watch over them, to assist them in times of need, and in death to escort them on their final journey to God. This feast of the 1500s speaks to what was once a common devotion. In the last decade of the twentieth century it experienced a brief — and mostly commercial — revival.

❧

A personal angelic spirit, however you imagine it, is an expression of God's presence and protection, which is ever present and lifelong. A thin film separates this world from the World of

Worlds. The belief in haunted houses is global, and confirms our deep-seated belief in the possibilities of otherworld entities, both beneficial and harmful. Charles Lindbergh spoke of being visited in his single-engine airplane while on the first solo non-stop flight across the Atlantic in 1927. Exhausted and lost in the last hours of his long flight, he reported that the cabin of his small plane was crowded with invisible entities who encouraged him not to give up and guided him onward.

The Great Future which arrives after death will hold a revelation for each of us. Consider today what surprises or confirmations that Future Day may hold for you.

3

Birthday of *Korrespondenz Karte*, Austria, 1869. The blank postcard was a novel innovation in correspondence; it allowed sending a message without an envelope and at a cheaper rate. In October of 1869 the first correspondence card appeared in Austria and quickly spread to other European countries, crossing the ocean to the U.S. in 1873. There this Austrian immigrant was adopted by many businesses for advertising purposes. Pictures on postcards were introduced in 1880 A.D. or 8 B.B.C. (Before the Brownie Camera – see the entry for September 4), and they became very popular. Prior to the small portable personal camera of George Eastman, people were fascinated by these inexpensive professional picture postcards. They were collected, exchanged and treasured. One famous stage actress bragged that she owned 73,445 picture postcards! Their world of great fame and profit ended before World War I, however, partly because the Brownie camera let people take their own souvenir vacation photos and partly because of the rise of the Hallmark company's folded greeting message cards. In our Super Image Age, in which one sees billions of color picture-images daily, pictures on cards have been retired to drug stores and souvenir shops.

Daily, whether with dramatic suddenness or in slow succession, the End of the World is coming to something. While some of us still consider picture postcards to be thoughtful remembrances, sending them home when we're on vacation as a way of saying "thinking of you," their day of prominence has come and gone. Collecting picture postcards is thought of as a quaint hobby today when television, computers, magazines and newspapers flood us with a deluge of images. Recently, a reviewer of an art show of small Medieval religious oil paintings regretted how easily the importance of these pieces could be missed. He observed how their impact upon those who first saw them was overwhelming, but that it is lost on today's average American, who sees more images in one day than citizens of the thirteenth century saw in their entire lifetimes. Likewise, it has been estimated that there is more information contained in an average weekday *New York Times* than average eighteenth century citizens would encounter throughout their lives.

Wise are those who know how to diet from both information and images. In this age of sensory overstimulation, be careful not to dull your senses or glut your mind lest your soul be smothered. Read smaller amounts, and think much upon what you read. See less, and be wide-eyed more often.

✺

4 **Feast of St. Francis of Assisi.** The little poor man of Assisi was a saint who has captured the world's imagination by a simple act: He took the Gospel literally. He lived from the 1180s to 1226, yet his spirit continues into the twenty-first century to inspire painters and poets, friends and followers, and even those of other religions. Francis is the patron of one-man revolutions and renewals, a model for personal conversions. He is the patron saint of environmentalists, having been a trail-blazer in "earth literacy," the art of knowing the language of creation. He has given a spiritual dimension to the urgent work of protecting the environment through his awareness of the Holy Family intimacy that connects humans with all creatures as brothers and sisters. He is the patron of those seeking to live in simplicity and those who seek a passionate, mystical, love relationship with God and the Risen Jesus.

His life was short but ripe with intensity. Two years before his death in 1226, seriously ill and half blind, Francis was visited not by a gentle, sweet guardian angel but a fiery seraph. This six-winged guard of heaven's throne pierced his hands and feet with the painful wounds of Jesus, the stigmata.

❧❀☙

In this month of angels, today could also be called Seraph Angel Day. These angels are the fierce, flaming serpentine agents of God who appeared in the First Testament at the call of Isaiah. One of these winged pinwheels of fire purified Isaiah's lips by burning them with a red-hot coal. Others trumpeted a triple call of "Holy," announcing a time of adoration of God. Seraphs are angels of adoration and executors of God's judgments. As in their appearance to Francis, who wanted to be in total communion with his beloved Jesus, they are agents of divine visitation, angelic replies to prayers of passion.

Moral of the day: Pray only for what you can bear to receive in your life, and in your body.

✡

Soap and Spic & Span Day. The term "spic and span" comes from a sixteenth century Dutch sailors' expression, *Spiksplinternieuw*, for every spike and splinter of wood on a new ship. The Dutch was Anglicized to "spick and spannew," and meant brand new and spotlessly clean. Soap, the agent of such cleanliness, was the invention of those early sailing merchants of 600 B.C., the Phoenicians, who made it from goat fat and ash. They marketed their new creation to the Greeks, Romans and others, and sold it to the Gauls as a laxative! Soap was so popular by the eleventh century in Venice that a tax was placed on it, giving rise to the bootleg business of selling soap in the dark of night under the many bridges of Venice.

A bar of soap is good for more than keeping things spic and span: Hang bars of soap around crops to deter hungry deer; make zippers glide with ease by rubbing soap on the metal teeth; soap nails and screws for easy entrance into wood; use it on furniture drawers and on windows to make them slide easier.

❧❀☙

Yes, the practical life and the spiritual life are one, and the wise draw no distinction between them. While purity has long held a high place among Christians, its exaggerated position can make it lopsided in relation to the other virtues. "Cleanliness is next to godliness" is often quoted with the same force as if it had been spoken by Jesus, when actually they are the words of John Wesley. They have become canon law for middle-class Western Christians, who sometimes consider those who are not spic and span, usually the poor, to be next to the devil.

Jesus said, "Blest are the pure of heart, for they shall see God." The early body-hating, sex-denying church leapfrogged those words into making blessed those who were "pure" of sexual activity. Like Wesley's soapy gauge of godliness, the church's sexless gauge for godliness or holiness is far from how Jesus measured what is important to God. *Loving others*, regardless of whether their clothes are dirty and they've slept under a bridge without a bath for four weeks, is the true gauge of who is godly.

Consider placing a bar of soap in your prayer corner, or on top of your Bible, today to remind you to seek a "spic and span" heart. Such a heart, by frequent washing and cleansing, would be free of the daily accumulation of the grime of greed and gossip, the easily acquired dirt of discrimination and divisiveness.

✸

6 Celebration of the First Millennium, 1000 A.D.

Today's festival of the year 1000 continues the entry of September 15, on the celebration of the First Millennium. While there was widespread fear of the End of the World and the arrival of the Last Judgment, this was also a year marked by the new and inventive.

In the Far East, for example, the Indian mathematician Sridhara recognized the importance of a critical number that needed to be added to existing numbers: the zero. In the Near East, the spiritual center of Judaism moved from Mesopotamia to Spain and found a fresh and new revival. The heroic epic poem *Beowulf* was written not in the customary Latin but in Old English. In Italy at this time of crossing there was an artistic revival of fresco painting and mosaics. In the early years of the First Millennium, Guido d'Arezzo, a Benedictine monk created novel musical innovations to make singing and playing music much easier (see the October 16 entry, **Gratitude to Guido Day**).

⁂

The frequency of warnings about the End of the World and the Last Judgment, while commonplace for decades on either side of the year 2000, will be less frequent than in the crossing of the First Millennium. The *Last* Judgment implies that there may be more than a single trial occurring at the moment of death, but perhaps a second, third or even a millionth judgment — before or after death. Daily our thoughts are on trial, our speech is examined and our deeds that flow from thoughts and words stand before the judge. Not just every thousand years — every day is a judgment day, a day in which God does not condemn us but rather in which we condemn ourselves by our actions or lack thereof. Yet this is not a reason for gloom, guilt or fear; it is, instead, cause for a daily auditing of one's life, an opportunity for accountability.

As you can pay a parking ticket fine by mail without having to go to court, be inventive in making restitution without waiting for the Final Trial. When aware of some failing, as soon as possible make restitution to anyone offended, to those robbed of joy or peace of mind or their good name or in any way injured by you. To daily attend to these matters in inventive and creative ways makes the Final Judgment nothing over which to be apprehensive or fearful.

✦

End of the World Day: Influenza Epidemic, 1918.

7

Could not the sudden and unexplained deaths of 400 to 500 Americans, baffling doctors, be called an ominous sign of the End of the World? That many died during September and October in 1918, causing the death rate in the major eastern American cities to jump over 700%. Panic spread like wildfire as newspapers were filled with outlandish explanations for this mysterious killer disease that was racing across the States.

The disease was transported to the U.S. on troop ships bringing American servicemen home from Europe after World War I. Altogether, in the two-year period from 1918 to 1919 as many as 20,000,000 died from it in Europe and America. This highly infectious disease is caused by a virus transmitted by secretions from the nose and mouth. Its common name is the *flu*, and it disappeared by the end of 1919, only to reappear in 1957 as a new virus named the *Asiatic Flu*.

This disaster disease was called *influenza*, an old name for plagues and pestilences, because these diseases were supposedly caused by the evil "influence" of the stars.

⁕⁕⁕

The end of October is spook season. Increasingly, as we see at Christmas time, homes are decorated, but now they're adorned with witches, evil spirits, ghosts, jack-o-lanterns and symbols of the autumntide. Stores and schools likewise are arrayed with these playfully fearful images and autumn symbols. Mindful of today's entry about the flu, why not decorate your house or school with stars!

If you get the flu this winter season, instead of blaming some invisible virus, maybe you should blame your unlucky star. The ancients so connected their calamities with the stars that they named them disasters: *dis*, meaning bad or dark, and *astro*, meaning star.

> Twinkle, twinkle, little star,
> don't star-dust me from afar
> with catastrophes that make life hard,
> with calamities in my back yard.

The next time some disaster drops into your life, point up to the sky and tell your friends that not you but the stars are to blame. Mindful that into every life some star-rain must fall, may the ✷ Star-Date below, and those throughout this Almanac, record far more good dates to remember than bad.

✷

Sports Worship Day. From the sport pages of newspapers to game by game saturation television coverage, along with sweat shirts, caps and other fan attire, a visitor from outer space would likely think that the religion of Americans is Sports. It is the religion of winners only, promoting the virtues of competition rather than communion, and whose attendance at worship is vast — or so it would seem. Interestingly, *The American Enterprise* magazine for November-December of 1995 stated that "Total attendance at United States religious services was 5.6 million in 1993 — 54 times the total admissions for all professional baseball, football and basketball games that same year."

8

⚜

While few people gather around the office water cooler to talk about what happened at their Sunday worship, the absence of discussion apparently is not from a lack of attendance. Here are a few October questions to ponder: Why do sports generate more enthusiasm (remember, enthusiasm literally means "inspired or possessed by a god") among us than does our religion? Do you enjoy your exercise of religion as much you do being entertained by sports? If some are so openly enthusiastic about their favorite sport's team as to wear sweatsuits, T-shirts, jackets and caps in the team's colors and emblems, never missing a game, are they fans or fanatics? If worshippers dressed in clothing and caps with the color and emblems of their religion and arrived hours before worship to have a tailgate party in the church parking lot for extra fellowship and visiting about God, would you call them religious fans or fanatics?

✠

Feast of St. Dennis of Paris, Patron of Long Journeys and Liberation from Fear, Frenzy and Headaches.

9

Blessed Dennis, pray for us who seem to be in perpetual frenzy, a state of wild excitement accompanied by manic activity, summed up in three brief words: busy-busy-busy. Today's saint was beheaded in the early centuries in the infamous Montmartre district of Paris. Legend said he walked — head in hand for six miles to the present site of the great Paris Cathedral that now bears his name. When he was asked about the most difficult part of this journey, his chopped-off head is said to have replied, "The first step was the difficult one."

❧❀❧

Today, if you have a headache, a heartache or a soulache, consider the wisdom of St. Dennis' remark whenever you seek a cure: The first step is always the most difficult. Whatever your first step, whether it be a step toward sobriety, a step away from being an alcoholic, a drugaholic or a workaholic — or a step toward counseling, seeking professional help with your marriage, life or vocation — take that step today with the firm confidence that the second and third steps will be much easier.

Fear beheads and behearts us, making us delay dealing with our problems. Fear beheads us and so we sit with head in hands and lament. The fear of _____ (fill in your own name for this evil warden who imprisons you) prevents us from taking that significant and sacred first step. The step, be it for conversion or recovery, is sacred since God is the Lord of Liberty. In ancient times it was said that if you knew the name of the dragon that held you bound you could escape. If you filled in the above blank, perhaps now you can take St. Dennis' Step, not a journey to some cathedral in Paris but the road to liberation.

✴

---

10 **National Alien Day.** This festival will not be one in which everyone will want to form a parade or hold a fiesta. Aliens are needed to do the hard work that nationals will not do; at the same time they are resented because they do not look like, act like or talk like nationals.

In 1995, worldwide, more than 16,000,000 men, women and children were classified as refugees, with 3,000,000 classified as aliens, all having crossed some country's border in pursuit of a safe haven. Displaced within their own countries were some 30,000,000, while another 30,000,000 had left their homelands to become migrant workers. War, revolution, civil and ethnic unrest, economic crisis and poverty had forced these many millions at the end of the twentieth century to become a "problem."

All these refugees, immigrants and aliens in the global millennium age are akin to the original refugees of America, the Native Americans. They were forced to become aliens in their own land, being pushed out of their native regions by the expansion of White immigrant Americans. The contemporary global attitude toward aliens and refugees is inherently American: to paraphrase an old U.S. saying, "The only good alien is a dead alien." In the United States, the Melting Pot has become the Boiling Pot the Romans once used to deal with "those damn Christians." Yet the Bible calls believers to remove hostility towards strangers who are strange looking and talking, and to practice tolerance and acceptance of aliens.

Each year at this harvest time of the year, the Israelites were to bring the finest fruits of their harvest to the Temple in Jerusalem and declare, "My parents were wandering Arameans who went down to Egypt with a small household and lived there as aliens" (Dt. 26: 5). In this season of autumn gratitude building to the festival of Thanksgiving, not only Jews but Christians, Muslims and all religious people should, as a family, pray that ancient Jewish prayer.

⚜

Whatever your personal feelings about foreigners, displaced persons and legal or illegal aliens, pray that sacred sentence from the Bible and be grateful. Like Abraham and Sarah, Isaac and Rebekah, your personal ancestors — whether in Colonial days or as recently as your great-grandparents — came to this land fleeing poverty, famine and hardship. Pray with all your passion that you will not promote a Homefront Holocaust of hate and rejection of "those" strange people who do not belong here. To not only respect but care for the needs of the aliens among us is a command God has written in bold print throughout the Bible. More weighty than sexual morality is the social morality God requires that practices love toward outsiders.

With great wisdom did the Jews place this prayer of alien awareness in their temple gratitude festival. True gratitude on any day requires remembering how once your ancestors were poor aliens who were hated and despised, outsiders and refugees from poverty and famine and religious oppression.

> Sts. Abraham and Sara, patron saints of aliens,
>   pray for us who so quickly forget our family history.
> Pray for us forgetters, who all too easily practice
>   the rejection and oppression of foreigners,
>   of those among us who are aliens.

✴

---

11 Trip to the Moon Day, or Perpetual Reinvention Feast.

In the jubilation after the Apollo 11 moon landing on July 20, 1969, one of America's great airlines announced it was taking reservations for the first commercial flight to the moon. The year 2000 was set for the first flight and among those who immediately reserved a seat was Ronald Reagan. The airline was the then-great Pam Am, which no longer is in existence!

Raytheon's Amana Division and Litton Industries were the great leaders in home microwave ovens. Believing their microwave oven was the oven of the future, they continued to build larger, more expensive and fancier ones, despite trade reports that people found them of only limited use. The future arrived, and foreign producers of small inexpensive microwave ovens took over the $3 billion market in the United States. Raytheon's Amana, while unlike Pam Am is still an existing business, has found its share in the microwave market reduced to a mere twelve percent.

While dreaming and inventive planning for your future is important, so is the work of daily reinventing. Reaching the future you envision requires perpetual change and adjustment to the realities of the present.

※⊕⊱

Have you made a reservation for a seat in your future? Perhaps it's a plan for retirement or some long-unfulfilled dream of unfolding an unused talent with a company or institution that may not exist in the future? Blueprints for tomorrow must be made with pencil that can be easily erased and redrawn.

By-product reflection: Do large institutions of business,

government and church, like Raytheon's Amana Division, refuse to listen to and believe field reports about their performance or products? If you belong to or depend upon such an institution, dwell a few moments on the possible implications of your institution's anti-extinction behavior.

✳

National Translation of Foreign Language Day. The computer has come to save us from the curse of the Tower of Babel. For seeking to make a name for themselves and build a cloudscraper tower, God turned humanity's one tongue into hundreds of different tongues. Today, computers at the click of a key can translate texts into almost any language you desire. Yet, perhaps the curse of Babel is still with us, for when "out of sight, out of mind" is translated into Russian by a computer and then back into English it becomes "invisible lunatic." **12**

᠉᠉

Today is also **Columbus Day**, which remembers the landing of Christopher Columbus in 1492 on the Bahamian island of Guanahani, which he renamed *El Salvador*, the Savior. Popular belief cites this as the discovery of America. However, 400 years before 1492, Pope Paschal II had named Eric Gnupsson as the first bishop of America and appointed him to the diocese of Greenland and Vinland (Newfoundland). Vikings had established a colony on treeless Greenland in 982 A.D., and the colonists routinely obtained their wood going by sea to North America. The colony died out through a combination of the Black Death of the late 1300s, the environmental cooling of the climate and raiding attacks by Native Eskimo Peoples.

᠉᠉

The next time someone quotes you the words of Jesus in English, which were originally spoken in Aramaic, remember what happened in the translation of "out of sight, out of mind." You can reply to them or to yourself, "Yes, or something like that."

Also reflect, today, on how "discovery" can easily be mistranslated. So, if someone praises Columbus for discovering

America, you can reply, "Yes, or you could say that Columbus was a Latter-Day Discoverer." This Almanac won't expand this Discover America Day with facts supporting the ancient Chinese discovery of North America. Suffice it to say that Columbus needs to share credit for "discovering" what was already well-known. (For a further reflection on the value of rediscovery, see the entry for November 26, **The Invention of the Needle.**)

✴

---

13 Flying Saucers with Aliens from Outer Space Day.

Since mid-to-late October is costume season, it is the perfect time for refugees, visitors and aliens from outer space to land and move among us. On this old feast of the saintly King Edward I of England (the patron saint of the author of this Almanac), we celebrate a day to honor UFOs and cosmic aliens. For hundreds of years people had reported seeing strange objects in the sky, but beginning in the 1940s the number of these sightings greatly increased. World War II fighter pilots called these strange moving lights seen in the night sky *foo fighters*.

The U.S. businessman Kenneth Arnold, flying in his own plane in June of 1947, reported seeing several saucer-shaped flying objects near Mount Rainier in Washington. His report to the press caused a tidal wave of reported sightings of flying saucers, referred to as Unidentified Flying Objects, UFOs. During some periods since then, the U.S. Air Force has received reports of UFO sightings on the average of one a day. Many of these sightings have been made by reliable and intelligent people who have rejected explanations that the objects might have been weather balloons, bright meteors, earth-made satellites or mirages caused by atmospheric conditions.

In 1997, the spectacular tail of the Hale-Bopp comet was believed by California's Heaven's Gate cult to be hiding a space-ship come to take the cult's members to a better life. Bags packed, they took their own lives as an act of escape to the Hale-Bopp UFO.

꙳ꙮꙭꙮ꙳

The existence of UFOs or alien visitors from space have

never been proven (to the public's knowledge), but this on its own should not be the basis for disbelief. Religion and daily life contain many things that have not yet been proved scientifically. What has been proven beyond any doubt is that Hollywood bank accounts have increased by billions of dollars from the making of movies about aliens from space rather than those from across the border. Aliens and flying craft from outer space are the raw materials of science fiction novels, TV programs and cult beliefs. Aliens are variously depicted both as enemies or as friends, as hostile or as benevolent, as humanlike or as unearthly in appearance.

Reflection: In the eyes of those he encountered, was Columbus an alien from another world as distant as another planet is to our mind today? Are there aspects of you that are as alien to your world, and perhaps as difficult for your family or neighbors to embrace, as an alien from outer space? Do you fear your own UFOs, those Unidentified Fear Obsessions that fly in and out of your thoughts?

✴

The Day President Theodore Roosevelt Is Shot in the Chest — but Delivers His Speech Anyway, 1912. 14

On this day New Yorker John Schrank shot President Roosevelt from a distance of only six feet. This attempted assassination occurred in a hotel in Milwaukee during Roosevelt's election campaign tour. The bullet first struck the bulky manuscript rolled up in the President's pocket and then entered his chest. Despite his wound, before allowing his bodyguards to take him to the hospital, Teddy Roosevelt insisted on delivering his speech.

꙳꙳꙳꙳꙳

"Bully" for those who put duty first in their lives. While today you may not be shot, as was Roosevelt, you may have other valid excuses that allow you to place your personal needs before your duties. If you are so tempted, remember the Rough Rider Teddy Roosevelt and say to yourself, "I'll attend to that when I've done my duty." Pray for the wisdom to know when to cancel and when to continue with what you've agreed to do.

Recalling John Schrank's deed on this day, make as part of your morning prayer the pledge not to assassinate anyone by attacking that person's reputation and good name. Also, be aware that long and bulky speeches and sermons make temporary bulletproof vests, even if they kill off their listeners.

✴

15 Feast of Electric Lights and Other Shocking Miracles.

On this day in 1878 the first electric light company was formed, The Edison Electric Light Company, which was located at 65 Fifth Avenue in New York City. In 1891 the White House was wired for the new invention of electric lights. At first President Benjamin Harrison and his wife were afraid of getting electric shocks from the light switches. At night, the lights in the downstairs parlors and halls had to be turned on at dusk by a servant. When the servant returned to work each morning, he found the electric lights still on.

~~~✦~~~

Flick a switch and you become like God, who simply said, "Let there be light, and there was light." God actually didn't have to verbalize the need for light but just thought it and "there was light." Just as President and Mrs. Harrison feared to touch their light switches, you won't have to touch yours — but not because you're afraid. As in the White House, a twenty-first century servant will perform that task for you. A small, inexpensive computer in your home can monitor your electrical needs, turning lighting on and off automatically whenever you enter or leave a room. You will not even have to create the thought, "Let there be light."

While miracles once possible only for God are happening each day, have you personally become more Godlike? With each new miracle of technology that becomes part of your life, are you also miraculously becoming as loving and compassionate toward all, as passionate about justice, as God is?

✴

Praising an Unsung Monk: Gratitude to Guido Day. **16**

The early years of the First Millennium saw the rise of wonders that are commonplace today. One such wonder is found on a page of music. Guido of Arezzo, born in the 990s, became a monk in the Benedictine monastery of Pomposa, where he invented a new method of education. By his own account, a pupil might learn in five months what formerly would have taken ten years to acquire. Although a musical genius, envy and jealousy drove him from that monastery. He went to Arezzo and from there seems to have been a resident at several monasteries, but still remaining ever creative. He revolutionized music, creating the lines of the staff and the intervals between them. Previously, musical notes had "floated" on white space. He introduced the names of the first six notes, still in use in Italy and France, and he is credited with the invention of the F clef.

＊＊＊

Perhaps in the first decades of the Third Millennium the world will be gifted with a teacher who can help students learn in five months what once took a college curriculum of four years. A thousand years ago, Guido of Arezzo had an educational inspiration greater than just giving musical notes lines on which to rest; he enabled a quantum leap in creating, playing and singing music. In light of his innovation we might ask if there is too much "empty" space in educational models that educators might reline in fresh ways to achieve better results.

Perhaps a revolution in education is waiting for the right moment to strike at the heart of learning, from grade school to graduate school. Guido of Arezzo proposed that he could teach ten years worth in five months. No wonder his brother monk-teachers sent him off packing to another monastery!

✷

Take Out the Trash or Junk Day. **17**

Peter Drucker said, "Nothing is less productive than to make more efficient what should not be done at all." Take a few minutes today to examine if you should trash some activity, program or behavior you've been thinking about doing more efficiently. This act of liberation is easier said than done, however, since we usually refuse to consider what we are presently doing to be junk or trash.

At first thought, junk or trash usually gives rise to negative rather than just neutral feelings. *Trash* means something worthless or to be discarded. *Junk* began as a sailor's term for old, worn-out pieces of rope and has a similar implication of being useless.

⚜

Organizations of all stripes are known for renewals of what might better be thrown overboard. Committees labor intensely to freshen up worn-out procedures, redecorate the obsolete and remodel what "should not be done at all." If you have in the past or presently serve on such a board or committee, use today to examine the use of your time.

On the water or in life, sailing with junk rope can be dangerous; when it snaps, be sure and stand clear! Failing to throw out the junk of frayed methods and worn-out procedures, however holy and ancient, can likewise be personally dangerous. So, sailing across the equator of the millennium into the decades across it, check your riggings and don't hesitate to take out the junk or trash.

⚜

Today is also the **Feast of St. Ignatius of Antioch**, who for the glory of God was eaten alive by lions about 107 A.D. He is known for saying, "The glory of God is a person fully alive." Considering what churches often claim gives glory to God, instead of giving money to support dubious projects, let the saint who was fed to lions inspire your investment in being fully alive.

✠

---

18 National Committee Day.

National Committee Day. Nothing is impossible in life — until it is sent to a committee! As the world experiments with democracy, with nations being governed and directed by public consent, churches likewise experiment. Committees are committed to a communion of opinions with decisions reached by voting and common consent. The smaller the organization, the better this system works. But how often does it really work? While teamwork and communal leadership can be products of a good committee, and while committees today abound in every institution, have you ever seen a statue to a committee? In any public park, in front of any government building or in any church, have you ever seen a group statue dedicated to a committee?

Of course, the absence of a statue to a committee isn't a sign that they do not contribute to society. Often statues are erected to unknown heroes, and so perhaps the twenty-first century will see a monument dedicated to those who have served heroically on various committees. There is hope that the new millennium may see truly creative committees. In the fields of science and technology new discoveries are increasingly made by teams rather than individuals. There are also collaborative teams of what Walt Disney called "imagineers," committees that are given the freedom to image and create something new and innovative. Many are the aging and stuffy institutions that could benefit from such a creative committee of imagineers.

There are many other kinds of committees, and the twenty-first century will surely find more rather than fewer forms. Much of the fate of our future may be in the hands of various committees. And so, it may be worth your time to do the valuable groundwork of discovering ways to make committees more creative and effective. If you are called to serve, however, consider carefully matching your gifts to the work of a committee. Before agreeing to be part of the team, it's wise to ask — and be clear — about its purpose, to help insure that its work can be fruitful.

Membership on a committee is often a heroic call to service beyond the call of duty. Statues, monuments or other appreciative signs of honor are very fitting, especially until that day in the new millennium when collaboration, consensus and communion become creative realities. Till then, rather than purple hearts, perhaps purple seats could be given to those who are forced to sit for hours at meetings that produce very little for the large amount of time and energy invested.

❧⳩⳩❧

As we celebrate National Committee Day, it's wise to be aware of the inherent limitations of committees. Consider, for example, whether a committee could write even one play of Shakespeare. Today is the traditional **Feast of St. Luke**, writer of one of the four Gospels. Consider what the Gospels would have been like if they had been written and edited by a committee of disciples and apostles. What would the life of any great hero, saint, inventor or revolutionary be like if it had been prenatally designed by the consensus of a committee? For a group to move by mutual consensus while still trying to follow the lead of a visionary can be as difficult a balancing act as walking a tightrope across the Grand Canyon. If you're seeking to create the *impossible,* make sure that before you take a proposal to a committee you follow Jesus' advice regarding prayer and "Go into your room, close the door and create in secret."

If you've ever served on a committee, you know they often have a dirty little secret. For committees can be clinics where abortions are quickly performed when something new, radical or different is proposed. Another deadly secret of some committees is that they like to kill an idea by discussing it to death.

So, if you are on a committee when something new and different is proposed for discussion, recall this rule of thumb: However outrageous the idea, like a bottle of good red wine, leave it untouched and breathing for at least five to ten minutes before making any comments.

---

19 **Remember Jenkins' Ear Day.** Today in 1739 the War of Jenkins' Ear began when England declared hostilities against Spain. Jenkins was the captain of a British ship who claimed that Spanish coast guards had cut off his ear in a raid on his ship which they suspected of smuggling. He displayed the ear before the House of Commons, and news of it so inflamed public opinion that the prime minister was forced to declare war.

This war between two countries that lasted from 1739 to 1742 was over the loss of one sailor's ear? Don't scoff or laugh, however, for a Jenkins' Ear War can erupt in your life today. In countless homes and offices minor wars will break out this day over issues as silly as Jenkins' ear. When next you are so "inflamed" as to declare a personal or domestic war over some minor injustice or personal insult, tug at your right ear and pray, "War, war, go away, and don't come back another day."

This reflection needs no further expansion, being so common to the experience of all of us. What does need enlarging is how to prevent not Jenkins' Ear War I or II, but JE War MCMXCIX, 1,999, if not JE War MMI, 2001 or MMXIV, 2014. The cure for the most frequent cause of war in history is humor and the humility to frame the offense within the big picture.

20

Grit and Patience Day. Today we honor SSt. Theodor Seuss Geisel, whose first children's book was rejected by twenty-three different publishers (see again the March 2 entry). Since publishers usually make decisions in concert with editors and in-house experts, Dr. Seuss was often a victim of the frequent sin of such committees: a lack of imagination (see again the entry for October 18). Dr. Seuss had grit (determination hard as flint stone) and patience, however, and did not accept the handwriting on the wall – actually, twenty-three different walls. He held firmly to his belief in his children's book and went on to become a great success, adding joy and fantasy to the lives of millions. So there, publishing experts, chew on that true story! Not only will you find this tale of fidelity to one's creativity "full of grit" as you chew, you will find your publishing houses poorer. Take heed, all so-called *experts*; remember the family history of your name. "Expert" comes from *expertus*, the Latin past participle of *experiri*, meaning "to try." So, experts always need "to try" to be open to the new, the untested and even the "impossible."

If today your ideas are not greeted with applause, remember Dr. Seuss: Be patient and don't give up. Pray for the gritty determination to go from door to door knocking. Knock, knock, knock, and one day it will be opened to you. Grit and patience is required not only when presenting the new and different but also in trying to keep the old and familiar vibrant. Love relationships, parenting and other such creative ventures require great measures of grit and patience as well as love.

✳

21 Fall Holy Spirit Feast of Imagination — H.C. Booth Day.

While physical exercise is extremely popular today, with a wide variety of clubs and programs offering a communal experience of exercise, have you remembered to jog your imagination too? In 1901 H.C. Booth was sitting in a rocking chair on his front porch at sunset watching the dust blow. As he observed the wind blowing clouds of dust down the road, he opened the eyes of his soul and said aloud, "What if we could reverse the wind? Then, instead of blowing the dust, we could pull up the dust." Later that year, H.C. Booth invented the vacuum cleaner.

❧❀☙

Today, if you feel the wind is blowing dust in your eyes and making your life unpleasant, consider reversing the wind so that it works for you. God's Wind, the Holy Spirit, is daily at your disposal; you only have to ask for assistance. If the Holy Wind were to be reversed, what would you like to see it suck up out of the church? Today could be called the feast of God's Holy Vacuum Cleaner, an occasion to reflect on the need for frequent housecleaning in all churches, mosques and synagogues.

In your personal spiritual life (which as we know is not separate from your practical life) and its exercises today, consider praying not so much for the Spirit to *descend* with something but to *ascend*. While eager for all the descending gifts of the Spirit, what needs to be cleaned *up* in your life today by the Holy Vacuum Cleaner?

✳

22 End of the World Day: Assyria, 2800 B.C.

Recently a clay tablet from ancient Assyria was unearthed. Written on the 4,800 year-old tablet was the following, "Our earth is degenerate in these latter days. There are signs that the world is speedily coming to an end. Bribery and corruption are common...."

Also, on this day in 1844, it was predicted that the world would end not for the Assyrians but for the Millerites. William Miller, an enthusiastic religious preacher, citing signs from the Bible, predicted that the world would end on April 3, 1843. Thousands gathered on hilltops and in cemeteries and waited. The sun rose beautifully on April 4 in 1843 and has every day since. Rereading his Bible, Miller then named today's date, October 22, in 1844, as the End for planet Earth. Again his followers prepared to depart, as did Noah before the end of his world, but again they had to return to their daily lives as the world refused to end. Cynics stated that on both of these apocalyptic dates, William Miller's pantry and woodshed were fully stocked. (You may wish to read ahead, or back, to the entry for January 4 for more recent reports of the End.)

⚜

The moral of Miller's prediction: Check the clothes closets, pantries and, most of all, the bank accounts of those predicting the End of the World. It's not the followers, but the prophets who should lead the way by disposing of all their belongings and money as a naked statement of their faith.

Also, if the world has been coming to a disastrous end for over 4,000 years, consider being a prophet of the End Times and predicting the End of the World in the year 8,002! Belief in the dogma that planet Earth is not about to be destroyed is an act of faith and hope — and an act of courage and determination to make God's dream grow. What Jesus began two thousand years ago is just a sapling tree that has only taken root; the future holds either a sunrise or a demise of his divine vision. Take care of the Tree of Life in your yard and it will grow into a great tree spanning the world in some far distant millennium.

✳

Day the Swallows Depart from San Juan Capistrano. 23

Today is the legendary day for the swallows' yearly departure from the monastery of San Juan Capistrano in California. This annual migration of swallows for the winter is among the more famous and accurate signs of the approach of winter. Consider keeping a record in this Almanac of the dates on which you observe the departure or arrival of birds at your home. Such log-like entries can be inserted in the ✣ Star-Date spaces.

While the migrations of various birds from your yard may not have the clockwork regularity of San Juan's swallows, they will assist you in keeping your body-and-soul clocks attuned to nature. Retaining the fullness of our humanity requires keeping in tune with creation, for Nature is intimately united with human nature.

If you live in an apartment or in the middle of a city, you can mark the changing of the seasons by the departure of the *unwinged* snowbirds for the South. While this annual migration of senior citizens may not fall exactly on this feast day, it is one of our society's signals that cold weather is in the forecast.

※◑◐◐⁂

This day in 1456 marked the death of the Franciscan priest for whom the famous mission in southern California is named. He achieved holiness while living on both sides of a century: 1386 to 1456 A.D. This century crossing was a time when one-third of Europe's population, along with forty percent of the clergy, were killed by the Black Death. It was also a time when three different men claimed to be the legitimate pope, and so it was an era of enormous religious confusion and division. War between France and England and the constant conflict between Italy's city-states added to the disaster of these times. John of Capistrano himself led the army of the Crusades against the Turks and so could be called the patron saint of those unwilling to sit around and worry about the world. While his choice of *warfare* as the means to confront the Islamic enemy can be questioned in light of the message of Jesus, his zealous enthusiasm and willingness to die in the process cannot. John of Capistrano was not a stay-at-home romantic; he embraced the likelihood of death by the plague, which was even more epidemic on the battlefield.

Today's patron, like many other saints of this period, had some less than admirable qualities. We don't need to dwell on his preaching that the End of the World was at hand or his service in the Inquisition, where he exercised zealous vigor in dealing with Jews and Protestant heretics. Also, we will overlook this saint's leading an army that slaughtered 120,000 Muslim infidels to save Belgrade from Islam.

Moral of the day: Saints of yesteryear and today do not have to be as pure as Ivory soap to be proclaimed holy. In saints and political or religious leaders, we should be compassionate in the face of seeming compromises in holiness.

24

Haunted House on Every Corner Day. As the celebration of Halloween approaches, haunted houses are popular as "fun houses." A truly haunted house, however, is not fun. The house of humanity is filled with ghosts that do more than merely frighten us. Ghosts of Injustices Past continue to condition how we create present realities. These specters inspire new and sometimes more severe obstacles to justice and equality.

Other Ghosts of Injustices Past demand the justice they were denied. Haunted during their lives by unjust attitudes, female Greek ghosts cry out, "In ancient Greece the age of a woman was counted not from the time of her birth but only from the date of her marriage. We were branded as nonbeings until we were married to a man." The ghosts of ancient European women likewise moan and weep, "While birthdays of pharaohs, kings and emperors were recorded from ancient times and most men's birthdays were kept from the fourth century on, it was not until the fourteenth century that those of women were celebrated." Ghosts of women dressed in the fashions of the early 1900s roar out, "Since the beginning of the American Republic in 1776, we women have been treated as incapable of making political decisions and forbidden to vote. It was not until we marched in the streets and demanded our rights that we were given the vote in 1920 through the Nineteenth Amendment." Then all the ghosts chime in, "An amendment! Our rights have to be *tacked on*? Amended to the rights and privileges of men?"

Two to three thousand years ago the Babylonians annually auctioned off to the highest bidder all girls of marriageable age. Part of the money was used to provide dowries for ugly girls to obtain husbands, since no one would bid on them. The Babylonians considered this to be a wise and practical custom.

Ancient attitudes about women still haunt us in this age: attitudes about women as property which can be purchased, as being of no value until they are married, as intellectually incapable of choosing their elected officials by the vote, as lacking the abilities to enter professions and work usually done by men. These false attitudes about women inhabit the heads of many in the Western world, and in some parts of the world they appear not as pale ghosts but as frighteningly alive and active forms of discrimination and oppression.

A true life parable: Charlie Parkhurst was a stagecoach driver in the days of the California Gold Rush who took passengers and gold shipments across dangerous roads. Charlie shot dead two highwaymen who tried to rob his stage; he smoked cigars, chewed tobacco, drank and played cards with a passion. He retired and went into the cattle business, running a successful ranch in Santa Cruz, California. On December 31 (notice a commemoration in this Almanac on that date) in 1879, neighbors found Charlie dead at home. When they were preparing the body for burial, they discovered that Charlie Parkhurst was a woman!

---

25 **"Don't Beat the Clock, Beat the Boss" Day.** The Matsushita Electric Company in Japan created what is called a Worker Control Room. This room is reported to be one of the reasons for the remarkable success of the Matsushita Company, which has grown an average of thirty percent each year over a twenty-five year period. Inside the Worker Control Room are bamboo sticks and full-sized dummies who resemble the factory foremen and bosses. Before leaving the factory at the end of the day, those workers who wish can enter the WCR and pound away on their bosses. This release of pent-up grievances and tensions before going home to their families, especially on Friday

nights, is credited with providing the employees with peaceful, relaxed free time, and thus more productive work time.

※◎※

While Christians, by Jesus' implicit word, are called to live lives of nonviolence and peaceful acceptance of conflict, this requires a rather elevated state of evolution — if the nonviolence is sincere and the anger not suppressed. If you feel you are still evolving as a true follower of Jesus the Nonviolent One and have not reached the stage of being filled with peace, why not have your own private WCR? You already have in your home a WC, or water closet, as the English call the bathroom. Even a closet can serve as a Worker Control Room if you install in it a dummy or dummies in the image of your boss, spouse, pastor, religious leader or whomever has the power to make your life difficult. You might also include an old baseball bat or broomstick.

Each night before sharing time with those with whom you live, go into your WCR and release all your suppressed anger and resentment. Perhaps like the Matsushita Company, your marriage and personal life each year will be thirty percent better.

✦

National Exercise Your Imagination Day. In 1876, shortly after Alexander Graham Bell completed work on the telephone, President Rutherford B. Hayes was told of this new American invention. President Hayes responded to the news by saying, "That's an amazing invention, but who would ever want to use one of them?"

26

※◎※

Take time on this day to exercise your imagination, which is another form of eyesight. What the eyes of the body perceive is processed by the mind. What is envisioned with the eyes of the soul is processed by the imagination. The imagination is able to see unlimited possibilities and a rich variety of new arrangements for existing things.

The exercise of your imagination results in creativity, a sharing in the divine activity. Such exercise requires the interplay of the trinity. This trinity is composed of tension, passion and conflict, whose mutual presence may appear to be a paradox. The wider world and our personal worlds seem full of tension and conflict in the course of daily life as we voyage into the Third Millennium. Yet it is rare to find creativity in either our personal or larger worlds. The usual missing element of the trinity is passion, the passionate desire to use the conflicts of life to create new alternates.

Normally we strive to remove the ever present pair, tension and conflict, from daily life. On this national day of exercising your imagination, turn that dynamic duo into a creative trinity by adding passion. Jesus gives us a model for such divine activity. When confronting the conflict created by outdated sacrifices and the tension created among devout Jews by money-changing in the Temple, it was said that zeal for God's house consumed him. Such passionate, consuming zeal in responding to tension and conflict gives birth to creativity, which in turn produces radically new life.

Exercise your imagination today. Turn off the TV, which leaves little room for imagination. Close the eyes of your body and open the eyes of your soul, and you may be amazed at what kind of possibilities you see. We all have such creative sight; all we need to do is exercise it.

As Jesus said, "Let those with eyes, see."

✳

---

27 **Don't Keep a Stiff Upper Lip Day.** Beards come and go, and in the days of England's Queen Anne (1665-1714), they all went. Being clean shaven was the fashion of the day for men, who replaced facial hair with the wearing of false head hair in the form of heavy wigs. When wigs went out of vogue, the style of hair on men's faces slowly returned, beginning with moustaches on young military officers. Yet this hair on the upper lip tends to draw the eyes of observers. The smallest movement of the lip in times of emotion makes the upper lip twitch, which in those days was seen as a sign of a lack of emotional maturity. Thus, when a young officer insisted on being stylish by growing hair on his lip, stern older officers would demand, "Keep a stiff upper lip." By 1833 this military command had become a popular phrase for self-control in both women and men.

⚜

A stiff upper lip, while giving the impression of being in control of one's emotions, makes laughter and crying difficult, if not impossible. From an early age, boys, especially, are required to control those emotions that are viewed as a sign of weakness. Yet, when experiencing either physical or emotional pain, even women are expected to keep a stiff upper lip. Tears shout what words can only stumble to speak, whether in sorrow or in joy. Even crying for joy makes many people uncomfortable since such a response to something deeply moving and beautiful is still crying, still losing that stiff upper lip. Examine your *Don't Do Department* today. See if by word, example or in any other way, you send the message, "Don't do that," when deep emotions are shown. To those with or without mustaches, to children or elderly, to those of any age or sex, do you promote a stiff or flexible upper lip?

✴

Feast of the Invention Factory in Your Basement. 28

Thomas Edison established the first industrial research laboratory with the intention of producing a new invention every ten days! In one four-year period he obtained over 300 patents, which actually comes out to a new invention every five days! During his lifetime, Edison patented nearly 1,300 inventions.

Every home, family, church or company should have an Invention Factory for research into new and better ways to do things. For the lack of creativity, of inventiveness, is the root of the dry rot that weakens home life and church life.

Christian churches, which proclaim with pride the "new" covenant and how their founder, Jesus, was adept at making all things new, usually live in mortal fear of newness and change. The vitality of religious ritual requires the balance of spontaneity and creativity with traditional values and practices.

⚜

The next time you experience a change in the traditional way of doing anything in your church or home, reflect on Edison's Invention Factory goal of a new invention every ten days. Realize in your daily prayer life that while ritual and repetition are of value, so is newness. Experiment with doing something new every ten days to bring freshness to your intimate times with the Risen Jesus and with God.

Whether in your work, marriage or prayer, also reflect today on the words of Isaiah quoted by Jesus, "Behold, I make all things new" (Rev. 21: 5). For anything new to remain new requires frequent visits to the Invention Factory, whether that workshop exists in your basement, garage or in your mind.

✵

---

29 Good or Bad Spirits Festival.

As the annual festival of Halloween nears, we see everywhere — in stores, schools and homes — images of citizens of the spirit world. These ghosts, demons and goblins were long believed to visit earth around this time of year. While fairies are usually only acknowledged around March 17, awareness and respect of them is good business on any day in any month. The *shee*, as the Irish called the wee folk, are actually the old fallen gods and goddesses of ancient days. While pictured as a merry lot, they can be mischievous. They are kind to people who are generous and considerate of them, and so the wise do not clean up dinner dishes before retiring at night. They leave their scraps of food and the few sips of wine still in their glasses for the fairies. In the old days, people would build a good fire in the hearth before going to bed to keep the wee folk warm. When you are kind to the *shee*, they are kind to you and become good spirits who make good luck smile on you. In return for your kindness and respect toward them, they will help you find lost articles, remember names and avoid mishaps.

In former times in Ireland, before throwing a bucket of water out of doors, it was customary to shout, "Take care for the water." You see, the fairy folk are a vain and fastidious lot, and if their bright-colored clothing would get drenched by mortals, the fairies could be merciless in their revenge.

Until recent times in Connaught, when a child would spill his or her milk, a mother would simply say, "That's for the fairies. Just leave it for them." Also, since unbaptized babies were thought to be easily kidnapped by the fairies, a small bag of salt was tied by a string to an infant's sleeping clothes to prevent such a tragedy.

⚜

If you're speed-reading this entry, not believing in the wee folk, be forewarned that it's dangerous to be an elf atheist. If you have never encountered the fairies, the reason may simply be the time of day when you were born. It was believed by the Irish that people born in the morning never have the power to see ghosts or fairies — for that ability one has to be born with night eyes.

What we see or don't see really belongs more to our beliefs and our fantasies. While few beyond early childhood believe in fairies, the loss of such beliefs can make life a rather dull machine gray. Before you pooh-pooh today's reflection, check your calendar to see if October 29 falls on a Friday. Never speak ill of fairies or cross their paths on a Friday for they are the most powerful on that day, and their hearing is especially sharp.

✴

The Great Make-Believe Festival. On this day before Halloween, millions upon millions of children can't wait to dress up in their costumes and masks and make believe they are someone else. Millions upon millions of adults are also eager to dress up in their costumes and masks for this popular adult festival of masking and making-believe.

30

Make-believe is not restricted to these few days at the end of October. Indeed, keeping up with the Joneses and keeping up appearances is a second job for all those who work harder trying to hide a problem than to solve it. In World War II, the Japanese soldiers defending Osaka, Japan, had a serious problem. They had two problems in fact; the first was insufficient ammunition for their antiaircraft guns and the second was to avoid being criticized for not trying hard enough to defend their homeland.

The solution was make-believe: To impress the population with their resolve, they fired blank ammunition. Even the limited real ammunition at their disposal was not of high enough caliber to reach the American bombers flying high overhead. At great personal risk, the Japanese soldiers remained at their posts in the open, keeping up a good appearance of providing an effective defense for Osaka.

⚜

Make-believe for fun is far different than doing it for profit, respectability or keeping up appearances. If you are going to a masquerade party tonight or tomorrow, take a few moments to hold your mask or make-believe costume in your hand. Then ask yourself whether on days or nights other than Halloween or Mardi Gras you dress up in a mask and costume for appearance sake.

✠

---

31 **All Hallows' Eve.** If your doorbell rings today or tonight, before you open the door be prepared to encounter one or several demons, ghosts, ghouls, witches, fairies or perhaps a few three-foot-high aliens dressed in Reynolds Wrap. November 1 was once the old Druidic New Year, and so for the Druids of the British Isles today was the end of the year. The end of the year, as with the end of an age or millennium, often brings out the worst in people. Unlike the contemporary year's end, in which New Year's Eve is a night for parties and dances, for the Druids this eve was a night on which spirits of the dead and lower worlds roamed the earth.

The wise Druids stayed indoors and did not go about. They also placed food offerings outside their doors as tokens of good will to the roaming demons and ghosts. Countless are the superstitions and customs on October 31 intended to protect one from harm and from being carried off by spirits and demons.

Today, demons have become an almost extinct species. Basically, the only demon that has survived the Industrial and Technological Revolutions is the devil, or Satan. Even so, tonight you may open your door to meet, face-to-face, a variety of ghouls as well as the devil dressed in red with a tall pitchfork and a long tail. Halloween almost makes one long for the good old days of demons. Space does not allow us to list the countless classes and species of demons in the ancient world. However, as one example, the Egyptians believed that forty-two different demons would be present at the Last Judgment of every human being. That number was chosen because there were forty-two districts in Egypt and there was a demon for each neighborhood. Thus, at least one demon could claim ownership over a person's soul, since being from his or her district he would know a person's sins and failings.

⁂

On this Eve of All Hallows, All Saints, treat yourself to a trick and invite into your home a neighborhood demon. Offer a treat to this local rascal from hell and ask in return what offenses the demon has recorded about you. Offer another treat and ask him or her to tear out that page, or pages, promising to reform your life while there is still time before the Last Judgment.

While the Egyptians selected a jury of forty-two, consider the implications of your Last Judgment jury having forty-two thousand demons: a demon watching over the office, parking lot, in traffic jams, checkout lines at the supermarket, your pew in church, the kitchen table, the bedroom, the neighbor's fence, the telephone..., and on and on.

The end of the month, like all things that end, is an occasion for a party, a private party of penance-conversion. Let each new year, each new month and each new day be a new beginning of feasts for all saints, as you strive to be one.

✳

THE

MONTH

OF

NOVEMBER

The Latin name for nine, *Novem*, reflects the place of this month in the Roman calendar, in which the year began in March. The Romans also gave their children numerical names according to their rank in birth. The Old Saxon name reflected how at this time of year fishermen drew their boats ashore until next spring. They called it *Wind-monath*, for "wind month." As most of North America begins to feel the cold north winds at this time, Wind Month would be a good name for this eleventh month of the year. Unlike the warming winds of March, the winds of November can often carry snow, freezing rain and ice.

Feast of All Saints, or All Hallows. This holy day for honoring all hallowed or holy ones had its first stirrings in the early seventh century and by the early ninth century was celebrated on May 13. It was transferred to November 1 in 840 A.D., becoming a universal holy day by 1484, and so is one of the venerable senior feasts. While a bit bland in this age, especially when compared to all the colorful customs and celebrations of its eve, Halloween, it wasn't always "fiesta-less." Graves were once decorated with flowers and lighted candles, with large processions of visitors going to cemeteries; throughout the day church bells pealed. In South America, Mexico and much of Latin America, these days still mark the festival of the dead.

Part of the beauty of this day, regardless of your religious preference, is that it is an occasion to honor the unnamed heroes and heroines of our families, our personal saints. While images of these saints in photographs may lack haloes, these family patrons were made holy by the very striving to be holy. Saints are sinners turned inside out, and by daily struggling with this divine inversion and holding fast to their faith they died in God. As many countries have a tomb-shrine to an unknown soldier, today is the feast of our unknown saints.

Rejoice that someday this will be your holy feast day too. May grace and all the talents of an acrobatic contortionist be yours today as you turn yourself inside out toward sainthood.

(You may wish to enter some of your family saints in the ✴ Star-Date space below.)

✴

2

Feast of the Holy Dead. In 1048 when the Second Millennium was but "hours" old, Abbot Saint Odilo of the monastery of Cluny decreed this celebration of all the departed ones. Over the next centuries this feast spread through Europe to England until in the fourteenth century Rome made it an official feast on November 2. Since Sunday is the day of the Resurrection, a little Easter, no funerals have historically been permitted on that high day of the week. So if this feast should come on a Sunday, it is transferred to November 3. This millennium-old celebration is an expression of the Christian belief in the Communion of Saints, the mystical solidarity uniting all of the Body of Christ living on earth with those who have died and are now one with God. This web allows spiritual energy to flow between the living and the dead by way of prayer, various good works and especially Holy Communion, which unites the Head and all the Body of Christ.

꙰꙰꙰

On this November Memorial Day, take time to remember in some fitting way all your holy departed ones. Besides prayer (which is not restricted to time and space but influences the past and the future as if it were the mystical Eternal Now), consider remembering your holy dead by some generous act of charity or volunteer service done in their name.

While it is common to think of the departed as gone forever, this feast can provide a wholesome meditation. Those who loved you while they were alive are bound to you by that mutual and mysterious cord of love. They are also drawn by that love to intercede for you whenever you are in need. Many would say, "It's impossible for those who are dead to be able to have an influence on their loved ones still living." To that you can respond, "With God, all things are possible."

> Eternal rest grant unto the holy dead, O God,
> and may perpetual light shine upon them.
> And may the faithful departed
> through the mercy of God
> come to our aid when we are in need.

✳

Day of the Big Pink Cloud. Recently in Louisville, Kentucky, a generous philanthropist, Mary Caperton Bingham, age ninety, rose to respond to a toast in her honor at a banquet. She remarked at how overcome she was by the toast and how "the best thing would be for a big pink cloud to come down and take me away." She then collapsed and died from a heart attack.

The Irish have an expression that everyone dies on the right day for that person, and, for Mary, her wish made her day. If you're having a great day, especially during this month of mindfulness of death, remember Mary Caperton Bingham and watch for the coming of the Big Pink Cloud.

꧁꧂

This third day in November is almost two months before January, and, if you're average, your appointment calendar already has at least a few future commitments for the new year. One future appointment which everyone has and which cannot be canceled is an appointment with death. Unlike those upcoming appointments during this month, in December or into the new year, the precise day and time of your ultimate appointment is blank — to be filled in by someone else.

Some future appointments just require your being present, while others require preparation. Your appointment with death is not a casual one in which you can come as you are. If you do, you may have to pay the consequences. Pray for a happy death, not one in which you die laughing, but one in which you die without regrets. Those who die free of the heavy weights of "If only I hadn't done that" or "If only I had made time to do what I always wanted to do" are ready, regardless of the day the Big Pink Cloud comes.

✳

---

4 **Famous Last Words Day.** The last words spoken are treasured as insights into a person and the person's state when approaching death. Albert Einstein's last words will never be known, even though he spoke them clearly before his death. For he said those last words in German, his native tongue, and the attending nurse did not understand German.

❧❧❧

Along with remembering your holy dead during these November days, an excellent assignment would be to select your final words. It is not necessary to create a poem of your last words — even though this was once a common custom — or to say some profound words of wisdom. Many baby books record the first words spoken by an infant, making them important words to remember. Since you do not know when death will arrive, say your last words, which are probably the most important words of your life, often — and each time with intense feeling. The effect will be twofold: You will have prepared to make that last significant statement, and you will be reminded frequently of how precious and unpredictable is the gift of life.

The baby book of this author records that his first spoken word — which gave a prophetic hint to his fondness of travel — was "Bye-bye." That's not a bad choice for a last statement too, especially if you add, "for now" or "until we meet in paradise."

❧❧❧

Remembering Einstein's dying message, this would be a good day to reflect on some other unspoken famous German "last words." On October 31, 1517, in Wittenberg, Germany, Martin Luther published his famous ninety-five theses. If you had the power to be transported to Wittenberg on this day in

1517, only five days after Luther's bold act, and could ask the residents, "Anything exciting or new happening around here these days?" you can be assured that the answer would not have been, "A great religious revolution began five days ago; the Protestant Reformation has begun!" What you would likely have heard is, "Today is like yesterday, rarely does anything new and exciting happen." Unknowingly, these would have been ironic, if not comical, famous last words.

Few who saw Father Martin Luther nail his ninety-five theses to the church door would have imaged the implications of the Reformation's famous *first* words for them and for the whole world. The same is true today; you may be on the cutting edge of a great revolution and be unaware of it.

5

Day of the First Flight Across the United States, 1911. This fifth day of November marks one of the major achievements of the first part of the twentieth century. To remember Calbraith P. Rodgers' feat of crossing the continent in a biplane suggests possibilities for the marvels of technology that will make headline news in the first decades of the twenty-first century – and that will likely be of only casual interest by the end of the century.

Today is also the old **Feast of Saint Elizabeth**, relative of Mary of Nazareth and mother of the great prophet John the Baptist. While the feast of St. Elizabeth may seem of minor importance today, she continues to have a significant place in the history of her relatives, Jesus of Nazareth and his mother Mary. When Mary came to visit her, Elizabeth is quoted by Luke as proclaiming, "Blessed are you among women, Mary, and blessed is the fruit of your womb." Like Mary, Elizabeth is a primary patroness of the *impossible*, for she became pregnant with a gift from God in her old age.

On this day you can recall how for millenniums it was deemed impossible for a human to fly, let alone fly across an entire continent as large as North America. Join that reflection to the case of an elderly barren woman who conceived an

extraordinary child, and realize how with God all things are possible! Consider some of the things you feel are impossible for you, and pray that in your case nothing will be impossible if God is for you. Also, today, take out old dreams you've stored in your mind's attic because they seemed impossible or out of reach and look forward to that historical day when they will fly.
✳

6

"Where in the World Am I?" Day. This could also be called NASA Window Day. The world is so large that we easily forget how small it actually is, especially when seen from space. To have a clearer picture of the world as seen from the window of a NASA spacecraft, reflect on this exercise. If the entire world were a small town of 1,000 people and you lived in that town, your neighbors would look like this: 564 would be Asians, 210 Europeans, 86 Africans, 80 South Americans and 60 North Americans. In your town 700 people would be illiterate and 500 would always be hungry, if not starving to death. As you look at the world through your NASA window, remember that you have been challenged to love your neighbor as you love yourself.

⚜

As our primary festival of gratitude, Thanksgiving, approaches, it is customary to give thanks by remembering those who are needy and poor. It is customary for churches, schools and other organizations to have baskets available to receive gifts of food for those who are in need. Interest is renewed at this time of year in soup kitchens and shelters for the homeless.

Be conscious, today, that you are a citizen both of a local community, which has its poor and homeless, and of a world community, where these and many other needs are present. In no prior age in history has it been so possible for the average person to be aware of belonging to a global neighborhood. The miracles of television and instant communication systems make disasters around the world present in your living room. That awareness and the knowledge of the massive worldwide need can sometimes stun and paralyze the human spirit.

Contemporary technology is decades, if not centuries, ahead

of our spiritual evolution and the capacity of the human heart to embrace and care for our global neighbors in need. As we spiritually catch up, make the world's suffering and poor *real* by taking them into your heart in prayer. Give aid to the millions of fearful refugees and starving people you see in your living room by donating to worldwide organizations that care for the needy across our globe. Most importantly, do something concrete for poor neighbors in your immediate community – volunteer at a soup kitchen or otherwise directly help someone in need.

God has given you two eyes. One eye is to look with love upon your nearby neighbor, the other is to look with love upon your neighbor in faraway parts of the world. To live fully alive in this age of the global neighborhood requires the cosmic heart of a Space Samaritan.

7

Select Your Symbolic Animal Day. On this day in 1874 a cartoon by Thomas Nast first featured an elephant to symbolize the Republican Party. The elephant, of course, has remained the GOP's image to this day.

Symbolic animals are very much a part of our culture. Our nation itself has the eagle for a symbol, even if Benjamin Franklin labored to have the turkey accepted as the national bird. It's a good thing he lost: Imagine the honored national bird as the main course at Thanksgiving dinner! All fifty states and many sport teams have birds or other animals as symbols. Perhaps each organization, church and institution should do the same.

On this day of the creation of the GOP elephant, take a few pennies out of your time-bank and select some creature – either real or mythical – a mammal, fish or bird you think might symbolize yourself. Such an exercise may assist you in seeing yourself in a new and revealing way. You might consider asking coworkers or family which creature they think best symbolizes your personality.

More fun could follow by asking them which symbolic creature would best symbolize their church. Responses might include a dove, a lion or perhaps a slow-moving turtle with a large heavy shell under which to hide in times of conflict, a dinosaur or an ostrich. The exercise has many other possibilities for organizations, institutions or families.

✳

---

8 **New Soap Day.** A new soap appeared over a hundred years ago in 1890, but it attracted no interest. A German chemist, A. Krafft, discovered that certain short-chained chemicals when mixed with alcohol made a lather-like soap from fat. "Ho-hum" was the common response. When the Allies blockaded Germany in World War I, none of the country was able to obtain natural fats. Two men named Gunther and Hetzer remembered Krafft's "useless" discovery and produced a German wartime substitute for soap, *Nekal*, a synthetic detergent that left no scum. In 1946 this synthetic detergent reappeared under the name *Tide*.

Today, or the next time you use detergent, you can reflect on this example of creativity born from conflict, tension and the passion to find a wartime soap substitute. As we have noted before, great evils have come out of war, but so have many useful products for daily life.

⚜

Yes, the practical life and the spiritual life are one. So, consider making a bright-colored box of Tide or some other detergent a holy symbol next to your Bible or in your prayer corner. The respectable English word *deterge* is seldom used in daily language, even though it owes much to its more famous Latin great-grandfather, *detergere*, to "wipe away." Yet like a box of Tide, it merits much more common usage in everyday life.

It is divine to deterge a friend, spouse or stranger's sin as soon as it happens. Without waiting to be asked to pardon whatever mess the offense might have created, deterge it, wipe it up at once with a love-soaked sponge. Deterging is difficult even when someone asks you to do it, and is really amazing when you do it before being asked. Yet life becomes more harmonious and full of grace the faster you go to work on deterging the spills, spots and stains others make in your life.

To paraphrase Gandhi, "To deterge is divine, and to refuse to deterge is diabolic."

✹

Day of the Forgotten 5,000,000 Holocaust Victims.

9

As we anticipate Veteran's Day, today is a day to visit not just the Tomb of the Unknown Soldier but the Tomb of the Unknown and often Forgotten Nazi Victims of Hate and Discrimination. Though we remembered Jewish Holocaust Memorial Day on May 17, along with the six million Jews who were killed in the Holocaust, there were also five million others. These included Christian pastors, priests and others who spoke out boldly against Hitler and his policies and against his persecution of Jews. They paid for their courage by joining Jews in concentration camps and in the ovens. Most of these five million were social undesirables: homosexuals, gypsies, the deformed, handicapped and other outcasts. In this month of remembering the dead, pray for these millions of often forgotten victims of hate and discrimination.

⚜

Recall that in the late 1930s as the Nazis were rounding up Jews to be deported or annihilated in the Holocaust, the United States was considered as a refuge for those victims. However, as we saw on May 17, a 1939 poll indicated that so great was the American prejudice of Jews that 83% opposed allowing them to find sanctuary here!

What would the polls in 1939, 1999 or even 2019 show if it were proposed that homosexuals and gypsies enter the country by the hundreds of thousands to escape a holocaust? That 1939 poll asked some questions about Jews which are just as valid for gypsies and homosexuals. For today's reflection, honestly answer a couple of those adapted questions: 1. Would you work next to a homosexual or gypsy? 2. Would you like to live next to a gypsy or a gay couple?

✹

10

Birthday of Holy Martin Luther, Reformer, 1483.
Filled with zeal for the Body of Christ, the church, the Catholic
Augustinian priest, Martin Luther, gave voice to the cry for
reforming the church in the fifteenth century.

Change is at the heart of the ministry Jesus began by
saying, "Reform your lives, the reign of God is at hand." This
reformation of Jesus is a continuous process for each of us as
individuals as well as for the church that bears his name. No
finer name could be given the disciples of Jesus than that of
reformers, perpetual reformers.

Today, join with all those of the Lutheran Church in this
day of remembrance of a great and holy reformer. Use this day
to continue the Reformation by reforming yourself. In each age,
each church is guilty of failing to live up to the ideals of its
original founder, Jesus Christ. The same is true for every mosque
or synagogue or temple. Institutions are reformed by individuals
who are perpetual reformers of themselves. While a church
council or some movement can begin the process, the true power
of reformation depends upon individual members' dedication to
perpetual reform.

꧁꧂

This is also the **Feast of St. Leo the Great**, another
reformer of the church, who confronted Attila the Hun in 452.
Unfortunately, Pope Leo had a sad bias against the blessings
and bliss of marriage, and determined that all marital intercourse
was evil. Holy Martin Luther, by his life as a married priest,
began to correct this negative theology which continues to have
an effect on how marriage is viewed by the church. If you doubt
this bias, count (on one hand or even one finger) how many
canonized married saintly couples you can name.

�֎

11

Feast of St. Martin of Tours, a Feast of Thanksgiving.
Martin was a famous early Christian saint. As a Roman army
officer he once cut his military cloak in two and gave half of it
to a half-naked beggar he met on the road. That night Jesus
appeared to Martin in a dream as the same beggar he had

befriended. Through that experience Martin had a conversion, left the army and founded several religious communities in France.

This feast was one of the greatest of all festivals during the Middle Ages, known as Martinmas. As a November feast, it was a harvest festival of gratitude and thanksgiving, and may well have been the origin of our Thanksgiving Day. Some believe that the Puritan colonists recreated this November festival they experienced in Catholic Europe. Martin's celebration began with a Mass in his honor, which was followed by feasting, games and parades. The main dish of the feast was the golden St. Martin's goose, which quite likely gave birth to Thanksgiving's use of another large bird, the American turkey. The substitution of a wild turkey for the European goose came later in the feast's history, however. As we will see in the November 24 Almanac entry, some authors suggest that the Puritan Thanksgiving table was made up of the simple local foods which were the gifts of the Native Americans.

⚜

Today also honors Sylan N. Goldman, the founder of the *Humpty Dumpty* supermarket chain. In the 1930s Goldman created one of the most necessary inventions for this approaching Thanksgiving feast — the grocery store shopping cart. Pause to thank Sylan today and the next time you go shopping for groceries. And consider what your life would be like without the shopping cart! Supermarkets evolved in the hard times of the 1930s, providing low priced food for a country in the grips of a depression. Among their clever advertising strategies was the motto, "At this store you may serve yourself."

Coming soon to your local supermarket: shopping carts with their own price scanners to eliminate wasted time in checkout lines. What's next? (You might want to look ahead, or back, to the February 8 entry.)

✴

A Window into the Future Day. Are you curious to know about the new inventions of the twenty-first century, which, as we have seen, will be far greater and more amazing than

12

those of the twentieth? If you are, don't consult a psychic or peer into a crystal ball. Rather, read a good novel about a future time, for a good novel is apt to have a window into tomorrow. In 1863, for example, Jules Verne's book *Paris in the 20th Century*, contained many of today's inventions. In his fictional new world of Paris, Verne depicted private cars, or "gaz cabs," of twenty to thirty horsepower which anticipated the automobile by a quarter of a century. He also foreshadowed machines like the telephone, fax and computer.

⚜

This ability to fantasize, to make images, which is an aspect of the imagination, is dearly needed at the crossing over into new millenniums. More important than envisioning new machines is the ability to imagine new ways of living together in peace and harmony. We need new visions of how to feed the millions of hungry and to lift the yoke of servitude and inhuman labor.

Each of us in our own world of family, friendship and work needs to spend time using the imagination to make blueprints for tomorrow. Then, we need courage and determination to begin to reconstruct our lives around these new images. Steal some time today to fantasize about your tomorrow.

Today's reflection: One is beginning to die when one has more memories than dreams.

✦

---

13 **Feast of St. Diego Alcala, Patron of Cooks.** Diego was a Franciscan lay brother of the early fifteenth century who lived on the Canary Islands off the coast of Spain. Brother Diego was given the humble tasks of being cook and doorkeeper for the friars. His kindness to the poor who came to his kitchen door and his gift of healing caused those who knew him to declare him a saint before his death in 1463 at Alcala. He later was also granted that status by the larger church through the efforts of the king of Spain, whose son's cure was credited to holy brother Diego.

⚜

In this month of Thanksgiving dinners and feasting, may cooks and all who tend the stove ask St. Diego to assist them to see themselves as being doorkeepers. To cook and serve meals with love is not only "good medicine," such activity opens the very doors to heaven. Jesus realized that all meals can be doorlike full-length mirrors of heaven, and so he made the meals at which he ate open to all who wished to come. Heaven is a love feast of inclusiveness.

Humble Saint Diego, be a blessing
  to all who prepare meals and work in the kitchen.
May all of us who take up that humble yet holy task
  strive to insure that not only the food
  but our hospitality and table conversation
  will make all meals doorways to heaven.

14

Waiting Till the Sacred Cows Come Home Day. This religious version of an old agrarian folk saying has ominous implications for our times. Waiting until the cows come home on their own could take a long time. It may not be until very late in the evening or early morning, when their utters are full and they need to be milked. Pray that our world will have time to wait for its sacred cows to come home!

A new sacred cow was born in 1996 on a farm in northern Israel, and her appearance has put the fear of God into many – for this sacred cow is a red heifer! Not since 70 A.D. and the destruction of the second temple has a red heifer been born in Israel, and her arrival has been greeted by some as a wondrous omen for the new millennium.

In the ancient days of the first and second temples, the ashes of a red heifer, butchered in her third year, were mixed with water and used to purify Jews before they could approach God's holy temple. Observant Jews see the newly born red heifer as a sign from God that the Messiah is near at hand. They feel that a third temple should be constructed so that the ancient sacrifices could be renewed. Others see the heifer as an ominous sign that the Muslim Al-Aqsa mosque on Jerusalem's Temple

Mount will be destroyed to make way for the construction of the new temple. Any such violation of one of Islam's most sacred mosques, the Dome of the Rock, would likely provoke an all-out war, and disaster for all living in Israel.

The site of the global and final war between good and evil is only fifteen miles from Jerusalem! Armageddon, *Megiddo* in Hebrew, is the site of several significant ancient Israeli battles and is the Book of Revelation's name for the War of Wars which many believe will be launched sometime around the year 2000.

⚜

Take heart, however, and be hopeful, for this red heifer isn't precisely a kosher sacred cow, since she is more auburn than immaculately red. Hope that she is unfit for the ancient sacrifice.

Indeed, hope is precisely the most needed virtue in the new century, for bleak is the prospect of true change in religious attitudes. The expression *sacred cows* comes from the Hindu religion where the cow is deeply revered as a source of life-sustaining milk. The real sacred cows, however, are the long-cherished practices, customs and ideas immune from criticism and protected from being touched or killed.

Hope and pray for the beginning of the slaughter of some sacred cows, the untouchable rituals and requirements, laws and regulations that separate Christian churches from each other and from other religions. Jesus quoted God saying, "My house is a house of prayer," it is not a barn!

On the future space station colony where in the not-too-distant future earthlings will be living, there will be no room for sacred cows! Nor will there be room for a church, a mosque, a synagogue, a temple, a shrine or meeting hall on every corner.

✴

---

15 **Senior Security Day and Other New Things Festival.** On this day in 1935 a historical event took place when President Franklin Delano Roosevelt signed the Social Security Act (see the entry for August 14 in this Almanac), providing insurance for old age and for unemployment. On this day in 1927 the first radio network, NBC, went on the air, broadcasting to twenty-five stations from New York to Kansas City. And on this day in 1806 Zebulon Pike's expedition of exploration reached a tall mountain in the Colorado Rocky Mountain chain now known as Pike's Peak.

⚜

Since this day is so rich in famous new beginnings and discoveries, consider doing something new so you can add a personal contribution to the famous day of November 15. Consider using your ✴ Star-Date line, found below, for your personal discoveries, inventions or anniversaries. Each life has its own history, and to remember personally significant events allows you to see a sacred pattern unfolding. It also marks occasions to party!

Remember Zebulon Pike and create in your life the habit of exploring the untried and untested, the habit of continually doing something new. The frequent practice of such exploration, even as simple an act as eating a new food or dish or going about some daily task in a new way, will add Zebulon zest to your life.

✴

Discover Yourself Day. Today's reflection continues yesterday's with a quote from the actor and director, Alan Alda. "Be brave enough to live creatively...and go into the wilderness of your intuition. You can't get there by bus, only by hard work, risking, and by not quite knowing what you're doing. What you discover will be wonderful: yourself."

16

Now that almost every remote place on the planet has been discovered and explored, earthlings are headed off the planet for space. Since children and cats love to explore the unknown, perhaps this is a primal urge that needs to be met. Instead of seeking some far-distant place, discover and explore yourself.

⚜

Each person has come into life as an original, but sadly most leave life as copies. God is a limitless creator, delighting in variety throughout all of creation, and so God created you as a unique person. Alda's quote is a call for each person to become an explorer, not like Zebulon Pike venturing into the uncharted terrain of the Rockies, but rather an explorer willing to go into the wilderness within. Such expeditions are difficult. There is a certain amount of trial and error involved in the process of discovery in a land with untrodden pathways and no maps. Yet dreams and aspirations give clues to what lies hidden; they can be departure points and guides for changes in course.

Do not be ashamed if you are fearful to begin such an exploration. Every unexplored place holds its own unknown terrors, monsters and variety of dangers. But each uncharted territory also holds buried treasures and great wealth of spirit for those brave enough to explore them.

Benjamin Franklin provides a thought worth chewing on:

> Hide not your talents,
> they for use were made.
> What's a sundial
> in the shade?

✴

---

17 The November Feasting Festival.

The great feast of Thanksgiving is at hand. It's a reminder and a model of what makes a holiday or holy day into a feast — eating in grand style. While it's common to speak of Christmas, Easter and even saints' days as feasts, in a diet-conscious society few of us really feast on those days, or on any day. Eating is required for survival, but feasting is required for joy, for the celebration of life. Eating can be done alone, but feasting requires the company of at least one other person.

A recent survey revealed the difference between just feeding the body and feasting the soul and heart. Among the questions asked was: "What is the key to a successful party: good food, good conversation, good company?" Good food rated 10%, good conversation 25% and good company 65%. When asked to pick three dinner guests they would like to share a meal with, common responses were people from the arts, politics, entertainment, religion and at least one good storyteller. The report of the survey stated that "the strangest threesome to emerge...was Jesus, Beverly Sills, and Ebenezer Scrooge."

⚜

Would you place Jesus of Nazareth on your Thanksgiving guest list? While inviting Scrooge, Sills and Jesus as dinner guests may seem "strange" because of the unusual combination, perhaps it is Jesus who would make us *feel* strange. Would you be comfortable with Jesus at your table? Would your friends enjoy having dinner with him, or would they find his presence threatening? Would you decorate or *un*decorate your home, dress up or dress down? Would your other invited guests be a few fellow parishioners and the pastor? Or perhaps a few dirty homeless souls, a couple of non-English-speaking aliens, a whore or two and an assortment of others with whom you might not want to be caught dead?

"Wherever two of you are gathered, there will I be" — Jesus of Nazareth, 30 A.D.

✶

Forbidden Math Day, 1300 A.D. The Roman number **XVIII** for eighteen is used on this day as a reminder of the good old days. Arabic numbers, so common today, were rejected when they first appeared in the European commercial world. The Hindu-Arabic method of numbering was adopted by Arab scholars around the year 800 A.D., and they carried it to Spain in 900 A.D. Slowly this new mathematical system of numbering was introduced throughout Europe by merchants and by scholars who had attended the universities of Spain. While the invention of printing aided the spread of this system, six hundred years would have to pass before these "foreign" mathematical numbers would be completely accepted in Europe, during the early 1800s. The reasons are various, such as religious prejudice toward this system as a *Muslim* invention and the fear of embracing anything new. In commercial dealings it was feared that these new numbers could more easily be forged than the ancient Roman numbers. For example, changing XVIII into CLXXX would require much greater craftsmanship than turning 18 into 180.

⚜

Give thanks today that the Roman sacred cow of numbering was finally replaced by the Arabic system. What would using Roman numerals be like in Millennium III, when dealing with hundreds of thousands, millions, billions and trillions becomes more and more commonplace. Imagine trying to decipher the symbols for the sum of 8,813,200,023,188? Or consider the mental calisthenics required to come up with the combination of Roman numeral letters necessary to indicate the number of atoms in a pound of iron: 4,891,500,000,000,000,000,000,000 — nearly five trillion trillion.

What do we reject in our day as offensive, as contrary to custom and tradition or simply as non-Christian? Would we resist the useful Hindu zero and the rest of the infidel invention of Arabic numbering?

Does the cultural source of a new creation or the religion of the inventor (or lack thereof) prejudice our determination of whether it should be accepted as valuable and useful? Shortly after the midpoint of the twentieth century the historic Vatican Council II stated, "The Catholic Church rejects nothing that is true and holy in non-Christian religions." *The Decree on Ecumenism* went on to say, "...Christians should also recognize, preserve and promote spiritual and moral truths as well as socio-cultural values found among these (non-Christian) peoples."

Have you recently observed any non-Christian spiritual or moral practices or values being promoted in your local church? Perhaps, as with Arabic numbers, it will require six hundred years before acceptance rather than rejection becomes the rule. If so, it will not be until MMDLXIII (2563) A.D. that Christians embrace and adopt what is true, holy and spiritually useful in non-Christian religions.

✺

---

19 The Feast of Forgotten St. Nerses.

Today's saint was a priest and bishop of Armenia in 363 A.D. He was forced to excommunicate one king for murdering his wife. St. Nerses then excommunicated the king's successor, whom Nerses was convinced was possessed by demons. The king loudly protested his innocence and invited the saintly bishop to dinner, whereupon he poisoned him. Nerses' own son, Isaac, succeeded him as bishop and also became a saint.

~~~~~

The Forgotten Saint Nerses was never named the patron of any profession or craft, nor was he called upon for any affliction, even unmentionable ones. Unlike the Irish hermit, St. Fiacre, who is the patron of gardeners and cab drivers and is also invoked for hemorrhoids (see the footnote below), poor neglected Nerses is called upon by no particular group — at least not until the Third Millennium. Would not St. Nerses make an excellent patron for those who have been invited to dinner only to find that their host or hostess is poisoning them?

During this holiday season of parties and dinners, luncheons and brunches, when you are apt to be often invited to dinner, remember St. Nerses, the proposed patron of those being poisoned. If you are a guest at a dinner (including Thanksgiving dinner) where the host, hostess or other guests are poisoning the food by their words of prejudice against those of another race, religion, gender or sexual orientation, pray to St. Nerses to protect you from this poison. Remembering his perception that the new king was possessed by demons, do not be surprised if St. Nerses helps you to sense the demonic in your table companions.

~~~~~

(Footnote) St. Fiacre is the patron saint of gardeners and those suffering hemorrhoids, as well as the patron of taxi cab drivers, for whom hemorrhoids is such a common complaint. Legend has it that St. Fiacre, an Irish hermit, had once become so exhausted by the long haranguing of a village wag that he had to plop down on a large rock. He sat so heavily on the rock that he left the imprint of his buttocks on it. It is said that this large rock was then moved to a nearby church, where generations of pilgrims suffering from hemorrhoids sat on it and prayed to be cured.

May St. Fiacre protect you from those who give you a pain other than in your neck.

✳

---

20 **Birthday of the Phonograph, 1877.** On this day in his laboratory in Menlo Park, New Jersey, the great inventor, Thomas Edison, constructed the first machine to capture the human voice with recognizable fidelity. Leon Scott, a French inventor, had experimented with but never perfected a machine he called a *phonautograph*. Edison's first recording was his own voice shouting, "Mary had a little lamb." Today's celebration honors the grandmother of the cassette and compact disc players. These machines have brought the enjoyment of music and recorded conferences and books into our lives.

❦

Use this day as an opportunity to sharpen your internal phonograph and tape recorder: your memory. Because of the ease of mechanically recording what we wish to retain, it is easy to neglect the ongoing development of our memory of what people say. Memory is strengthened by repetition and by association. Studies indicate that our memory more thoroughly retains information that is repeated only once every hour for several hours than what is repeated continuously for a shorter period of time. Yet, although we may know more about how the memory works, our memories don't work nearly as well as in the past. Because of the technology that enables a vast storage of printed matter, most people's memories are far inferior to those of our ancestors who lived in an oral tradition.

It is said that God gave us memories so we could have roses in December. How is your rose garden growing?

✳

---

21 **The Celebration of Forgetfulness.** To forget something in contemporary culture is commonly an occasion for apologies as well as for fear. With greater awareness of the afflictions of

Alzheimer's disease and other difficulties of an aging population, any sign of forgetfulness is disturbing to most people. On the other hand, it is important and necessary for the mind to forget in order that it can remember new significant things and events. An example of this gift of forgetfulness is your inability to remember what you had for dinner a week or two ago. Such knowledge is excess baggage for your memory bank; it quickly jettisons such information when more pressing needs arise. The mind in a healthy person remembers those events and data that are truly significant and those that are frequently repeated by choice or circumstance. As the ancients taught, "Repetition is the mentor of memory."

The ability to forget is also spiritually necessary in forgiving others, even though a common expression says, "Forgive your enemies but remember their names." To both ask for pardon and to grant it requires a healthy use of the grace of forgetting. Those who say they've forgiven you for some fault, but weeks, months or years later remind you of it, have not really forgiven. The next time, and each time, you recall some offense done to you in the past, be quick to pardon the offender as fully as possible. Repetition is the mother of pardon.

Rejoice, today, in the gift of forgetfulness and how it creates fresh space for new life experiences and new perspectives. Rejoice also in the ability of the mind and soul to forget actual feelings of pain and to remember only that something was painful. And the next time you realize that you've forgotten a name or event, instead of feeling guilty, ask yourself how significant in the big picture is the thing you forgot.

22

The Festival of "Good-bye." Today is the holiday of Good-bye, one of those accordion contraction words. When compressed, it is a farewell. When expanded to its original, it says, "God be with you." In England, Charles Davies, age 67, had just concluded a solo of "Good-bye" at the annual dinner of the Cotswold Male

Voice Choir with the words, "I wish you all a last good-bye." He bowed as the audience applauded; then he immediately collapsed and died.

※※

In much of North America, these last days of November are stark and gray. Trees slumber in late autumn rest, undressed of their leaves, which now blow in the cold wind. It is the season for letting go and taking leave. Nature, while only sleeping, appears to be dead, and a consciousness of death, scribbled in invisible ink, is written between the lines of each day. For those who are awake to the mystery of life and death in daily life, "Good-bye" is a better parting expression before retiring than merely saying, "Good night." Whether it is spoken to our children, spouse or friends, "Good-bye" has the power to remind us of how fragile is the gift of life. A conscious, love-filled "Good-bye" spoken at the door as a loved one is departing is both a blessing in secular disguise and a sacred sign that you are indeed awake.

✷

---

23 *Sayonara* or *Arrivederci* **Exchange Day.** Instead of "See you later," "Take it easy" or "Have a good day," our partings could be freshened up by exchanging them for other ways of saying farewell. The Japanese and Italian words for "Good-bye" both have richer meanings. Since we are rapidly becoming global citizens, these two foreign farewells could well become more familiar and more fitting terms of departure. The Japanese *Sayonara* (sigh-a-nar-ra) entered the American vocabulary after World War II, but few know how poignant it is as a parting expression. Its literal translation is, "If it must be so."

The Italian *arrivederci* (a-ree-va-dare-chee) means, "Till we meet again" and so carries the blessing that our farewell is not final but only temporary. By adding a simple spoken or silent "in paradise," in English or Italian, we express our hope and belief that all good-byes have a secret compartment containing those beautiful words "Hello" and "Welcome home."

※※

Recalling yesterday's entry about what happened in Charles Davies' "Good-bye" makes one mindful of how important a greeting it is. Repeated day after day to those we love — often with other thoughts and demands shouting louder in our heads — good-bye can easily become a ghost word. Hollow as an old tin can, it needs to be constantly refilled. Today is a good day to ask: With how much "good" did you fill your last "Good-bye"?

A cousin ghost-expression is, "I love you." It also suffers from the strain of frequent use and so constantly needs to be refilled. For adult men it suffers from the social stress of not seeming manly enough to use with other men, being the private property of opposite-sex lovers. Even with married couples it often seems too dangerously intimate, and so it is said quickly and as empty of feeling as possible.

This reflection is like a drive to a gas station to fill your car's fuel tank, and it *is* time to fill up. Make it a practice today to fill your common expressions with real meaning and emotion. You might even want to "top 'em off" with a little extra love.

✴

Thanksgiving Day - a Movable Feast. Today — in fact, every day — could be Thanksgiving Day. If this year the 24th falls on the fourth Thursday in November, then you will be reading this Almanac entry on the actual day of the feast. While this day officially begins the Christmas shopping season, it should also launch a yearlong season of gratitude.

The story of the first Thanksgiving has been heavily doctored with large measures of legend and myth and with a reversal of roles. The classic image of Thanksgiving has the white Anglo-Saxon Puritan Pilgrims all dressed up in their starched Sunday best, sharing their food with the almost naked, red Indian aborigines. Authentic history tells another story, for how could the Puritan's have shared foods unknown to them, foods like pumpkins, turkeys, corn and squash. And Governor William Bradford, tradition says, invited the Indian chief, Massasoit, to the feast, and he came with ninety men who joined 140 Pilgrims for a dinner cooked by four women and two teenage girls! That first Thanksgiving dinner included a surprise desert when

Quadequina, the brother of Massasoit, disappeared into the woods and returned with a bushel of popcorn.

It was not the Christian Puritans who introduced the pagan Indians to the tradition of an autumn harvest gratitude feast, since the Native Americans of eastern North America had observed such a celebration for centuries prior to the Puritans landing at Plymouth Rock. While the art images and stories of this day may, like most of history, be a blending of fiction and fact, the celebration itself is not. Ancient is a harvest festival of gratitude, belonging to peoples of almost every age, culture and religion. Thanksgiving, then, is a deeply human expression whose tradition continues, even if threatened, into our time.

❧⦿❧

Thanksgiving is an endangered holiday as a holy day, as it yearly loses more and more the sense of gratitude to God, from whom all good things come, and becomes a secular celebration of family, food and football. It is also an endangered festival for expressing gratitude for a good harvest, a full pantry stocked to last through a long cold winter. It is endangered by modern industrial society's divorce from the land, from growing our own food, from the personal sense of pride in the hard work that produces a good and rich harvest.

As we journey into the twenty-first century, old-fashioned Thanksgiving is in the intensive care ward. Since visiting the sick is an act of mercy, on Thanksgiving Day show mercy to this old, frail celebration and invest your Thanksgiving with a profound sense of gratitude for what God has done for you in this past year. Make a pilgrimage to the full pantry of your life: Count the gifts of comfort, the blessings of food and shelter, of education and a job, of the good things you so easily take for granted. Be thankful for all that fills your pantry to overflowing.

Also, in some personal way, like the generous and hospitable Native Americans at the first Thanksgiving, share your food with those who are hungry or find themselves threatened and alone in a strange new land.

✺

Day to Remember the Public Sin of Segregation. It was not until on this day in 1955 that racial segregation was banned on all interstate trains and buses by the Interstate Commerce Commission. This government ruling, however, did not affect state or local buses, which continued to force African-Americans to ride in special sections in the rear of the bus.

※※◆※※

Today, other inequalities and violations of justice based on various prejudices continue to exist in our society. Remembering past injustices such as segregation should inspire each of us to work for full equality toward all persons, without any "yes, but" conditions. Thanksgiving for the gift of being a citizen in a free and democratic country requires giving thanks by showing segregation-free equality to all persons you encounter. By such behavior you profess and live out your national creed.

Today is thus a good day to pause and examine your prejudices. Be cautious about skipping over this examination, saying, "I don't have any prejudices," for we all do. Who can say without question or doubt that he or she is free of the affliction of xenophobia, the fear of the stranger or foreigner? What is different in others arouses a primal fear, which then often leads to assumptions and prejudgments lacking in evidence and based on feelings, rumors and fears. While these assumptions of others who are different may exist in all of us, each of us is free to decide whether or not to act on them. Being honestly non-prejudicial means refusing to react and rising above our fears.

※※◆※※

Today also celebrates the **Birthday of Angelo Roncalli** in 1881. On October 28, 1958, at the age of seventy-seven, he was elected as an "intermission" or "caretaker" pope taking the name of John XXIII. He took good care of the Catholic Church and convened the Second Vatican Council and the modern renewal of the Church.

✸

26 The Invention of the Needle, 30,000 B.C. (and B.W.).

Before the invention of the wheel (B.W.), there occurred the marvelous invention of the needle. An unnamed Cro-Magnon genius conceived and made the first needle out of animal bone with a hole, or eye, in one end. Using animal sinews as thread, it was possible to stitch together animal pelts into clothing. A new age had begun.

Yet like many inventions that were brought to light and then misplaced only to be rediscovered centuries later, perhaps this was true of the needle as well. Among these previously discovered inventions is the 1775 flush toilet P.D. (Previously Discovered). As early as 8000 B.C. the inhabitants of the Orkney Islands off the coast of Scotland had built latrine-like plumbing systems connected to nearby streams; these "toilets" allowed people to relieve themselves while inside their homes. A greatly refined bathroom system was in operation by 2000 B.C. at the palace on the island of Crete. It included hot and cold running water for baths and a type of flushing toilet. In 1500 B.C. the Egyptian aristocrats were using copper pipes to carry hot and cold water.

Is it possible, then, that the needle's invention 30,000 years ago should also be dated with a P.D.? Could Eve, the mother of all the living, have been the true genius who discovered the needle? Upon discovering that she and her husband Adam were naked, she "...sewed fig leaves together and made them loincloths" (Gen. 3: 7). If so, perhaps her name should be linked to her creation, making them known as Eve needles.

❦

Also today, in 1832, the **First Streetcar** in the world was put into operation by the New York & Harlem Railroad in New York City. Designed by John Stephenson, this horse-drawn carriage named *John Mason* "ran" on lower Fourth Avenue. What do you think, should a P.D. be placed on this discovery date as well?

What marvelous new medicine, invention or creation will appear in the coming years that should carry the letters P.D.? If you feel the urge to be an inventor, perhaps you should consider doing some historical research to find any one of a number of things itching to be reinvented.

✯

Awesome Mysteries Day, 2001. While more of daily life is becoming beyond comprehension, people are less inclined toward religion or to a God who is beyond understanding. Few who daily use computers understand how they function or even how their car, TV, telephone and other electronic machines operate, yet some of these same people demand that God be "understood" before they will place belief even in God's existence. 27

Increasingly it is necessary to abandon understanding how something works and to simply use it and repair it once it stops working. The paradox is that in an age of shrinking religious faith and growing doubt, the contemporary person places blind faith in a multitude of machines, forms of transportation and means of communication without experiencing any doubt.

Perhaps a new spirituality is needed which could call us to stand in awe of technology as the All-Knowing Spiritual Master. Our mysterious machines could be priestly servant-gurus, leading us into greater and greater wonder about an unknowable, unexplainable, yet real God. Technology could be the electronic usher to show us where to kneel.

As Thomas Carlyle said in *Sartor Resartus*, "Wonder is the basis of worship." We need to continue to cultivate a sense of wonder and awe to live our lives fully alive.

✯

The Life Expectancy of Religions Day. Among today's religions, which ones are middle-aged, which ones are on their last legs and which ones are already dead? At the birth of Jesus of Nazareth two thousand years ago there were religions that once had dominated the Near East for two thousand years or more that today are dead and buried, including those of the 28 ancient Egyptians, Greeks and Romans. Religions that were prominent four thousand years ago are being dug up by archeologists, and their ritual objects exist only in museums. And the religions of five to six thousand years ago are lost in the dust of blowing sand or only pale images on the walls of caves and tombs. What is the life expectancy of a great religion — two, three, four thousand years?

Today's age of world religions can be figured by their date of origin: Judaism, 1800 B.C. or B.C.E. (Before the Common Era), Hinduism, 1500 B.C.E., Shintoism, 600 B.C.E, Confucianism, 551 B.C.E. and Buddhism, 534 B.C.E. Christianity began in 28-30 C.E. (A.D.) and is presently the largest with 1,700,000,000 estimated members among its various denominations. At the beginning of the Third Millennium, Islam, begun in 622 C.E., is the fastest growing and second largest religion in the world, with slightly over one billion followers. While the last two decades of the twentieth century saw a decline in membership and vitality of America's major mainline Protestant churches, the Roman Catholic Church reported an increase, as did fundamentalist Protestant denominations.

The worship and knowledge of God historically appears to be an evolutionary reality and so never remains static. Not only do old religions die, so do young ones and new offshoot sects of established religions. By the year 3000, how many existing religions will be vital or even still living? Old theologies are called mythologies, but they are not myth or fantasy, simply the dead belief systems of a once dynamically religious people.

⚜

Revelation appears from history to be evolutionary. For Christians, does this mean that "The Word became Flesh" from John's Gospel should better read, "The Word is Becoming Flesh"? Jesus did indeed promise to be with his followers until the end of the world. The question as the season of Advent begins is: Of which world was he speaking? Also, in that promise he did not say in what form he would remain till the end of the world.

✳

End-of-November Holiday of the Message Sender. **29**
Books contain many messages, some of which are correct and
others which are not, some messages reflecting the thought of
their day and others ahead of their time. Today celebrates the
birth date of two renowned message senders who were authors
and visionaries, one American, the other British. On this day in
1832 in Germantown, Pennsylvania, Louisa May Alcott was born.
While a tomboy in her youth, she wrote the enchanting novel
Little Women. This day in 1898 in Belfast, Northern Ireland,
also marked the birth of C.S. Lewis, who wrote *Out of the Silent
Planet* and more than thirty other books filled with magical
messages.

Today also honors a creative composer who sent all of his
messages by music, Giancomo Puccini. The great Italian opera
composer died on this day in 1924 in Brussels. By happy accident
on this same day, Thomas Edison demonstrated his hand-cranked
phonograph, whose first message was Edison reciting the simple
poem, "Mary Had a Little Lamb" (see the entry for November
20). The grandchildren of Edison's phonograph, the record player,
tape deck and CD player, would carry to millions beautiful
messages of music and literature, like the operas of Puccini and
the recorded books of writers like Alcott and Lewis.

In 1929 on this day, the *wrong* message was sent by
Commander Richard E. Byrd when he said, "My calculations
indicate that we have reached the vicinity of the South Pole."
While Byrd miscalculated, the nation rejoiced at his success in
reaching the goal of his South Pole expedition.

❦

In these days after Thanksgiving and before the gift-giving
of Christmas, take a brief moment to reflect on the necessity of
sending good and correct messages whenever you are given a
gift. When someone says, "Thank you," for some favor bestowed,
the customary response is, "You're welcome." This phrase must
sound confusing to a foreigner, since *welcome* is used to greet a
guest or as an adjective for something agreeable or good, as in
"welcome news." It might surprise most of us, however, to learn
that in response to thanks, the dictionary meaning of "You're
welcome" is "You are under no obligation for the favor given."

Such a reply is indeed welcome news, for most gifts carry long and heavy strings attached which bind the receiver of a favor to the giver. Usually an honest response when thanks are spoken would be, "Now you owe me one." To say, "You're welcome" but to mean, "I expect something in return for my gift or favor," would be a message as inaccurate as Commander Byrd's. But to say, "You're welcome" with full meaning, implies that the receiver has absolutely no obligation for the gift. One who gives as Jesus intended gifts to be given — freely and out of love — will only send this *right* message.

✳

---

30 The Longing to be Famous, or Infamous, Day.

Psychologists have stated that acts of random violence, like attacks on celebrities, mass killings, hijackings and bombings, are crimes committed for notoriety. The need to be noticed is nothing new. In 356 B.C. the great, elaborate temple of Artemis in Ephesus, one of the seven wonders of the world, was destroyed by fire. The fire was the result of deliberate arson, and the culprit was captured. When asked why he had committed such a terrible deed, he replied that he wanted his name to live in history. The man was executed for his crime, but it was ordered that his name be removed from all public records and never be spoken again. Despite this firm instruction, however, history does know his name: Herostratus.

Perhaps in our contemporary world it is impossible to have a total news blackout of the names of those responsible for acts of mass murder or the attempted killing of famous people. Yet, what purpose is served in making their names and identities known?

※

The telescope was invented in 1608 when a young apprentice was playing with the lenses belonging to his master, a spectacle-maker named Hans Lippershey. While his boss was away, the young man was amusing himself with a variety of optical lenses and accidentally stumbled upon a combination that made distant things look closer. He showed the result of his play to his master, and Lippershey thereupon placed the lenses in a tube and created the telescope.

Play around with the idea of society having a law that forbids the release of the names or photographs of those guilty of a crime, especially the more spectacular and infamous kind. Perhaps when those arrested are taken to court, the police could cover their heads with black bags to prevent them from being identified on the evening news. In 1722, James Bradley used a telescope that was 212 feet long; consider the use of a Reverse Bradleyscope for news about criminals. By this means a criminal's name and identity would shrink to a mere speck, so small as to barely exist.

The Reverse Bradleyscope might be of value not only for criminals but also for saints! Jesus praised and blessed those who prayed in secret, who gave to charity with such secrecy that even their other hand did not have knowledge of the generous deed. As the season of Advent begins, play around with schemes for how to disguise your acts of kindness and generosity – schemes for a microscopic spirituality – and so become famous for nothing!

The paradox is that your name can live in history by committing a terrible crime more easily than by performing deeds of great charity. Yet how important is it to live on by having your name etched forever on bronze plaques, stain glass windows and over the entrance of college buildings? Consider seriously playing with Advent Anonymity as one of the excellent ways to prepare for the birth of Jesus, who loves secret saints.

Now, as easily as you slip into bed at night, slip into a new month.

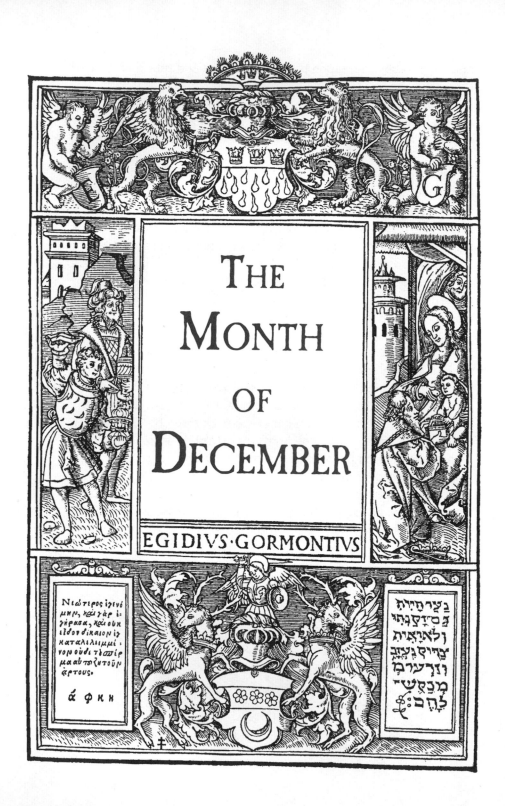

THE
MONTH
OF
DECEMBER

EGIDIVS·GORMONTIVS

Originally the tenth month, this twelfth one retains its old Latin name of *Decem*, for "ten." Yet, the number ten is most appropriate for this month filled with shopping for gifts, decorating your house and tree, sending Christmas cards, attending school programs, going to holiday parties, balancing your end-of-the-year financial affairs, making Advent a holy and prayerful season — to mention but a few of December's activities. If you wish to keep your patience, remain calm and retain your spiritual center amidst the tensions and conflicts of this month, don't forget to count to *decem* before reacting to any stressful situation. For obvious reasons, the Anglo-Saxons named this the *Winter-monath*, or *Yule-monath*. After they became Christian, they also called it *Halig-monath*, "holy month" because of its high holy feast. May this truly be a holy month for you.

The Festival of Advent Snake and Spinach Time.
On a shifting date in the last week of November the year ends — at least the worship year for mainline churches. Four Sundays before Christmas a new worship or liturgical year begins with the Season of Advent. While a contemporary Westerner views time as a line with a termination point, many ancient peoples saw it as a circle, often using the image of a snake swallowing its tail. The ideal almanac would be printed not as an oblong book but in a round shape. To help in entering the cyclical flow of time, use your Almanac as if it were a circle book, a natural form for feeling how days, weeks, months and years flow into one another. On this first day of December feel yourself beginning to curve time around toward the coming months of January and February. As you circle in this endless flow of time, realize

1

that it's not simply a cyclical path but a spiraling one. Each time a month or season recycles, it's not just a rehashing of last year. Rather, it's a reopening and expansion of possibilities along the same arc. It's the difference between return and resurrection — it opens to a true rebirth.

⚜

The Advent season of preparation for the birth of Christmas that we are flowing into can seem schizophrenic; it's a season with a split personality. In Italy for a thousand years it was celebrated as a two-to-four week season of joyous preparation for the feast of the Nativity. In Germany and France it was a forty day season for fasting, doing penance and confessing one's sins, an attitude influenced greatly by the massive fear of the End of the World at the time of the First Millennium. The Gospel readings about the End of the World in the last weeks of the worship year and the first week of Advent reflect this fearful anxiety. With time the Franco-Germanic Advent approach of penance became the focus of the entire church. This northern European approach is clearly reflected in an Advent regulation made by the bishop of Worms, Germany: "In the *Quadragesima* (40 days) before Christmas you must abstain from wine, ale, honey-beer, meats, fats, cheese, and from fat fish." At one time this first day of December was a purple fast from food and fun.

⚜

Contemporary Christians are adopting more of the old Roman Advent of festive, joyful preparation, swimming upstream against the purple pre-millenniumism of the recent Advent. While you decorate for Christmas and listen to carols, you can still keep the spirit of penance by serving a special Advent dish — spinach. Monks in the Middle Ages ate it in seasons of penance when the diet was lean. Nutritionists in the early 1900s preached its benefits, especially for children. In 1930 Elize Segar created Popeye the Sailor, whose legendary source of superhuman strength was spinach. With so much to do in these December days, consider making this wonder food part of your daily diet.

Once it was said of this vegetable, "Eat spinach and be calm." These pre-Christmas days are among the most hectic, and so it would be a good time to test out this claim for calmness. An Advent dish of spinach could do marvels as you stand in the checkout line. Spinach was also once believed to arouse romantic feelings; eat a bowl before praying or giving gifts to the poor so your love for them will inspire you to great generosity. Instead of a coffee break, think about taking a spinach break at work and see if interoffice relations don't become more friendly.

The old northern European Advent was a time to do penance and to confess one's sins, a practice still promoted as necessary for Christmas by today's clergy. Spinach can again come to the rescue. For centuries spinach was also called "the broom of the stomach," since it was thought to sweep out all impurities from the body. Seated before a big bowl of steaming Advent spinach, you could pray:

> Come, holy Advent food,
>> cleanse me of all impurities in these coming days,
>> so that I can truly be ready to celebrate Christmas,
>> the birth of Jesus Christ.
> Cleanse me of impatience so as to make me calm;
>> cleanse me of anger so as to make me more lovable,
>> cleanse me of selfishness and blindness to the poor
>> so as to make me more generous.

✳

The Advent of an Age of Justice and Peace. Not a preparation, but the arrival or coming, especially of something long awaited — this is the first dictionary meaning of advent. The classic Latin meaning implies something that is to come rather than something already arrived. Yours is the choice, then, as to how to use the word. Adventists, the religious denomination, believe that Christ's Second Coming, and the End of the World, are near at hand.

❧⚘❧

You can be an Immanuel Adventist by living as Jesus lived when he said that God's age of justice and equality had already arrived, that it is here and now. Or you can live as if it were still to come, abiding in the hope of its full flowering. Shoplift some precious time in this busy season of shopping and preparing for Christmas to reflect on what your behavior would be like if you were an Immanuel Adventist. To assist you, here is an Islamic parable on justice.

Once, a wise man was approached by four children with a problem. "Holy man, we need your wisdom. The four of us have gathered walnuts together and want to share them equally, but after dividing them among us only three walnuts remain. It seems one of us must have one less, but we cannot decide which one it should be. Help us with your wisdom to do what is just."

The old man replied, "Would you like God's justice or human justice?"

The children were puzzled by his question, and went apart to discuss the problem of two kinds of justice. "We know human justice," said one. "Bribes must be paid to judges, and whoever pays the least loses the case. We'll surely lose some of our walnuts if we ask for human justice. I say we ask for God's justice." One of the other children agreed, saying, "God provides for all, rich and poor. Perhaps, the holy man will shake down another walnut from the tree, and we will all have the same number." Now all in agreement, they returned to the holy man.

"We have decided," said the leader of the children, "to choose God's justice, and now ask for your judgment on our problem."

With a smile the old man replied, "You have chosen well." And to the first child he gave fifty walnuts, to the second thirty, to the third he gave three, and to the fourth none at all!

The end of the parable — or is it the end? As an Immanuel Adventist of the reign of God's justice and peace, how will you live out the ending to this parable?

✵

---

3 **"To Decorate or Not to Decorate, That's the Question" Day.** This Advent day ponders, in the style of Hamlet, the problem of when to decorate for the holidays. The Joneses across the street had their tree up the day after Thanksgiving, and most of the chain stores had theirs up by Halloween. These days you can live simultaneously in two time zones as you attend church and attend to daily life; one is festively attired early for Christmas, while the other is starkly draped in purple penance.

The green and purple Advent Wreath doesn't hold a candle to a six-foot, magical, tinkling lighted, baubled Christmas tree — alas what to do?

❧✥❧

When Christmas trees had real candles, they could be dangerous. So can rushing your Christmas decorating. As this year curves around into the next, you might want to read the Almanac entry for January 8. Before you determine when you want to put your decorations up, ask yourself this question: How long do you want to have your tree and house decorated? Even into the mid-nineteenth century it was believed that if you removed your evergreens and Christmas decorations before February 2nd, the feast of Candlemas, someone in your house would die before next Christmas! Decorating can be hazardous to your health, or, more correctly, *un*decorating too early can be dangerous. Some more liberal interpreters held that you could safely remove your decoration after the Twelfth Day, or Epiphany, without fear of a curse or bad luck.

❧✥❧

Today is also the **Feast of St. Francis Xavier** (1506-1552), a Spanish Jesuit missionary who carried the Gospel to India, Malaysia and Japan, the first European to land there. He was sailing to China when he died, abandoned by the ship's crew on an island a hundred miles southwest of Hong Kong. Francis Xavier could be the patron of Immanuel Adventists, who decorate for Christmas by being willing to give their lives in decorating with Christ those places most in need of the Light of the World. 'Tis the season to decorate — the question is: What?
✥

First Millennium Celebration, 1000 A.D. This day continues the reflection on the celebration of the first thousand years after the birth of Christ. On the eve of that date, in the year 999, Gerbert of Aurillac, a philosopher and inventor, a gifted man in all fields of education and the arts, was elected

4

pope and took the name Sylvester II. He was the Bishop of Rome at the crossing of the millennium until 1003. (Note: Pope Sylvester I lived as Christianity was emerging from the catacombs, and died in 335. His feast day is December 31.) During Sylvester II's reign, the church in the northern territories of Gaul and Germany was proclaiming Advent days of fasting and penance in preparation for the approaching Last Judgment. The new millennium was witnessing frightening things in every area of life. Perhaps foremost was the arrival of a new and terrible weapon that would change the casual pace of war. The atomic bomb of that age came in the form of charcoal, sulfur and potassium nitrate as the Chinese perfected their invention of gunpowder.

Meanwhile, across the great western ocean, potatoes and corn were planted in South America as the Tiahuanaco civilization extended all over Peru. While one South American civilization was thriving, it was the End of the World for the declining Mayan civilization in the Yucatan peninsula. One by one their great cities were being abandoned, and their life and religion were undergoing great changes under their new rulers, the Iltzas from Mexico. The Mayans were highly advanced; for example, they had so precisely calculated the path of the elusive planet Venus that they had an error of only fourteen seconds a year! Their study of the stars and planets led them to make the following prediction: the End of the World would occur on December 23, 2012!

⚜

This could be called Check Your Calendar Day. Will history repeat itself? Will a new and more deadly weapon than the nuclear bomb be invented early in the Third Millennium? Will a new pope be elected a thousand years after Sylvester II to preside over the church in the new century? Like Sylvester, will he also be an inventor, and, if so, might he reinvent an entirely new Catholic Church? Regardless of your denomination, such a reinvention could have wonderful consequences.

✻

Walt Disney's Birthday, 1901. Today marks the birthday of the creator of Disneyland and those globe-trotting American ambassadors, Mickey Mouse and his girlfriend Minnie. Mickey was featured in an early talking movie called *Steamboat Bill,* and a few years later, in 1932, went to Technicolor.

Disney's miracle was to take a despised little creature, a rodent, and have the entire world fall in love with it. Mice and rats are dirty, disease-spreading animals who eat up grain supplies. A pair of them like Mickey and Minnie can leave 18,000 droppings in a month! A 150 pound man would have to run 20,000 to 30,000 miles a day to equal the relative distance a mouse moves its body mass in the same period of time.

Mickey travels even farther and faster than that, spanning the entire globe with dizzying speed. Like many rodents, he also carries a virus, Americanitis, being a prophet-forerunner of McDonald's golden arches, Levi jeans and an array of other American products that are spreading quickly across the world. An Advent question: Was Mickey Mouse a prophet, a kind of John the Baptist of contemporary America, who made straight the crooked cultural ways for twentieth century American symbols of Christmas to spread rapidly across the globe?

❧❀❧

'Tis the season to write a letter with your wishes to Santa Claus. Today, perhaps you can take up an old-fashioned custom instead and write a letter to your household mouse or mice. Some old-timers believe that such rat-letters are more effective than a cat or poison to rid your house of rodents. They suggest giving your unwanted guests an address or place for them to take up new quarters. Such rolled-up rat letters have been found in the walls of old houses and buildings.

Since our practical and spiritual lives are so closely intertwined as to be one, you may wish to experiment with this December exercise: Write a letter to some restless, disease-carrying, dirty little attitude living inside the walls of your heart. If the rat chewing away at your ability to love lives in your pocketbook or billfold, place the note there. If the rat that chews away at charity lives inside your telephone, place your note under it. Place your note in the kitchen, at work or wherever you find a disgusting behavior leaving its trail of unpleasant droppings. Mindful that this is Walt Disney's birthday, you may even wish to address your relocation letter to Mickey or Minnie.

✳

---

6 **Feast of St. Nicholas, Patron of Children.** Nicholas, the fourth century bishop of Myra, is the patron of children, pawnbrokers, sailors and several nations, including Russia and Greece. Having immigrated from the Netherlands to America, Sinter Klaus has become the cultural symbol both of Christmas and of gift-giving. By the end of the twentieth century over twenty-three million children annually visited Sinter Claus in U.S. shopping malls, an average of about 12,000 per mall — sixty percent of all children ages one through ten.

Santa, with his heavy fur-trimmed suit, as well as snowmen, ice and other wintry symbols are now global in their use, even in tropical areas of the world. The "crooked cultural ways" we spoke of yesterday have been made straight, but to what end?

⚜

The kidnapping of children for ransom, abuse or in custody cases is a great concern. Saint Nicholas, who is the patron of children and of Christmas, is also kidnapped in the increasing commercialization of religious rituals, symbols and greetings.

In the mid-1990s, the official China Daily newspaper reported that Chinese consumers were buying millions of Western-style Christmas cards! What is amazing is that many Chinese do not understand what the holiday messages on the cards mean. Yet the English greetings, "Merry Christmas, Happy New Year, and Season's Greetings," said the newspaper, "are becoming household words in China." Not only do the Chinese use Christmas greetings without knowing what they mean, even those who understand English can use them as if they were in a foreign language. "Merry" as a Christmas wish implies "jolly" and "happy," yet it originally meant "blessed, peaceful and pleasant," as in the old Christmas carol "God Rest Ye Merry, Gentlemen." And terms like "Happy holidays" are broad, ecumenical and generic, politically correct greetings, covering not only Jewish and

Christian festivals but also purely secular celebrations.

As you write or speak wishes for Christmas, fill your "merry" with as much peace and blessing as possible. While tainted by commercialization, allow the holy symbols of this season to be instruments of grace and blessing for you and your household. Faced with the overwhelming task of trying to rescue a holy day from the ruthless gang of commercial kidnappers, you may feel as little and poor as a church mouse. Remember that Jesus promised it was the little ones God loved and cared for the most, that they hold the ultimate power in this world.

7

"Praise the Lord and Pass the Ammunition" Day, 1941. On October 16, 1922, former U.S. Secretary of the Navy Josephus Daniels was so impressed with a new wireless invention that he said, "Nobody now fears that a Japanese fleet could deal an unexpected blow on our Pacific possessions....Radio makes surprise impossible." On this day in 1941, an Advent Sunday echoing with songs about God's vision of an earth where even natural enemies like the lion and the gentle lamb would rest side by side in peace, another chant was being sung. While under attack in Pearl Harbor, Hawaii, Chaplain Howell Forgy, on board the U.S. cruiser *New Orleans*, created his own prayer and sang out, "Praise the Lord and pass the ammunition." He was attempting to encourage weary and fearful sailors to keep up their antiaircraft barrage as 353 carrier-based warplanes were bombing U.S. warships.

Earlier on that Advent Sunday morning, the Hawaiian Opana radar station reported incoming aircraft 136 miles from Hawaii. Higher authorities at the information center told the privates on duty to disregard the information. It was not radio but radar which detected the invasion, but it was new and not entirely trusted yet. Five hours after the successful surprise attack, a message sent through ordinary commercial channels reached Pearl Harbor with a message from Washington that the island's defense forces should be on alert.

On this anniversary you can consider the parable of "higher authorities" failing to heed the warning of an approaching disaster. If you are like the privates on that day and have no rank or authority, don't be afraid to trust your own judgment about what's happening in your world. Let the historical event of this infamous day remind you that those in authority can be blind and can give wrong and disastrous orders.

Jesus the realist says to us who are longing for Isaiah's lion and lamb vision of Advent peace, "My peace I leave you, my peace I give to you" (Jn. 14: 27). Two thousand years of war and violence have shown his gift to be either empty or something steeped in mystery. The peace Jesus gave to his followers is not the absence of conflict, but the presence of God in the very midst of strife. Shalom, the Hebrew word usually translated as peace, is so rich in meaning that no single English word can render it. While perfect peace is the expectation of the Messianic Age, in this Age of Immanuel (God with us) peace implies communion with God, and Jesus is the cause and the very presence of that communion. To live in peace is to live in God in the midst of tension and conflict as you daily work toward perfect peace, toward a world of justice, a world without war.

For two millenniums the followers of Jesus who have declared the Messianic Age to be a present reality have sung "Praise the Lord and Pass the Ammunition" as they slaughtered heretics, infidels, pagans and each other. As a follower of the Prince of Perfect Peace, do you sing "Praise the Lord" as you wage holy wars against your enemies in your household, neighborhood, church or society? If so, what ammunition do you pray God will pass to you? Also ask yourself if you find Pearl Harbor style "surprise" attacks on others to be useful and effective.

(Note: Peace takes longer than war. On August 15, 1978, China and Japan signed a treaty of "peace and friendship," which formally ended their mutual antagonism from World War II. That was thirty-three years after V-J Day and the end of hostilities! Does it take you that long to make up and be at peace with your enemies?)

Feast of the Immaculate Conception of Mary. Today's Advent-Christmas holy day celebrates that Mary, the mother of Jesus, was "full of grace," or as a new translation says, "highly favored of God." Mary of Nazareth's unique role in God's plan of salvation as the young girl whose womb would be seeded with Jesus is honored today and is the source of joyous song and prayer. If you feel less than holy or slighted for being maculate — flawed and spotted — chew on this Chinese proverb, "Water which is too pure has no fish" (Ts'ai Ken T'ah).

8

⚜

This season rejoices in the birth of our Savior Jesus Christ. A savior is one who brings *salvation*, which is a baptized word; it once had the secular meaning of "freedom." Isaiah and the other Jewish prophets saw salvation in terms of a "New Israel," an entirely new world liberated from communal and personal evil. That new world of freedom, proclaimed by Mary's son, Jesus, seems so foreign a world as to be rejected by many Christians.

In Maryland in 1671, a law was passed declaring that baptism as a Christian did not mean freedom from slavery. In 1664, the Slavery Act of Maryland stated that slaves could not convert to Christianity in the hope of obtaining freedom, reversing an English court decision requiring that baptized slaves must be given their freedom. Laws similar to Maryland's existed in Virginia, North and South Carolina, New York and New Jersey. Christian slaveholders feared that if the Gospel were taken seriously they would lose their slaves, and so they denied that baptism was the entrance to salvation-freedom.

Holy Mary, Mother of God, pray for us slaves. Pray for all of us baptized Christians, birthed in the salvation of your son, who are still not free.

What are the names of your personal slave owners?

✳

The Birthday of the Credit Card, 1950. Necessity is the mother of invention, and her half sister, Embarrassment, is the mother of the credit card. Francis Xavier McNamara, while

9

attending a business lunch with clients in an exclusive Manhattan restaurant, couldn't pay the bill because he had left his cash at home. Red-faced, McNamara frantically called his wife, who rushed his money to the restaurant. Mother Embarrassment inspired him to resolve never to be caught cashless again, and he created the *Diners Club*, a multipurpose charge card to cover food and drink, entertainment and travel.

The Gold Rush was on, and his credit card was adopted by others, many of whom failed. *American Express* cards appeared in 1958, and soon millions would not leave home without them. Once IBM began to computerize the business of credit card companies, McNamara's creation became the prophet of a new cashless society. What would Christmas shopping be without the credit card? The answer is the three S's: Safer, Saner and Simpler.

In 1996 over one million Americans filed for bankruptcy, up forty-four percent from 1994. Americans in 1997 were borrowing money more than ever and were in debt almost $1.2 trillion, a good part of which was owed to credit card companies. Does your personal future hold the possibility of bankruptcy? Estimates indicate that by the year 2010, there will be more than 100,000 Americans aged 100 years or older, and by 2020 there will be more Americans over the age of sixty-five than under the age of thirteen. A "2010" dollar is estimated to be worth only sixty-three cents compared to its counterpart of thirteen years earlier. As you look at your savings account or credit card bill debt, look over the horizon at the year 2020 and these estimated prices: A gallon of milk, $5.96; a postage stamp, $.71; one room apartment, $1,010 per month.

⚜

If you will be among that multitude of those over sixty-five in 2020 and on social security or a fixed income, or among those over one hundred years old in 2010, does your financial future look frightening? If you found it difficult to make ends meet in 1996 when a gallon of milk was only $2.64 and a postage stamp for your Christmas card only thirty-two cents, what will you do as we progress into the Third Millennium? Sending far fewer Christmas cards, eating bread and drinking water could be the answer. Another answer comes from Immanuel Jesus, who said to us, "Do not be anxious about tomorrow, about what you will drink or eat or wear" (Mt. 6: 31). Remember how God has taken loving care of you in the past when you have trusted in God. So fear not concerning tomorrow. Do not be anxious, but be wise as serpents and clever as squirrels and prepare for tomorrow as best you can.

Remember how God cared for you throughout the Exodus, how God fed you in the desert; remember the past half century. In 1950, a Sears three-piece bedroom set cost $49.98, a round-trip ticket on North American Airlines from New York to California was $88.00. In 1958, a brand new Oldsmobile was $2,933, and a pair of blue jeans was $3.75. In 1960, milk was twenty-six cents a quart, a Black Angus eight-course Christmas dinner was $3.75, and you could rent a car for $119 a month. As the cost of living increased from decade to decade, you did not perish. Remember, and do not be anxious as you move into the Advent of the future.

✹

Prophetic Law Day – U.S. Women's Suffrage, 1869. 10

Today in 1869 the Wyoming Territory was the first place in the United States where women were given the right to vote. To many this was shocking, as shocking as women serving tables in a restaurant. A decade earlier in 1853, prophetic women began working as waitresses. American feminist Amelia Bloomer was delighted to see graceful women in place of "(men) in their heavy tread and awkward motions." In a discussion with the proprietor, however, Bloomer learned that while the change in table servers was generally satisfactory, it was not universally accepted, "...the only objectors being a few women...preferring black men."

≈⅌⅌≈

The two great prophets of Advent, St. Isaiah and St. John the Baptist, knew from their personal experience that some crooked ways do not enjoy being straightened. Many are the hills that resist being leveled, even if that is required for God to enter daily life with justice and equality. And surprisingly, many are those valleys, while a depressed lot, that are not interested in themselves or their sister valleys being raised up.

Laws — as well as men and women — can be prophetic instruments of God for change and justice. When you are given a chance to work with God, do so; vote for those prophetic laws that make flesh God's slowly emerging vision for our world.

Do you have any crooked ways, hills or valleys that are eager to be reconstructed? Which of them might resist being altered?

✦

---

11 Christmas Gift-Giving: U-Turns Forbidden Festival.

Mid-December is shopping season, when gifts are purchased and wrapped in preparation for the feast of gift-giving, Christmas. Consider, today, making the *No U-Turn* red arrow a new symbol of this season.

It's already a familiar sign in the age of automobiles, an age that surprised the president of the Michigan Savings Bank. In 1903, Horace Rackham, who was Henry Ford's lawyer, was advised by the bank's president, "The horse is here to stay, but the automobile is only a novelty — a fad." Rackham ignored this professional advice and bought $5,000 worth of stock; he sold it several years later for $12.5 million.

There's no going back to the horse and buggy days. In the same way, each gift you give this Christmas should bear on it a small sticker with that familiar *No U-Turn* symbol, meaning, "There's no going back — no return of gratitude is expected." That symbol says that your gift is marked, "No strings attached. This gift has been given feet to walk away, and can be given away to whomever you wish."

⚜

Gift-giving, Jesus admonished, is an art involving such secrecy that even the other hand, left or right, does not know about it. It's no easy matter to give a gift without strings, expecting no expression of gratitude from the person to whom it was given. It requires dealing with the common affliction known as *gift-itch*. This is an itching of one hand to feel the appreciation from the gift given by the other hand. *Gift-itch* has us daily watching the mail for a thank you note or letter. *Gift-itch* is also manifested by the need to get something back, a favor or a gift in return for what is given. Invisibly wrapped in each gifts-with-strings-attached is a small IOU intended for the receiver of the gift.

In the last decades of the twentieth century, letter and package bombs were a dangerous threat. Any gifts that come with strings that bind the receiver to some future obligation are forms of package bombs. Refrain from sending them this Christmas and be cautious whenever opening such gifts.

✳

Feat of Our Lady of Guadalupe, a Fiesta Festival. **12** On this day in 1531 the Mother of God appeared to a fifty-seven-year-old, recently baptized Aztec convert peasant named Juan Diego on the Aztec holy hill of Tepeyac located just outside present-day Mexico City. Dressed as an Aztec princess, she filled Diego's poncho with roses and told him to go and show them to the bishop. When he released the roses and presented them to the bishop, imprinted upon his cactus fiber poncho was the now-famous image of our Lady of Guadalupe. That image has inspired the revolution for Mexico's independence as well as more recent labor-justice protests.

This is truly a feast fit for a *fiesta*, the Spanish word for party or celebration that also means a holy day or holiday. Fiesta is a smile-producing kind of word, for it is impossible to think of a frowning fiesta. If all holy days were occasions to party, their popularity would soar in our society of perpetual work. On this feast, consider making all your holy days into homemade fiestas.

᠅

Gift yourself with a day of smiles and find yourself gifted by happiness. Research has shown that by simply smiling an artificially induced smile the same brain changes occur as in moments of spontaneous joy and delight. What better gift to give yourself — and others — than a smile. A smile can be as miraculous as the appearance of the Virgin Mary and her gift of special roses to Juan Diego. A smile can imprint upon your heart the rosy glow of happiness.

For mature adults the satisfaction and joy of giving a gift is far greater than the thrill of receiving one. Giving is one of the measurements of maturity and the foundation of a satisfying life. Along with the joy of giving gifts, especially secret gifts, treat yourself today and smile as much and as often as possible. Practicing both gift-giving and smiling this Advent will allow you to say and truly experience the Fiesta Festival of a "Merry Christmas."

✠

---

13 **Feast of Saint Lucy and Frozen Foods.** A rejected Sicilian suitor accused the teenage Lucy of being a Christian in 304 A.D., and she became an early witness-martyr for her faith. Her feast is popular among Lutherans of Sweden; on this day the oldest daughter, wearing a crown of lighted candles, brings coffee and rolls to her parents in bed. Her brothers follow wearing cone-shaped hats decorated with stars; then come her sisters carrying lighted candles. In Lucy's name, and to honor the Light of the World, let candles and lights blaze forth in your home on this feast.

In the dark of winter, only a few days from the winter solstice on December 21, what better time for a comment on the work of subzero temperatures that give us the gift of frozen foods. In 1945 A.TV. (After Television), *Consumer Reports* stated, "Precooked frozen foods have a brilliant future." 1940s refrigerators were short on freezer space, and so this new/ancient food storage process was limited. Television prompted the arrival of precooked meals for those who were magnetized to their TV screens. Swanson dinners were renamed TV dinners, and as TV audiences grew so did the market for frozen food.

❧⚬❦

Give thanks in this Ice and Fire Age, when both freezing and heating makes daily life easier for those in the industrial world. Freezing, although immobilizing on some levels, does preserve food from spoiling. Fire, even as small as a candle flame, while it can burn, brings warmth and light into the world. On this Advent day, ask yourself what parts of you need to be defrosted, and what aspects of your personality need to have a flame put beneath them? Defrosting and warming up are challenging Advent activities.

✳

A Jubilee Rest Stop Day. These days before Christmas are often extremely hectic and busy, so declare today as a personal Jubilee rest day. The biblical Jubilee year of grace, to which Jesus compared himself in his shocking sermon in his hometown synagogue, was a year to let fields rest, unpaid debts be forgiven, slaves set free and liberty proclaimed for all. (See Lv. 25: 8-17, 29-31 and Lk. 4: 16-21). A Jubilee, proclaimed every forty-nine or fifty years, was a year with 365 Sabbaths.

14

Old-fashioned Christian Sabbaths were weekly rest stops on the highway of life. In 1656, the burgomasters of New Netherlands, which was shortly to become New York, made a law to insure the rest of Sundays. Their Rest Law forbade drinking, sowing, mowing, building, sawing, smithing, bleaching, hunting, fishing, dancing, card playing, bowling, jaunting in a boat or carriage and ticktacking. A year later, in 1657, the sheriff of Fort Orange, now Albany, New York, arrested men for playing *kolven* — believed to be an early form of golf — on Sunday.

❧❦❧

Ah, for the good old days of the seventeenth century, when Sunday meant a chance to catch your breath and have a mini-Jubilee. Yet the clock can't be turned backwards, especially since it is racing forward at supersonic speed. Perhaps you feel a bit like the man who owned a large hunk of the world in the eighteenth century, the emperor Napoleon Bonaparte, who said, "You can ask me for anything but time."

To be able to have an Advent Jubilee Day of rest requires saying that "vulgar" two-letter word, "No." In this season of countless gatherings, parties and programs, just say "No." Yet, if you do so, be prepared to be made to feel guilty. Regardless of the request, when pressured to say "Yes," experiment with the response, "Are you trying to make me feel guilty?" Without doubt this question will be answered with a "No." However, you may want to ask that question again to help the other person do an honesty check. You may need to repeat it even a third time to help the other check for unconscious motives.

'Tis the season to be jolly, and 'tis the season for guilt. Beware of acting and decorating your halls not with holly but with guilt, guilt, guilt.

✸

---

15 Christmas Season Day to Beware of Clip Joints.

These clip joints are not barbershops, but those establishments where you are cheated by unfair prices or hidden charges. The term *clip joints* originated in the sixteenth century, when pickpockets were plentiful. Among their prime targets were expensive pocket watches the wealthy carried in their vest pockets. To protect the considerable investment in those watches, watch chains were invented as an anticrime device. Thieves — especially, it was said, gypsies — began to use small metal clippers by which a watch and its proud owner could be separated. And so, coffeehouses, taverns and social gathering places where gypsies and pickpockets were known to mingle were called *clip joints*.

⚜

Beware being mauled at the mall, and beware of letting your home become a clip joint. Joy can easily be stolen by the pickpockets of exaggerated expectations about Christmas. Joy can easily be clipped out of your heart by expectations that the house must be spotless, every dish home-cooked and "just the right" gifts found for everyone. Clip, clip — there goes your peace and joy when all the family must be together, everyone must have a good time and love and peace must abound. Clip, clip, goes your peace and contentment when you live alone and television shows are filled with parties, dinners and happy celebrations of loving, caring families and friends.

Sixteenth century owners guarded their pocket treasures

with chains. Not a gold or heavy iron chain, but a watchful eye over your expectations and assumptions about this holiday season is the best anticrime device to protect you from pickpockets of the heart.

✷

The Toy Festival of St. Sergius of Radonezh. By the age of twenty, this Russian Orthodox hermit was living in a forest north of Moscow. Drawn by his charm and prayerfulness, others joined him there, and he founded a monastery. Sergius was known as a mystic who had visions of Mary, the Mother of God, and was renowned for his skill at settling arguments among fellow monks and between neighbors. The mystic's hobby, and good mystics have them, was making toys for children. St. Sergius thus joins St. Nicholas as a patron of children and their toys.

16

Toys are playthings, often seen simply as objects to amuse children, having no practical value. Santa's bag is overflowing not with practical winter clothing, shoes and school books, but with "useless" toys. But good toys are not useless. Toys arouse the passion of imagination: To operate early toys required not batteries but the indispensable power of make-believe. Joshua Lionel Cowen's electrical-powered train of the 1920s was the grandfather of electronic toys and video games that for many a child spelled D.O.O.M. for their imagination.

⁂

Toy Shopping for the Future: the Year 2020. An ideal gift for your child this year is PAL, Personal Ally-A-Lone computer. It will act as a teacher, mentor, moral guide, confessor and, most importantly, a companion. Gone is the need for some imaginary friend and playmate; PAL is now available in small, medium and large doll shapes, or in a portable pocket-size.

Due out for Christmas 2021 is MATE, a computer companion for adults. It will feature interactive conversations as with a friend, a personal twenty-four-hour-a-day slave that will remind you of appointments, when to take your medicine and when to shop, eat, sleep and pray each day. As your personal secretary it will give you updates on messages, give directions for a variety of tasks and make reservations. MATE is also a perfect nighttime companion; it can read to you, tell bedtime stories or hum softly as you fall asleep, and then gently awaken you at any appointed hour. As God said to Adam, "It is not good for one to be alone" — so buy a MATE today.

> St. Sergius and St. Nicholas,
>> protect us from the runaway train of technology.
> Holy saints of toys, arouse us to prayerfully play
>> and to waste away part of every day
>> in totally "useless" activity.
> Electrify our imaginations
>> and lead us to make room for make-believe.

�֎

---

17 The Eight-Day Jewish Festival of Hanukkah.

Today remembers the Jewish movable festival of lights, and of several spellings. Chanukah, Hanukah or Hanukkah begins at sundown, as do all Jewish feasts. It commemorates the victory of the Maccabees in 165 B.C. over the Greek Syrians. The rededication (from which the name comes) and lighting of the temple lamps is traditionally remembered with the lighting of eight candles, with feasting and the giving of gifts.

The well-known Yiddish greeting and toast of "*Mazel tov*" literally means "Good luck." It has come also to mean "Congratulations" or "Thank God!" While *tov* means "good," it is interesting and appropriate for this season that *mazel* is actually the Hebrew word for "star." Thus, *mazel tov* can mean "Good star" or "May a good star shrine upon you."

In 1910 the General Electric Company registered its lamps and light bulbs with the name of *Mazda*, from Ahura Mazda, the Persian god of light from Zoroaster's sixth century B.C. religion of Zoroastrianism, one of those nearly extinct religions sited in the November 28 entry. In the mid-seventh century when Persia fell to Islam, it virtually disappeared. Today, only 10,000 people in Iran are thought to practice Zoroastrianism.

According to this old Persian religion, the god Ahura Mazda created all the 486,000 good stars, or lucky stars, under which people are said to be born. While there were an equal number of bad stars, or disasters (See the entry for October 7 on *disastro*, bad stars), this is the season of good stars, particularly the good star of Bethlehem.

～～❀～～

Perhaps a good, new season's greeting could be, "May 486,001 *mazel tovs* be yours" (the added one is for the star of Bethlehem). In the second half of the twentieth century, the Japanese also gave the name of *Mazda* to one of their automobiles. Few who own one may even know that their car is named for an old god. Reflecting on the November 28 entry, will the year 4999 likewise see the ancient names of *Moses* or *Jesus* being used on products?

～～❀～～

Also on this day in 1943, a "good star-*mazel tov*" shone on the Chinese people living in the U.S. For too long they had suffered under many of the 486,000 bad stars. In 1943 President Franklin Roosevelt signed the bill repealing the Chinese Exclusion Act. Initiated in 1882, this act banned all Chinese immigration for ten years and was extended until 1924, when Congress banned all Asians. So great was American anti-Asian discrimination that even Roosevelt's repeal allowed for only 105 Chinese to immigrate to the U.S. annually, a quota not abolished until 1965 when a better star appeared.

How many of the stars in the flag of the United States are good stars for some and bad stars for others?

✡

Death Day of Sitting Bull, Chief of the Sioux, 1890. On this day in 1890 Chief Sitting Bull of the Sioux was killed by U.S. Indian Police in a mysterious skirmish in his house in South Dakota while allegedly resisting arrest. Murder may be a more accurate term for the death of Sitting Bull who had been victorious over General Custer at the battle of Little Big Horn in 1876. The great chief had appeared in Buffalo Bill's Wild West Show, and as a parting gift Buffalo Bill gave him the trick

18

horse he rode in the show.

Shortly after he returned to the Dakotas, Sitting Bull was taken under arrest by the U.S. Army, which was alarmed by the spread of the Indian Ghost Dances. A confused scuffle broke out on that fateful day in 1890. Shots were fired, and Sitting Bull was killed. Outside the house, his horse heard the gunshots, thought they were the cue for his act and began to do his tricks. The horse sat down and raised one hoof — to the horror and terror of those gathered outside. They supposed that the spirit of Sitting Bull had entered his horse.

✦

Like Sitting Bull's horse, all of us can easily respond to old cues and begin to perform routines learned by practice over the years. While you may not sit down and raise one hoof, you may raise your dander, your voice or your fist when given the right cues. The prayer of this season is to make the crooked ways straight. This could be translated as learning how to respond differently to old cues that initiate negative behavior, anger and distress. Habitual ways of behaving are cued not as in the theater by some overt action but by unconscious signals. The more you know what your cues are, the easier it is to make straight ways.

Consider this practical example: Whenever a speaker pauses in the midst of a sentence, that empty space can seem like a cue for you to jump in and finish the thought. Putting words into other people's mouths is unsanitary, impolite and unloving. Finishing another's sentence by supplying a word or name without being asked for assistance could be taken as a rude way of saying you are smarter and quicker than the speaker. Another cue is the clock; when time is squeezing your wrist by tightening the strap of your watch, that can be an unconscious cue causing you to cut someone off in mid-sentence, in a hurry for the speaker to get to the point.

This is the season to practice how to respond differently to old cues, unless they are cues that signal the need for a patient saint or a generous Santa Claus to step onto the scene.

✴

Anniversary of *Poor Richard's Almanack*, 1732. This entry commemorates Benjamin Franklin's publishing of his almanack (with a "k") in Philadelphia on this day in 1732. It was in continuous publication for twenty-five years and was one of the most popular writings of Colonial America. "Early to bed and early to rise, makes a man healthy, wealthy and wise" is one of Franklin's more famous Almanack proverbs. Franklin, it appears, named his almanack after *Poor Robin's Almanac* (without a "k") by Robert (or Robin) and William Winstanley, first published in England in 1663. An earlier Colonial almanac was printed in 1639 by William Pierce, a shipowner who wanted to attract more English passengers to the Colonies. The familiar *Old Farmer's Almanac* was established in 1792, and today contains — along with planting tables — Zodiac secrets and useful astronomical calculations that hold "new, useful and entertaining matter."

Almanacs take their name from the medieval Latin word for calendar and are stuffed with astronomical data, with tidbits of information, jokes and proverbs. The first almanacs were issued before the invention of printing, as early as a hundred years after the First Millennium.

♠♥♦♣

For more on Ben Franklin, lean ahead around the corner on the circle of time and read the entry for January 17th in your *Old Hermit's Almanac*. After this voyage around the curve of time, close your Almanac and ponder. The book you are holding is an antique, a relic from an old and slower age. Almost half the Americans polled in the late 1990s, forty-one percent, said they believed that in a hundred years books would become collectors' items.

Five hundred years ago books were so scarce that the bishop of Winchester, England, whose entire library counted only seventeen books, had to leave a large deposit to guarantee that he would return, uninjured, a Bible borrowed from the convent of St. Swithin. In two or three decades, books printed between 1900 and 1940 will be scarcer still, since they are self-destructing. The acid in the paper used to print books in that era, together with pollutants in the air, are eating them up. Books whose paper was made from rags, as was the case before 1900, are holding up well. What, however, will be the effect of recycled paper — even faster disappearing books? Yet, a more immediate factor that will make your Almanac a relic is electricity. A copy of your *Old Hermit's Almanac* is in the U.S. Library of Congress, which has over 16.5 million books. That entire library of books could be reduced to photochromatic mircoimages that can be stored in six four-drawer filing cabinets!

Does the Third Millennium mean the End of the World for books? Is it *sayonara* to books because of television, internetting, new forms of electronic books and, most of all, the death of leisure? At the crossing of the century, sixty-four percent of your fellow citizens believe the twenty-first century will have less leisure time. This Hanukkah-Christmas, give yourself the gift of a book to read, and the gift of a resolution to carve out more leisure time for yourself — so that *you* won't become extinct!

✳

---

20 **Feast of the Christmas Tree, 1521.** The evergreen tree has an ancient Germanic tradition; the first recorded Christmas tree — without lights — was in the German region of Alsace in 1521. Candles began appearing on the evergreen tree from the seventeenth century when it immigrated from Germany to France in 1837. Prince Albert, the husband of Queen Victoria, set up a German Christmas tree in Windsor Castle in 1841. German Catholic and Protestant immigrants then carried the Christmas tree to America in the mid-1800s, where it first appeared in the homes of German-Americans. In 1850 Charles Dickens called it "a new German toy," and by 1891 President Benjamin Harrison called it "an old-fashioned" Christmas tree.

As early as the 1700s, the alien Christmas tree may have been smuggled into the Colonies by German immigrants. It was, in fact, reported that German Hessian soldiers who served in George Washington's army had Christmas trees. Generally, however, these smuggled trees were kept hidden — and for good reason. In 1660 the celebration of Christmas was forbidden by a law in Massachusetts, carrying a fine of five shillings for violators.

Not only was Christmas banned but also Christ's Mass, from which the holiday is named. In 1700 all the colonies but

Maryland and Pennsylvania had enacted laws forcing all Roman Catholic priests to leave within three months. If a papist priest were found after that time, he would be arrested as an "incendiary and disturber of the public peace and safety and an enemy of the true Christian religion." If caught, a priest faced life imprisonment, and if he escaped and was caught again, he would be executed. To understand the cause of this intense bigotry, follow the curve of time either forwards or backwards and read the entry for August 24 in your Almanac.

⚜

Perhaps as you frantically race to get your last Christmas cards in the mail on your way to the mall to finish your shopping before you attend the office Christmas party, you may wish for a renewal of the 1660 law forbidding Christmas. Yet, instead of bemoaning the numerous obligations of this season, remember that once it was legally banned here in the United States.

Let each brightly lit Christmas tree, every decorated home and the freedom for Catholics to attend Christmas Mass be reasons to sing out loudly the joy of your religious liberty.

✻

Winter Solstice, the Long Night of Fear. For our ancient ancestors these days around the winter solstice were times of great fear: Would the sun die or refuse to return, casting the earth into icy darkness? Would the great glaciers return, destroying all life? Yet, the evergreens, mistletoe and holly plants that remained green were signs from the gods that spring would return. Fires were kindled, prayers were chanted and spells cast to lure the sun back from today's journey to its northernmost point. *Holly* is actually another word for *holy*, for it was godly green in the darkness and cold of winter.

Among the beliefs of the Germanic peoples was that at the advent of the End of the World, the great glaciers of the north would begin to creep southward, relentlessly overwhelming everything in their path. All humans would be destroyed in a great cataclysmic disaster of crushing ice and the raging flames that would follow earthquakes. Only two humans, it was believed, would survive, the last boy and girl on earth. They would be hidden in the trunk of an evergreen tree to be kept safe until the destruction of the earth was complete and a new sun and moon would appear. Then the meadows would turn green, and the young couple would come out of the evergreen tree to begin life all over again. From this belief arose the custom of burying people inside tree trunks, which is the supposed origin of coffins.

Ancient fears linger, even if far beneath the level of consciousness. Freud held that in our blood still lurk fears of prehistoric beasts and the fear that the sun will die. But there are more immediate dangers to fear, like snow, ice and even fog. "Beware the *Pogonip*, my child," an uncommon occurrence of frozen fog. *Pogonip* was the name given by the Native American Indians for the needlelike icicles of the frozen fog that might form in these early winter days. Breathing any kind of fog, the Native Americans believed, would injure the lungs.

⚜

Obtain some real holly, today, and hang this green holy symbol in your home as a sign of hope during this winter of frozen possibilities, stalled reforms and renewals of religion and government. Celebrate this night in a warm circle of family and loving friends, and drink a toast to spring. Light a fire, even if only the flames on candles, and let all declare that spring is greater than winter, fire stronger than ice and love stronger than death.

✳

---

22 **Solemnity of the Feast of St. Wenceslaus.** The patron saint of Czechoslovakia and Bohemia — and of beer brewers — his feast is officially commemorated on September 28. Today is the solemn celebration of his feast as the saintly subject of the Christmas carol, "Good King Wenceslaus." While murdered by his brother, Boleslaus, whom he forgave as he died, crying out, "God forgive you, brother," he became a Christmastide hero for another reason. Wenceslaus, the duke of Bohemia, was once out walking in the snow on the night after Christmas, the feast of St. Stephen, December 26. When he saw a poor beggar freezing in the snow, he removed his heavy fur cloak and covered the poor shriveling man with it. Later that night he was awakened in his sleep by the same beggar, who appeared to him in a vision as Jesus Christ.

⚜

As we hurry about to complete our Christmas shopping for ourselves and those we love, let us not forget to gift those unknown poor. They may not appear to us in a vision as Jesus Christ, but they truly are members of the body of the Risen Jesus. Blessed are those who see Christ in the least and poorest.

These last days of Advent are days to both forgive and to be forgiven. Long ago in China this was a time to sweep and clean the house to greet Tsao Wang, the spirit of the hearth and chimney. He wore a pointed red cap and a red jacket. Each year at this time he returned to heaven to make an annual report on the lives of people. It was customary for young and old to smear syrup on the lips of Tsao Wang in pictures or statues to seal them, keeping Tsao Wang from reporting their sins and thus insuring heaven's good fortune and blessings.

The need for house and heart to be cleansed at this darkest time of the year seems to be a part of our human heritage. Instead of smearing syrup or glue on the lips of Jesus Christ in pictures in your home or using syrupy words about being sorry for your sins, like good king Wenceslaus you can actually forgive your brothers and sisters, forgive them even as they are inflicting pain and injury on you. This is a good feast to forgive, which is the best way to be forgiven for the failings of this past year.

⚜

This day is also the **Feast of St. Thomas**, the bold doubter of the resurrection, who gladly laid down his life in proclaiming what he once doubted.

✦

Birthday of the Toast, 600 B.C. *"Cheers"* and *"To your Health"* or *"Mazel tov"* and other toasts so associated with this season are believed to have originated with the Greeks as a

23

precautionary step before drinking. To insure that those drinking the wine would not be poisoned — a longtime favorite way to dispose of an enemy — the host first sipped the wine, and then all raised their cups and drank. This ritual soon became a sign of friendship, since if the wine were poisoned the host was willing to take on a dark fate for his friends. The Romans adopted the custom as a precautionary step but added a piece of toasted bread to their cups, giving the ritual its present name. The burnt toast provided charcoal which reduced the acidity of slightly vinegary wine.

By the early eighteenth century a new tradition was added to the custom: to drink to the health of a famous person, king, pope or a very beautiful woman. This, as you may have already guessed, was the origin of being known as "the toast of the town."

⁂

To raise your glass in a toast is a sacred action as well as a gesture of friendship. The raising up of a glass of wine while making a toast is linked to the priest at Mass raising up the chalice after pronouncing the words of consecration. The lifting up of that chalice is an offering of *the* sacrifice to God. So too, when friends and family toast on Christmas by raising their glasses, they are offering up their love and friendship to God.

In the ritual of toasting, what is symbolically lifted up is blessed by God above. As the glass is lowered, the offering is returned, enriched by heaven's blessing. Then all drink of the consecrated love and friendship, enriched by heaven's blessing. Since the practical life and the spiritual life are one, I propose a toast: "Here's to the eternal wedding of those two lives."

※

---

24 **Christmas Eve, Orthodox Feast of Sts. Adam and Eve.**
Christmas begins at sundown today with a liturgical feast, as is the custom with Jewish holy days. Tonight is not only the holiest night of the year but also the richest in music, magic and enchantment. The following are some of the beliefs about the enchantment of this night of nights: It was held that cattle in

stables fall to their knees at midnight, birds sing all night long, all trees and plants — especially those along the Jordan River — bow in reverence toward Bethlehem. On this night, water in wells and fountains is said to be blessed by God with healing powers. Mysterious bells chime joyfully in the depths of mines, while cheerful lights can be seen in caves.

It was once believed that at midnight the gates of paradise are opened and anyone dying at that hour would enter heaven at once. Children born on this night are especially blessed; they were believed to have the power to see spirits and even command them. Animals were thought to be able to talk like humans at midnight, and even in Latin, while witches, evil spirits and ghosts had their powers suspended and could work no harm to humans, beasts or homes.

Shakespeare, in Act 1, Scene 1 of *Hamlet*, echoed some of those common beliefs:

> Some say that ever 'gainst that season comes
> Wherein our Saviour's birth is celebrated,
> The bird of dawning singeth all night long:
> And then, they say, no spirit dare stir abroad;
> The nights are wholesome; then no planets strike,
> No fairy takes, no witch has power to charm,
> So hallow'd and so gracious is the time.

❦

Make this night both magical and mystical by your efforts to let the enchantment work in your household. Mindful that legend says all evil spirits are impotent on this night, extend that power to those dark spirits of anger, impatience and hate. Work with the magic and perform miracles of healing and reconciliation between family members. Work with the magic and perform acts of restitution, so that whenever you die the gates of Paradise will be wide open. Work with the magic and add your voice to those of the birds, singing your praises of God by attending worship. Work with the magic and bend down with the trees in adoration that two thousand years ago God became flesh so that you could experience God in your flesh.

Also, tonight, at your evening meal you can celebrate the Orthodox Church feast of Saints Adam and Eve and their famous fruit. By eating the forbidden fruit, usually named as an apple, they lost paradise. Apples and Christmas Eve go together like apple pie and cheese. The bright globes on your Christmas tree took the place of apples, which were once hung on fir trees called Paradise Trees. On Christmas, apples were replaced with round Holy Communion wafers and later by pastry and candy, and then by metallic balls.

At table with family or friends, pass around an apple and let each person take a bite out of it. By this ritual you can join in solidarity with Adam and Eve and express your personal responsibility for the sins that the Savior born this night came to remove. Then you can rejoice with a festive meal that Immanuel has come.

✳

---

25 **Christmas, Feast of the Nativity of Jesus Christ.** About the year 330 A.D., after Christianity had emerged from the catacombs, it began to observe a feast of the Nativity of Jesus. While his birth was celebrated by some on January 6, it was moved by Rome to December 25, where it is known as Christmas, or the day of the Christ's Mass. Some early theologians, called Church Fathers, and writers claimed it was the actual date of his birth. Others, more historically correct, stated that the actual date was unknown. The feast fits well near the winter solstice since the Bible had called the Messiah "the Sun of Justice." The ancient cult of Mithras (another extinct religion) celebrated this day as the "Birthday of the Sun" with great festivity in the Roman world, and so it was baptized and made the birth of the Son of God.

While our calendar is dated from the birth year of Jesus, the present number is incorrect. In the sixth century in Rome, Dionysius Exiguus, a monk scribe, made a mistake of four or five years in determining the birth of Jesus. He counted backwards thirty years from the beginning of the public life of Jesus given by Luke's Gospel. However, that was not a precise figure, but rather was intended to mean "around thirty." Scholars today believe a more accurate date for the birth of Jesus would be 4 B.C. With that correction in place, this Almanac is being written in the year 2001, which means that the Third Millennium has already come and that you are reading today's entry as a citizen of the twenty-first century.

⚜⚜⚜

So significant is Christmas that it could be celebrated each day of the year's 365. Images of the crib should have year-round presence as reminders that God became flesh in Bethlehem and nothing has been the same since. The greatest gift on Christmas is to open wide God's gift to Earth: Ended is the ancient divorce between the sacred and the secular; all life and matter has become enfleshed with God. The vision proclaimed by the prophets predicted as coming "...in those days" has arrived — the reign or age of God has begun. Not only is it proper to count time from Christmas' day and year, it is fitting to count your blessings in being so gifted as to live in this time of the reign of God on Earth.

Perhaps some day in this new century a new denomination will arise, the Church of Christmasites. They will celebrate Christmas daily with family meals and the giving of a gift each day. They will keep their Christmas trees and decorations up in their homes the entire year, and carols will be the chants of their worship gatherings. Most importantly, people of this new church will be extremely generous to the poor and homeless, all 365 days of the year. They will work tirelessly for peace on earth and will practice perpetual good will toward all. While this might seem tiresome to some, perhaps that is because they are only halfhearted Christians.

✳

Feast of St. Stephen. In the Acts of the Apostles the first followers of Jesus created an office, or ministry, of a servant to care for the widows and the needy. Perhaps the most famous of these deacons, Stephen, was martyred for his faith. Deaconesses also appeared in the New Testament, Deaconess Phoebe for one, and they had a full and respected standing as ministers into the fourth and fifth century. In 692 the minimum age for a deaconess was set at forty, and their role was limited to works

26

of charity and pastoral service to women. They became an extinct ecclesiastical species a hundred years after the First Millennium. Deaconesses saw a revival in German Lutheranism in 1833. The office of the permanent deacon was revived in Roman Catholicism in the 1960s. In those churches that have the office, deacons and deaconesses perform outstanding service in countless ways.

⚜

Using the ugly word "slave," Jesus called all his followers to be deacons or deaconesses, to be servants to one another. Today there are clerical deacons, permanent as well as transitional, who are part of the hierarchical church, and there are also catacomb deacons and deaconesses. These unofficial servants wear no special clothing or symbol of their honorable calling, and they receive no additional ordination other than their baptism and confirmation. They are not treated with any special respect or given any privileged place in processions. Like the ordained deacon, they *preach* — but only by their lives. They *baptize* their workplaces by bringing to them the fullness of Christ. And they *perform marriages* as they wed together the sacred and secular again and again on the assembly line, at the office or at home. Catacomb deacons and deaconesses perform lowly tasks in parish life and in the world with humility and great love of God. Today is also their feast day.

In these Twelve Days of Christmas gift-giving, if you are an ordained or a catacomb deacon or deaconess, go out of your way to care for the poor.

✳

---

27 **Feast of St. John the Beloved.** This is the feast of friendship, in honor of St. John, the beloved disciple-friend of Jesus. The Gospel of John and the epistles that sing the song of love so beautifully make him the patron saint of friendship. Gift yourself today, this Third Day of Christmas, with time to remember in prayer those whom you have called by that sacred and beautiful name, *friend*. The blessing of St. John's wine and toasting with friends was once a part of this holy day (see again the entry for December 23 on the **Birthday of the Toast**) and is still a perfect way to celebrate this feast of friendship.

Saint John was the only one of the twelve apostles who was denied the gift of being a martyr, dying instead at an advanced age on the island of Patmos. His embracing as the will of God a death in old age could be called "White Martyrdom," for that truly is a difficult calling. Legend says that John dug his own grave, in the shape of a cross; laying down in it, he died. Then, the legend says, a bolt of lightning shot from heaven, and John, both body and soul, was gone.

⚜

Good diet and medical care in the Western world have helped create an ever increasing population of elderly people. Recall the research showing that by 2020 there will be more Americans over sixty-five than under thirteen. St. John could be the patron saint of seniors, inspiring them to embrace Wrinkled or White Martyrdom with grace and good humor.

Many elderly, worn out by sickness, aches and pains, and the loneliness of old age, may feel inclined to dig their own graves and like John be caught up to heaven in a blinding flash of light. To die young is often viewed as a blessing — assuring one of a packed church for one's funeral — and old age as a curse. The question is: What is the purpose of old age? One answer may be found in the story of a Japanese senior-senior citizen.

Looking back on his artistic career, the painter Katsushika Hokusai, who lived from 1760 to 1849, made this comment: "I have been in love with painting ever since I became conscious of it at the age of six. I drew some pictures I thought fairly good when I was fifty, but really nothing I did before the age of seventy was of any value at all. At seventy-three I have at last caught every aspect of nature....When I am eighty I shall have developed still further, and I will really master the secrets of art at ninety. When I reach a hundred my work will be truly sublime, and my final goal will be attained around the age of one hundred and ten, when every line and dot I draw will be imbued with life."

God has made you, and each of us, an artist of life, and it

seems to take a long time to be imbued with the fullness of life.
✴

---

28 **Feast of the Holy Innocents.** On this Fourth Day of Christmas, we reflect on Herod's slaughter of the innocent children of Bethlehem and the surrounding area at the time of Jesus' birth. Seeking to kill the child king of whom the Magi spoke, he resolved the problem of a potential heir by killing all boys two years of age and under. Matthew's Gospel records this regal deed and so identifies the first martyrs of Christianity.

Today is the feast of the millions of innocent victims of infanticide and abortion. It is also the feast of those who have had their childhood slaughtered by being enslaved in sweatshops and factories in third world countries to make cheap clothing and other products. Their enslavement by King Greed makes them victims as were the Holy Innocents.

The stark reality of human slavery is still with us. The fact that the poor are forced to slave away so the wealthy and those of the first world can have inexpensive products is a failure of resolve on the part of good people everywhere. The failure of governments, the U.N., of churches and organizations to prevent this injustice haunts this festival season of Christmas. May this bloody feast of the Holy Innocents help us find hope in the midst of failure, light in the midst of darkness, success in defeat.

⚜

Success, Winston Churchill said, was "going from failure to failure without loss of enthusiasm." Only the truly innocent can maintain that kind of stamina. If your life is more a festival of failures than a holiday of success, find encouragement in Churchill's words and pray for great enthusiasm. Don't count your failures, or those of Christianity; count instead your home runs.

The baseball career of the Sultan of Swat, Babe Ruth, echoes Churchill's wisdom, for he struck out more often than he hit home runs. To recall how he never lost his enthusiasm based on his success rate, coil around the circle of time to the February 6 entry for his birthday.

Talking of the "Babe," today's feast of the Holy Children of

Bethlehem once gave rise to a monastic tradition of serving baby food to monks on this day!

✯

The Death of *Life*, 1972. On this day in 1972 *Life* magazine, which had been a pioneer of good photojournalism, suspended regular publication after being a weekly fixture in American life for over thirty-six years. This pioneer magazine did reappear again, but not as a weekly. Photojournalism is the technological expression of the first language, communication not spoken but seen. Rock paintings and carved figure images in stone cliffs date back 26,000 years. Paintings and images express a universal language which can be understood by all, regardless of one's spoken language. To paraphrase Confucius, "a picture is worth a thousand words — in any and all languages."

29

Today's commemoration provides an opportunity to consider other things that are in the act of being suspended, becoming extinct. Magazines, prehistoric animals, religions and languages all die. By the year 2020 it is estimated that ninety percent of all world languages will be extinct!

English, which is presently the language of motion pictures, international air travel and of the computer revolution, will dominate as the world's most-spoken language. Which languages will make up the remaining ten percent could make an interesting discussion at your coffee break today.

⚜

Yes, like the now-extinct diplodocus, brachiosaurus and tyrannosaurus rex dinosaurs, languages also disappear from the earth. Among those whose bones are already housed in the museums of religious or literary texts are Sanskrit, ancient Greek, Latin, Gothic, Saxon, Norse and Old English. No longer are these classical languages spoken as a common tongue among people. Likewise, along with many of today's major languages, thousands of ethnic dialects are rapidly going the way of the passenger pigeon and the dodo bird.

⚜

Today is also the **Feast of Saint Thomas à Becket**. The famous pilgrimages to his tomb in the Cathedral of Canterbury inspired one of the first wonderful uses of the English language in Chaucer's *The Canterbury Tales*. Becket is also the subject of another magnificent use of English by the poet T.S. Eliot in his "Murder in the Cathedral." Worth your reflection today is T.S. Eliot's four tempters who come to Becket as he waits for Henry II's overzealous knights on their way to kill him. The most diabolic of the four seducers is the last, who tempts Thomas to do the right thing for the wrong reason. He slyly tries to persuade him to embrace becoming a sainted martyr whose tomb will become a shrine of pilgrimage for the faithful.

Watch well, today, and any day, for that same tempter to come and encourage you to do the right thing but for the wrong reason, for that tempter can speak to you in any number of languages.

✻

---

30 Day of the Gadsden Purchase, 1853.

On this day in 1853 the U.S. minister to Mexico, James Gadsden, acquired from Mexico 29,644 square miles of territory in the southwest for $15,000,000, which later was reduced to only $10,000,000. The purchase established the final boundaries of the continental United States by including the land of present-day Arizona and New Mexico. The purchase was prompted by the Southern Pacific Railroad, which had sought the territory for a proposed new railroad line to the Pacific coast.

꧁ꙮ꧂

Prepare for the approaching new year and make your own purchase today, not of land, but of a brand new broom. As your decorated evergreen tree and other holiday decorations have helped you celebrate Christmas, a new broom can be an ideal and useful New Year symbol. Tomorrow night, your New Year's broom can be the centerpiece of your party if you are having friends come to your house, or if you are going to someone else's house you can take your broom along. As the old proverb says, "A new broom sweeps clean." Here, then, is a personal or communal ritual prayer for your New Year's Broom:

> O God, you are ever-new and forever ageless,
>> and we who live in space and time
>> are about to begin a new year
>> as the wheel of time turns round
>> again for one more try.
>
> With the coming year, we also wish to be new;
>> may this New Year's Broom sweep clean this house
>> of last year's grudges and reservations
>> and any residual acts of unkindness.

(Symbolically sweep your broom several times)

> Sweep clean this our home of old dusty routines,
>> of tired ruts and dead-end patterns,
>> which prevent us from a greater love
>> of each other and of you.
>
> New Year's Broom, sweep from our hearts
>> all fears and angry memories,
>> and the pieces of broken dreams.
> May our hearts, now swept clean,
>> have room for fresh new dreams,
>> for all the new beginnings of the new year,
>> with which you, our God, have gifted us.
>
> Let the new year,
>> rich with God's holy blessings,
>> now come into our lives.

(The broom can be passed around, allowing each person present to make several symbolic sweeps with it. A dust pan filled with the old year can be ritually dumped outdoors.)

New Year's Eve and the Feast of St. Sylvester. While traditionally a night to bid farewell to the old year and welcome in the new with parties and noisemaking, this is also a night to watch your step. If there is an east wind on this Saint Sylvester's Night, it is an omen of a disastrous twelve months of calamities. **31**

Another belief is that whatever you are doing as the bells ring in the new year you will be doing for the next twelve months. For this reason it once was common, especially for the elderly, not to go to bed until after midnight. Also on this night of the changing of years, it was held that just before midnight every door should be opened to allow the spirit of the old year to exit from your home.

The custom of shooting guns and firecrackers, banging pots and pans — and, in Denmark, the breaking of dishes and crockery against the door — is an relic of pre-Christian times. Noisemaking was not done to salute the new year but to drive away the demons. An ancient Roman custom is to give presents at the beginning of the new year, a practice which has survived in many Latin countries, although it has been moved to January 6. In some places children and any guests who come to your home are given gifts of money, in the form of bright new coins. In Scotland this night is known as *Hogmanay*, and it is believed that the first person to cross your threshold, who is called, "the first footer," will foretell the year. If the person is tall and dark, the year will be a good one. Consider having some tall, dark (and preferably holy) friend insure your household of a good year by coming to your door at 12:01.

⚜

Of course, these old traditions, and every tradition and ageless custom, was once brand new. A night as rich as this one deserves to be celebrated with more than eating and drinking. Perhaps one of the customs mentioned above will inspire you to recreate it as a new one. For example, the old Roman custom of giving presents is an excellent one to recreate. You can breathe a longer life into your Christmas tree by laying beneath it special gifts to be opened only on New Year's Eve or Day. These gifts could be placed under the tree at the same time as your Christmas gifts but left untouched until this night.

Creating a new tradition on New Year's Eve or gifting your home or apartment with something new would be two good home-church rituals for this night. The presence of anything new is a way to celebrate the new possibilities that exist for you and those you love as the ancient circle of time comes full circle

— yet opens to a wiser, holier new beginning. Happy New Year and Happy Circling Around to January, February, March and the other nine months of this new year.

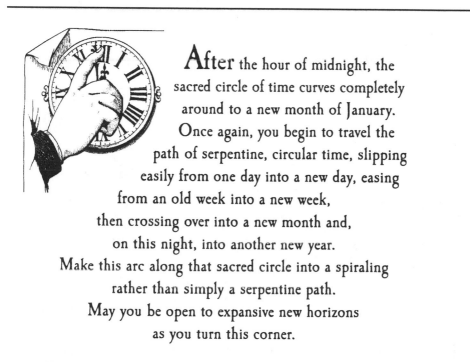

Also on this death day of one year, remember the famous Charlie Parkhurst, who was found dead on this day in 1879. You may wish to ride the circle of time back to October 24 and read the Almanac entry for that date. You may find Charlie Parkhurst's story to be inspirational, especially if you are going to a New Years' Eve costume party.

After the hour of midnight, the
sacred circle of time curves completely
around to a new month of January.
Once again, you begin to travel the
path of serpentine, circular time, slipping
easily from one day into a new day, easing
from an old week into a new week,
then crossing over into a new month and,
on this night, into another new year.
Make this arc along that sacred circle into a spiraling
rather than simply a serpentine path.
May you be open to expansive new horizons
as you turn this corner.

Happy Circling and a Happy, Fresh and Brand-New Year
as you change calendars, soul clocks and yourself.

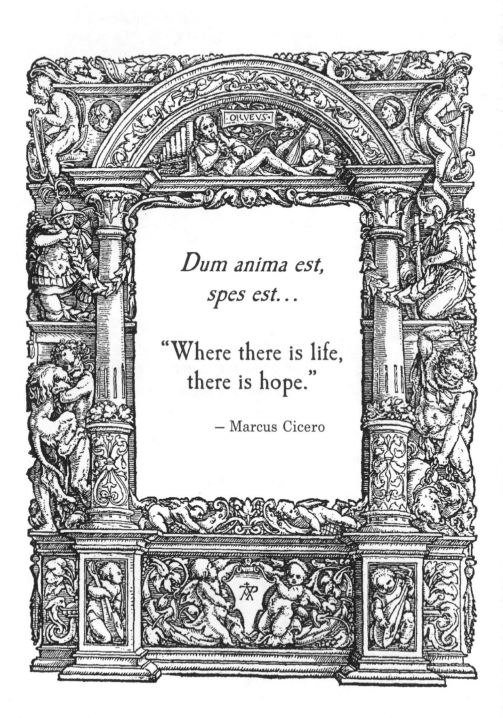

Dum anima est,
spes est...

"Where there is life,
there is hope."

— Marcus Cicero

Bibliography and Resources

ASIMOV, ISAAC, *Book of Facts.* Hastings Books, Mamaroneck, N.Y., 1992.

BARTLETT, JOHN, *Familiar Quotations.* Little, Brown & Co., Boston, 1980.

BURNAM, THOMAS, *The Dictionary of Misinformation.* Ballantine Books, New York, 1975.

CALDER, NIGEL, *Timescale.* Viking Press, New York, 1983.

CARRUTH, GORTON, *What Happened When.* Penguin Books, U.S.A. Inc., New York, 1991.

The Concise Columbia Encyclopedia. Columbia University Press, New York, 1983.

DEEDY, JOHN, *Catholic Fact Book.* Thomas More Press, Chicago, 1986.

DESMOND, SEAN, *A Touch of the Irish.* Michael O'Mara Book Ltd., and Quality Book Club, New York, 1995.

EVANS, IVOR H., ed., *Brewer's Dictionary of Phrase & Fable.* Harper & Row Publishers, New York, 1981.

FARGIS, PAUL, AND BYKOFSKY, SHEREE, eds., *The New York Public Library Desk Reference.* Webster's New World, New York, 1989.

FINK, JOANNE, *Greeting Card Design.* PBC International Inc., Glen Cove, New York, 1992.

FOLEY, LEONARD O.F.M., ed., *Saint of the Day.* St. Anthony Messenger Press, Cincinnati, 1990.

GREEN, JOEY, *Polish Your Furniture with Panty Hose.* Hyperion, New York, 1995.

GREEN, JOEY, *Paint Your House with Powdered Milk.* Hyperion, New York, 1996.

GRUN, BERNARD, *The Timetables of History.* Simon and Schuster, New York, 1982.

HENDRICKSON, ROBERT, *Encyclopedia of Words and Phrase Origins.* Facts on File Publications, New York, 1987.

HIGHWATER, JAMAKE, *The Primal Mind.* HarperCollins, New York, 1982.

HIGHWATER, JAMAKE, *Ritual of the Wind.* Methuen Publs., Toronto, 1984.

JOHNSON, OTTO AND DAILEY, VERA, *The 1993 Information Please Almanac.* Houghton Mifflin Co., Boston, 1992.

KELLY, SEAN AND ROGERS, ROSEMARY, *Saints Preserve Us!* Random House Inc., New York, 1993.

LAUX, JOHN, *Church History.* Tan Books Publishers, Rockford, Il., 1945.

LOWEWN, JAMES W., *Lies My Teacher Told Me.* The New Press, New York, 1995.

MCKENZIE, JOHN L., *Dictionary of the Bible.* Bruce Publishing Company Milwaukee, 1965.

MCKENZIE, JOHN L., *Source.* Thomas More Press, Chicago, 1984.

OPIE, IONA AND TATEN, MORIA, eds. *A Dictionary of Superstitions.* Oxford University Press, Oxford, England & New York, 1989.

PANATI, CHARLES, *Browser's Book of Beginnings.* Houghton Mifflin Co., Boston, 1884.

PANATI, CHARLES, *Extraordinary Origins of Everyday Things.* Harper & Row, New York, 1987.

PANATI, CHARLES, *Extraordinary Endings of Practically Everything and Everybody.* Harper & Row, New York, 1989.

PANATI, CHARLES, *Parade of Fads, Follies, and Manias.* HarperCollins, New York, 1991.

URDANG, LAWRENCE AND ABATE, FRANK, eds., *Dictionary of Borrowed Words.* Wynwood Press, New York, 1991.

RAWSON, HUGH, *Wicked Words.* Crown Publishers, New York, 1989.

ROGERS, JAMES, *The Dictionary of Cliches.* Ballantine Books, New York, 1985.

SANDERS, E.P., *The Historical Figure of Jesus.* Penguin Books Ltd., London, 1993.

SCHERMAN, KATHARINE, *The Flowering of Ireland.* Little, Brown & Co., Boston, 1981.

SCHLESINGER JR., ARTHUR M., *The Almanac of American History.* The Putnam Publishing Group, New York, 1983.

THOMAS, ROBERT, *The Old Farmers 1997 Almanac.* Yankee Publishing, Dublin, N. Hamp, 1996.

TULEJA, TAD, *The Cat's Pajamas.* Fawcett Columbine, New York, 1987.

VANONI, MARVIN, *I've Got Goose Pimples.* William Morrow, New York, 1989.

VON STRAALEN, ALICE, *The Book of Holidays Around the World.* E.P. Dutton, New York, 1986.

WESIER, FRANCIS X., *A Handbook of Christian Feasts and Customs.* Harcourt, Brace and Publishing Co., New York, 1952.

WHITCOMB, JOHN AND WHITCOMB, CLAIRE, *Oh Say Can You See.* William Morrow & Co., New York, 1987.

WURMAN, RICHARD SAUL, *Follow the Yellow Brick Road.* Bantam Books, New York, 1992.

England's Famous Discoveries

Capt. Davies · Sir Walter Raleigh · Sir John Hawkins · Capt. Smith

Sr. Fran: Drake

Mr. Tho: Candish

THE
Coasting Pilot:
Or the Index Pointer

If setting sail on an expedition
to revisit an island of intriguing
information, to return to the
site of a buried treasure of
ancient wisdom or any port of
call encountered on your journey
through this Almanac, let the
pilot of your index finger
point the way.

LONDON

Index

389

390

Edward ? Hays

The author of *The Old Hermit's Almanac* informs his publisher that he is both old and hermetical, and so can legally use the title for this book. He presently shares his reclusive contemplative life with the many readers of his books and with his brothers who are prisoners at the Kansas state penitentiary, where he serves as their priest chaplain.

Edward Hays has been a Catholic priest of the Archdiocese of Kansas City in Kansas since 1958. His college and theological education were at the hands of the Benedictine monks at the Immaculate Conception Abbey of Conception, Missouri. In addition to his parents, the monks of Conception are credited by the author with instilling in him a love of prayer and contemplation, along with a Renaissance love affair with the arts and knowledge. As a result of this romance with learning, his friends have nicknamed him "Edward the Curious." The author enjoys this nickname and has requested that it be appropriately acknowledged with the above question mark as his middle name.

After ordination, he served in parish ministries for thirteen years, including seven years as pastor to the Pottawatomie Indian Tribe at Mayetta, Kansas. In 1971, he undertook a prayer pilgrimage to the Near East and India after which he began Shantivanam, a lay contemplative community at Easton, Kansas. After twenty-three years he resigned as director of the house of prayer and departed on a sabbatical of prayer and study in the desert Southwest of Mexico and the United States. He was then appointed to a dual ministry of Prayer and Writing, and Prison Pastoral Care.

Father Hays is the author of twenty books on spirituality, prayer and original parable-stories (see page 4 for a complete listing). A self-taught artist, he enjoys illustrating his own books and painting. Now in his senior years, while in good health, he tells friends that he is sick — homesick — and compares himself to a salmon who has begun swimming upstream.

Editor's Note: While preparing for his third and final great pilgrimage, Edward the Curious is rumored to be also working on several unpublished manuscripts and other projects in various stages of creative chaos!